The Great Cat and Dog Massacre

ANIMAL LIVES

A series edited by Jane C. Desmond, Barbara J. King, and Kim Marra

The Great Cat and Dog Massacre

*The Real Story of World War Two's
Unknown Tragedy*

HILDA KEAN

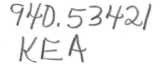

The University of Chicago Press

CHICAGO AND LONDON

The University of Chicago Press, Chicago 60637
The University of Chicago Press, Ltd., London
© 2017 by The University of Chicago
Published 2017.
Printed in the United States of America

26 25 24 23 22 21 20 19 18 17   2 3 4 5

ISBN-13: 978-0-226-31832-5 (cloth)
ISBN-13: 978-0-226-31846-2 (e-book)
DOI: 10.7208/chicago/9780226318462.001.0001

Library of Congress Cataloging-in-Publication Data

Names: Kean, Hilda, author.
Title: The great cat and dog massacre : the real story of World War Two's
   unknown tragedy / Hilda Kean.
Other titles: Animal lives (University of Chicago Press)
Description: Chicago : The University of Chicago Press, 2017. | Series: Animal
   lives | Includes bibliographical references and index.
Identifiers: LCCN 2016027115 | ISBN 9780226318325 (cloth : alk. paper) |
   ISBN 9780226318462 (e-book)
Subjects: LCSH: Animal welfare—Great Britain—History—20th century. |
   Human-animal relationships—Great Britain—History—20th century. |
   World War, 1939–1945—Food supply—Great Britain. | Animals—Social
   aspects—Great Britain—History—20th century.
Classification: LCC HV4805.A3 K43 2017 | DDC 940.53/421—dc23 LC record
   available at https://lccn.loc.gov/2016027115

♾ This paper meets the requirements of ANSI/NISO Z39.48-1992
(Permanence of Paper).

For Sidney Trist, Tommy Atkins, and Albert Chevalier
and in memory of their London ancestors

Contents

CHAPTER ONE

Introducing Animals, Historians, and the "People's War"

A significant section of Britons, by the way, thought first of their pets. [1]

I never intended to write a book about the war. I say "the war" because in my London childhood of the '50s and '60s this was the only war my family and community discussed—and it was the only war depicted in the weekly visits to the cinema with my parents on a Friday evening. Like many of my generation I grew up on particular images and stories emanating from those years of warfare from 1939 to 1945. Those born after the war have belonged to a generation suffused, as Geoff Eley has discussed, in the effects of war but whose "'memory' of them came entirely after the fact."[2] I can still remember the tales of the church raffle for a slice of banana (a real rarity given the difficulty of importing food); my grandfather refusing to go to the Anderson shelter in the back garden and next morning waking up to find shards of glass from bomb-blasted windows on his bed, having slept through the air raid; my aunt walking through glass-strewn streets of Hackney to check whether her elder sister had survived a bombardment she had heard a half mile away. I experienced none whatsoever of these events but they were nevertheless part of my childhood through the stories relatives told. There would also be food that my parents—normally not fussy eaters unlike their daughter—disliked eating, particularly rabbit and butter beans, since it reminded them of wartime deprivation. Such accounts are not just my own family stories but ones now shared by several generations who never directly experienced the war. This war remains so popular in British national memory and culture that scarcely a week goes by without a television or radio program centered on this time.[3] Such programs include documentaries around the buildup to the war, the evacuation of nearly 340,000 troops retreating from the German advance at Dunkirk in May 1940, or the subsequent role of Churchill as Prime Minister until his defeat in the postwar election of 1945. More recently recollections of the now diminishing numbers of elderly people who had served in the armed forces have been broadcast to sympathetic audiences. Fictional narratives of this time remain popular, including several series of *Foyle's War*, a Hastings-based detective, or *Dad's Army*, a humorous series first aired in 1968 and still engaging Saturday night audiences with its gentle satire of the antics of a thoroughly class-based Home Guard. It is no wonder that we think we "know about" the war.

Underpinning such documentary and fictional narratives is the idea that the Second World War was generally, as Sellar and Yeatman might have summarized in *1066 and All That*, a "good" war.[4] While obviously it was a war in which millions of military forces, civilians, Roma, Sinti, and, of course, Jews were killed it has nevertheless been reinterpreted, with the benefit of hindsight, as being primarily a battle against fascism (rather than German expansionism) and a war in which Britain was correct to fight (certainly more correct than in recent adventures in the Middle East and Afghanistan). Significantly, the 1939–45 war, particularly on the Home Front, is seen as a "People's War" when, so the story goes, people pulled together and stood firm against the Nazis—despite being isolated in Europe as a consequence of not being invaded or surrendering—and withstood aerial bombardment with resilience. This time is "remembered" as one when the interests of the nation allegedly overrode those of classes. It is recalled as some sort of golden age not only by right-wing extremists hostile towards immigrants but by those distressed by the breakdown in community cohesion caused by aggressive neoliberal politics. There is a search for "lost reassurances."[5] The BBC's creation of its People's War website with requests for "storygatherers" indicated not only the ongoing importance of the war within national memory and identity but also "the fear of losing this imperative at the death of the last survivors."[6]

The story of my grandfather refusing to go into the shelter was by no means unique: in his own way he defied Hitler to do his worst while he lay in his own bed as shattered glass landed on the blankets. The state deliberately fostered such language and an image of standing firm for purposes of morale. Indeed "by the time war broke out in September 1939 the myth had been all but scripted."[7] The phrase "People's War" at the time applied to the period of the so-called Blitz from September 1940 to May 1941. Of particular significance then (and subsequently) were the first months of the bombing, when Londoners endured bombing for 57 nights in a row.[8] As Paul Addison has characterized the Battle of Britain of 1940, the aerial fighting in the skies in the summer of 1940 that preceded the Blitz, "it was fought over landscapes painted by Constable, churches designed by Wren, and the London of Dickens, Pepys and Shakespeare."[9] At that time London was appropriated for propaganda purposes as a national landscape with which to mobilize the nation.[10] People saw images of St. Paul's Cathedral surrounded by smoke and flames symbolically not only of London and the city but also of the country as a whole. Despite academic debunking, myths of the "People's War" "remain lodged in the public imagination."[11]

All nations, of course, have their own stories about their pasts they wish to remember and pass on to future generations. Scandinavian noir fiction in the hands of Asa Larsson, Hening Mankell, or Jo Nesbo, for example, has foregrounded their respective nations' myths of the Second World War in which, apparently, there were no Nazi sympathizers and the resistance was the dominant force. Jo Nesbo has recently explained that his novel *The*

FIGURE 1.1 St. Paul's Cathedral surrounded by smoke c. 1940 (LHW/18/16, Bishopsgate Institute)

Redbreast is both his most personal novel and one that undermines "the mythical self-image of the Norwegian people as a nation actively resisting Hitler."[12] It draws on the stories of his own Nazi-supporting father, who was one of some 6,000 young Norwegians who had volunteered to fight on the Eastern Front, as a device to expose the long legacy of this politics in Norway today. Tellingly the unrepentant fascist in this novel compiles his own memoir of the Second World War and includes amongst his victims a historian who promulgates the sanitized version of Norway's past, neglecting the traces of Nazi alignment. The popular memories that need interrogating in Britain are rather different but nevertheless still merit critical attention.[13]

Like adults of my generation and those who have followed us it is not surprising that I thought I "knew about" the war. But this changed several years ago when I was researching for *Animal Rights: Political and Social Change in Britain since 1800*.[14] I came across a phrase in Angus Calder's key work, *The People's War*, that stuck in my mind as I had never heard of it before. "[At the start of the war] there was no stoning of dachshunds in the streets. But a holocaust of pets occurred as homes were disrupted; outside vets' surgeries 'the slain' lay in heaps."[15] The phrase "holocaust of pets" was not unique to Calder. In his book *The Phoney War*, analyzing the first months of the war, E. S. Turner also talked of the "holocaust of pets" during September 1939, arguing, "Most of this slaughter was unnecessary, from any standpoint."[16] I would later discover that the term "holocaust of pets" or "massacre" were not post-hoc constructions but contemporary descriptions. The *Oxford English Dictionary* carefully describes the different meanings of the word holocaust, noting that its modern meaning of the "mass murder of the Jews by the Nazis" did not start to be used until 1942. An earlier meaning of the word meaning a sacrifice or massacre on a large scale was used to describe the unnecessary killing of at least 400,000 "pet" cats and dogs in London in the first week of the war in September 1939. The word may have had a different meaning but it still nevertheless indicated a "great slaughter or massacre" or a large-scale sacrifice wholly consumed by fire.[17] This was no routine killing. The government, state, veterinary profession, and animal charities were all opposed to this "sacrifice." It was not required by the state even at this initial moment of war.

This animal killing is not part of the popular memory of the "Good War," the unified "People's War." Animals' role in the war has not been the focus of scholarly accounts and the popular books that do exist tend more towards human emotions rather than analysis of what companion *animals* actually did. Missing to date from both popular and scholarly accounts of war on the Home Front is any serious analysis of the role of nonhuman animals (hereafter animals)[18] either in propaganda or visual representations although they performed key functions here. More significantly, animals as beings living and dying alongside — or because of — humans and human decisions have been written out of such history. As I shall explore later there are good reasons for this. Although the killing does not necessarily show human panic, the shocking events that would happen in the first days of the war were the complete antithesis of the promoted spirit of steadfastness and resilience. Scholarly historians are at one in arguing that "there was no evidence of any significant increase in neurotic illness or mental disorder in Britain during the war."[19] These unremembered events do demonstrate the utter disposability of companion animals in what become constructed as times of human crisis. This war act is "forgotten" — but so too are the subsequent animal-human relationships that grew and developed during the war in which the distinction of killer and victim become blurred into common beings sharing hardship and proving mutual support.

However, I am not attempting to simply "add in" animals to the existing trope of the "People's War." I am seeking to do more than that. This book attempts to shift focus away from humans onto animals. It also explores the changing animal-human relationship but not in the spirit of "roundedness" or of some twenty-first-century sense of "inclusion." Rather, I will argue that an awareness of animal presence and activity — and of how humans engaged with this — can challenge and disrupt our somewhat lazy assumptions about the war and the role of our ancestors in this "Good War." In a nation that often chooses to define itself as "animal loving" — irrespective of the reality of the situation — the acts perpetrated in those September days confront the stories we like to tell ourselves and suggest that the term "People's War" is a misnomer.

THE DISTINCTIVENESS OF ANIMALS — AND THEIR METAPHORICAL REPRESENTATION — IN BRITAIN DURING THE WAR

Certainly, animals existed in the Second World War outside Britain — and were recorded as such in different countries. Thus the anonymous author of *A Woman in Berlin* reminds us that companion animals in Germany were also sheltering from bombardment — by the allies:

> I slept until the bombs woke me up. My hand was dangling over my bed and I felt something licking it — Foxel, our absent landlord's terrier. There, Foxel, good dog, don't be afraid, we're alone here in this front room.[20]

In the accounts of American journalist William Shirer we can read of the plight of both companion and farm animals:

> Denmark's three million cows, three million pigs and twenty-five million laying hens live on imported fodder, mostly from North and South America and Manchukuo. These supplies are now cut off. Denmark must slaughter most of its livestock, one of its main sources of existence.[21]

Or we might imagine the sounds of the lowing of cattle, abandoned by human refugees passing from the countryside, heard in Paris as the Germans entered on 14 June 1940.[22]

The situation in Britain was rather different. The extent—or almost saturation—of the notion of a "People's War" means that we are looking at a "representation" that is (still) an important part of popular and cultural memory.[23] To understand what happened to animals in Britain at that time and the nature of the animal-human relationship in the war we also need to think about *these* events "representationally" precisely because they occurred within another "representation," that of the "People's War."

It was not a war experienced just by humans: animals were an integral part of the domestic parameters of warfare. They not only suffered (as did humans) but also actively played a role in their own and their human companions' physical and emotional survival. However, in discussing human treatment of animal companions particularly at the start of the war, I will also question whether our assumptions about this being a "good" war can remain when we realize how thousands of people treated the animal members of their families. Philip Howell has noted that in the 1914–18 war, "dogs were uniquely vulnerable to the revocation of their privileged status as human companions."[24] This statement is just as relevant to their position (and that of other companion animals) in the 1939–45 war, as I shall show in later chapters.

As the outbreak of war drew near, animals (and their supposedly benign treatment by British people) were seen metaphorically to represent civilization under attack from Nazi barbarism. This idea was embodied, for example, in different ways in Louis MacNeice's poem *Autumn Journal*. Here he reflected on losing his dog on London's Primrose Hill and recorded a taxi driver's comments on soldiers gathering in trucks, "it turns me up." But in the police station order was restored with the discovery of his dog:

> I found my dog had vanished
> And thought "This is the end of the old regime,"
> But found the police had got her in St. John's Wood station
> And fetched her in the rain . . .[25]

Later, in prose, MacNeice expressed similar sentiments of both the human and animal world affected by an impending disaster. While working in the British Museum reading room, he had observed the birds outside, "The colonnade of the British Museum is the quintessence of peace. Many people come in from the streets to eat their lunch upon the steps and the pigeons pick up their crumbs. There are already many refugees beginning to hibernate."[26] Animals were—and would be—seen throughout the war as symbols of fidelity, stability, civilization. Contrasts would continue to be drawn between the righteousness of the allies' cause typified by the apparent British attitude towards companion animals and those of the Nazis. But, as Jonathan Burt has argued, treating an animal *only* as an icon or image places the animal outside history: "The role is purely symbolic; it reflects historical processes without truly being a part of them."[27] Too often such animals become written out of the actual processes of history.

Certainly animals—or more accurately their representations—did play a part in war stories. Humans appropriated them for different purposes. This happened at a national level—and within families. It is without doubt the case that Chummy, whose paw print "signed" a letter to a child evacuated to Canada, did not understand the contents of the letter.[28] Asta, another dog, regularly "wrote" to the child of the family who was told he had gone to the country, away from the Blitz where he was safe and happy—although the dog had been killed. The little girl's aunt typed "Asta's letter."[29] In particular, images of dogs in the popular press were constructed as peculiarly British devices to boost morale. American journalist William Shirer had regularly reported from Berlin in the late 1930s, watching the behavior of Germans and foreigners alike in the buildup to war. He lamented the sudden loneliness of the Adlon hotel bar in Unter den Linden once the British journalists had left towards the end of August. But even this experienced commentator found the conversations of the British Embassy staff odd once war was declared: "They talked about dogs and such stuff."[30] British journalists found such sentiments entirely understandable.

Thus Sir Nevile Henderson, the British ambassador to Germany, was photographed returning home on the weekend war was declared, disembarking with his tiny dog, Hippy, a Dachsbracke—a relatively new breed of tracking dog developed in Southern Austria in the late nineteenth century—held closely to the chest of a member of staff.[31] For propaganda purposes, however, Hippy was portrayed as a dachshund, showing that the British were a mature people no longer given to the apparent hysteria that overtook them in animosity towards the small dogs, vilified as German, during the 1914–18 war.[32] Less attention was paid to the fate of the actual dog, collected

FIGURE 1.2 Sir Nevile Henderson with Hippy when Ambassador in Berlin

by an employee of Spratt's, the dog food company, and taken, in accordance with procedures of the time, to quarantine in West Hackwood for some six months. When collecting Hippy in March 1940 Henderson observed that this experience had affected the dog considerably: "His resilience and buoyancy were not there." Hippy was to die shortly after from jaundice, causing his human companion to declare, " For nine years and more he had been part of my life and a very big part of it, and when he died something went out it which I know that I can never find again. None can ever take his place and I can hardly conceive of another life unless Hippy be waiting there to share it with me."[33] Despite the obvious importance Hippy played in the life of Henderson, the relationship portrayed in his moving book is defined by his official biographer as an " eccentric study," apparently not being an appropriate show of emotion for a man of Henderson's standing.[34] The image of Hippy in the *Daily Mirror* [35] was in stark contrast to that included in the previous day's edition of Baerchen, the Chow dog belonging to Ribbentrop when ambassador to Britain, who was apparently abandoned when the German embassy staff quit their London premises. The paper gave words to the dog accusing his master of cruelty: "His was a smell of hatred and cruelty. It sent to my mind something that made me cringe."[36] The different treatments of these particular dogs typified, according to the *Daily Mirror* in a leading story, the cause of the war: "That's what Britain is fighting—the inherent brutality of Nazi-ism, that has no justice or human feeling—even for its pets."[37] As if to exemplify this differentiation in practical ways, some two hundred people purportedly competed for the honor of taking in Baerchen.[38] Humans privilege the visual sense in contrast, say, to the sense of hearing and smell that dominate the lives of cats and dogs. Here the image of Baerchen and the sight of the accompanying text apparently resulted in a morally motivated response.[39] But Baerchen and Hippy were not just symbols but actually existing animals specifically affected by the start of the war. Both of them had lost their previous homes. Ironically the abandoned German dog, being quickly re-homed, would have enjoyed a more pleasant next few months than Hippy, imprisoned in quarantine. But these dogs, seemingly so important and so representative of the allies' cause at the start of the war, are no longer remembered. Precisely because their stories were *subsumed* within the broader extant story of a "People's War" and Britain "standing alone," the human story has inevitably dominated. In the course of time their intrinsic elements and potential capacity to disrupt such a narrative as nonhuman beings have been largely ignored.

To further illustrate how incorporation can lead to oblivion I turn to the story of Faith, a cat. Faith lived in St. Augustine's and St. Faith's Church then opposite St. Paul's cathedral in the City of London. During the first nights of the Blitz in September 1940 she sheltered her newborn kitten amidst fire and falling masonry. And, like her offspring, she survived. The photograph that had hung in the church showed Faith sitting upright, paws calmly closed in front of her. The accompanying text describes how the "roofs and masonry exploded . . . Yet she stayed calm and steadfast and waited for help."[40] The image of sitting upright and being "steadfast" serves to incorporate the cat within the human story of the People's War. Living cats, even with newly born kittens, tend to hide and "go to earth" in the event of danger and attack. They are not necessarily waiting for human help since they have already found safety. Because of hiding in this way, as the National Air Raid Precautions Animals' Committee (NARPAC) would report later in the war, injuries to cats and dogs were fewer than had been anticipated.[41] Faith became an epitome of the image of St. Paul's Cathedral itself (and indeed Britain at this time) standing alone and steadfast. Through such myth-making Faith was recognized at the time but subsequently has almost disappeared as a discrete living being and morphed into a mere symbol or human myth.[42] Her distinctive animal characteristics have thereby been obliterated. She is just an image that conveniently demonstrates that "animals are like us" and mimic our ways—even in war. But the war did not just encompass representations of animals. It also was a framework for animals' very existence as living beings and for their interactions with humans.

THE DIFFICULTIES AND POSSIBILITIES OF WRITING A HISTORY OF ANIMALS THAT GOES BEYOND REPRESENTATION OR HUMAN HISTORIES

Histories that discuss animal-human relationships have not been numerous. While military and economic historians have long embraced animals within their broad subject areas, works on war have focused on the frontlines of military activity, maneuvers, and strategies.[43] Within an economic history of industrialization the role of horses has been widely discussed—and analyzed. In a key inaugural lecture over 40 years ago Professor F. M. L. Thompson expanded on the hard work conducted by horses "so hard for so long, historically, that of course horsepower naturally became the measure of the strength of the steam engines and internal combustion engines."[44] More recently McShane and Tarr have characterized horses in American cities as "four-legged workers."[45] But it is only in the recent past that animals have started to be the subjects of social and cultural histories. In some ways, this is surprising. The 1960s and 1970s saw, for example, ground-breaking work subjecting new topics and people to historical scrutiny by highlighting actions that had been overlooked or written out of standard histories. In his *The Making of the English Working-Class*, E. P. Thompson had sought to "rescue" his subjects "from the enormous condescension of posterity."[46] Similarly, *Hidden from History: Three Hundred Years of Women's Oppression and the Fight against It* of 1973 was innovative because Sheila Rowbotham made a neglected subject matter valid within the discourse of history. (It was left to later works to develop the impact of a history of women that would challenge the structures and concerns of existing notions of history by arguing that women could not just be "added in"—acknowledgment of their existence profoundly altered existing histories. That is, work on historiographical processes developed later.)

But works on animals as serious objects of historical study did not develop alongside books on class and gender at that time. As recently as 1974, as Animal Studies expert Erica Fudge has discussed, a spoof article appeared in the *Journal of Social History* entitled "Household Pets and Urban Alienation" criticizing the new subjects of that time:

> It seems brash to suggest that pets become the next "fad" subject in social history but, after running through various ethnic groups (and now women), historians may need a new toy. . . . Left-handers, another large group long subject to intense social discrimination merit attention, but again their collective consciousness has lagged. So why not pets? Here, clearly, would be the ultimate history of the inarticulate.[47]

Although clearly satirical and inevitably saying more about the author's hostility to women and ethnic minorities rather than companion animals, the lack of coverage *was* well observed. There has been a striking absence in scholarly discussion on the role of companion animals in, for example, the changing nature and composition of the family or women's lives, even in the period after this satirical offering. For example, the part played by animals in constructing the British royal family positively, for example, has been strangely neglected although popular photographic collections make clear the importance of the physical presence of dogs as companions within the nineteenth- and twentieth-century British / German royal family.[48] Earlier in the twentieth century, some 100,000 copies in a few weeks were sold of *Where's Master?*, the tome purportedly penned by Caesar, the dog living with Edward VII who preceded his funeral cortege marching behind the late king's horse; these sales probably say as much about the British nation's interest in dogs as in royalty: "I'm marching in front of the kings. I've no history. I've no pedigree. I'm not high-born. But I loved him and I was faithful to him."[49] As images in the Royal Photograph Collection also suggest, dogs not only were popular subjects for posed photographs but also played an active part in the daily life of successive royal households.[50] An absence of scholarly analysis is somewhat surprising. No wonder Animal Studies scholar Jonathan Burt can state, without fear of rebuttal, "We have not to date been particularly well served by the history of animals in the twentieth century."[51] Burt's frustration with the direction of some work in Animal Studies was expressed forcefully in his plea to "emancipate the animal" from the "concept of the human methodologically." Instead, he has argued, "we need to bring the animal center stage."[52] Such a shift in focus has been seen in the work of Harriet Ritvo or Kathleen Kete, influential in creating "holistic history" in which "the presentation of the animal is offered as a way of rethinking culture."[53] However, this is not quite the same as subjecting "already known" and conventional historical topics such as war to an "animal lens."

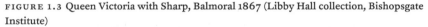

FIGURE 1.3 Queen Victoria with Sharp, Balmoral 1867 (Libby Hall collection, Bishopsgate Institute)

While believing that the role of animals in society is important and certainly worth analysis, some scholars in the Animal Studies world believe that it is not possible to even contemplate trying to write *histories* that privilege animals. Cary Wolfe, in particular has been dismissive of this possibility:

> So even though—to return to our historian example—your concept of the discipline's *external* relations to its larger environment is post humanist in taking seriously the existence of nonhuman subjects and the consequent compulsion to make the discipline respond to the question of nonhuman animals foisted on it by changes in the discipline's environment, your *internal* disciplinarity may remain humanist through and through [original emphases].[54]

In other words, the very structure of the discipline of history overrides the intentions of the historian to write about animals in a way that makes them the focus of history. This tends to ignore both the extant material about animals' past lives and the fact that history is an evolving area of study embracing many aspects of other "disciplines" in the way that the past is summoned up—and imagined.[55]

Certainly much of the historical work on animals that has developed within the past twenty years has often privileged research that focuses on "distinctive" aspects of animals' lives, such as vivisection or zoos, because of the absence of previous attention to such subjects.[56] However, to date research that has revisited "human-focused narratives" from an animal "perspective" has been less evident. Acknowledging that an animal presence can disrupt and challenge conventional ways of seeing historically is still a fairly new idea. In standard British social history, the 1911 Insurance Act, for example, has usually been seen as the first step on the way to constructing a modern welfare state, as later realized by the 1945 Labour Government, with limited pensions and welfare benefits. But this was also the Act that instituted for the first time a state-endorsed medical research committee with implicit support for experimenting on animals.[57] What might have been seen as unproblematic and positive (and totally human-centered) becomes disrupted when approached in this way. The institution of the National Health Service (NHS) in 1948 took welfare provision a step further, but as some animal campaigners argued at the time, the government was now also

FIGURE 1.4 Caesar at the funeral procession of Edward VII (Libby Hall collection, Bishopsgate Institute)

officially "sanctifying" the "cruel and immoral practice" of vivisection.[58] Asking different questions about such a key piece of social legislation may well result in demonstrating the role of animals in welfare policy, but more significantly it may also challenge the exclusively benign ways in which the NHS as such is seen and the not-so-benign nature of the animal-human relationship that helped create it.

THE ISSUES FACING HISTORIANS WHO WANT TO PRIVILEGE ANIMALS

The writing of history—of whatever sort—involves both materials and a writer to analyze and present them to a reader. To date those working in animal-human history have tended to pay more attention to the nature of materials for the making of history rather than interrogating the role and responsibilities of historians. Dorothee Brantz, for example, has written about the problem of using materials written by humans: "Writing the history of animals demands negotiating our desire to recover the *historical* [my emphasis] lives of animals vis-à-vis the fact that all of the available records of those lives have been produced by humans. Whether such a history can be anything *but* [original emphasis] representational is thus one of the key debates in the emerging field of animal studies."[59] Here she elides the past—in the sense of events happening before the present—and the writing of history as (usually) writing or/and analysis that gives a status to chosen aspects of the past. This may be an unconsidered elision but it is an important one. An acknowledgment of the existence of a "past"—whether considering animals or humans—needs to precede the making of a history. Most working in the field of Animal Studies would not dispute that (at least certain) animals have *past* lives. Whether past lives become "historical" lives depends not on the subjects themselves—be these people or animals—but on those writing about them who then choose to construct a history. This is an important distinction.[60] Even the most conservative of historians would agree animals played a role in past *events*. Whether one sees history as a construction or reconstruction, a historian—of whatever sort—is key to its creation. An elision of "the past" with "history" leads to a lack of clarity. It implies empirical approaches that inevitably promote materials or so-called sources as the only components of value in the history-making process. It also denies the way in which various nations, communities, and individuals, as well as historians in different times and places, have created different histories for the present.[61] When social historians such as E. P. Thompson

or Sheila Rowbotham, whose work I referred to earlier, chose to write po-
litically engaged histories about working class women and men, they were
not deterred from so doing by what was often regarded as a comparative
lack of material written by the protagonists themselves. They were clear
about their own role in writing new histories. It would now be a very brave
(or foolish) historian who would attempt to write, as Rowbotham did, about
three hundred years of women's history in less than two hundred pages. It
would be seen as not only methodologically dubious but also physically impossible because of the amount of material that, of course, has been found
to exist on women's lives once a historian decides to look for it.[62] Despite
the supposed lack of material, in different ways pioneering historians of
class and gender, such as Thompson and Rowbotham, boldly promoted the
role of agency in their subjects' actions.[63]

WARTIME PUBLICATIONS INCLUDING
ANIMALS ON THE HOME FRONT —
AND MATERIALS AVAILABLE NOW

Etienne Benson has suggested, "Human-authored texts can still provide
valuable insights into the past that are not reducible to the human perspective."[64] Contemporary material about the war does still exist and can be
mined for animal traces. Some material, inevitably, is specifically incorporated into overarching "human" mythologized narratives of the war. But
even in some "public" accounts written at the time, the war was not just
a human story. Animals were not seen as separate from the events of the
war or a sentimental diversion; rather they formed an integral part of the
war narrative. Thus some official accounts acknowledged an animal presence throughout the war. *Front Line 1940-1941: The Official Story of the Civil
Defence of Britain*, published in 1942, is typical. It notes, for example, a firefighter in London's East India docks observing:

> Occasionally we would glance up and then we would see a strange sight. For
> a flock of pigeons kept circling round overhead almost all night. They seemed
> lost, as if they couldn't understand the unnatural dawn. It looked like sunrise
> all around us. The pigeons seemed white in the glare, bird of peace making a
> strange contrast with the scene below.[65]

Official accounts written to document the role of the local state in wartime
also recalled animals. Frank Lewey, mayor of Stepney in east London, highlighted the role of NARPAC, the official body established for "the preven-

tion and alleviation of animal suffering."[66] Indeed the uniformed services gained status by rescuing animals. As Lewey explained:

> [NARPAC] has received very little limelight; most people outside raided areas do not know that it exists; yet its members have shown their mettle. It needs as much—perhaps more—pluck to wander among blazing and tottering ruins, looking for a maddened dog or trying to pick up a crazed cat, as to go to try to help sensible humans.[67]

In another quasi-official account George Vale described the impact of a bomb in October 1940 on the Great Eastern stables in Hare Marsh. Stabled here were horses working for the railway company that operated out of the nearby Liverpool Street terminus: many horses were killed both because of the initial bomb blast but also because of severe injuries caused by falling debris.[68] Their deaths were seen to be sufficiently important to be acknowledged at that time. Even local Home Guard accounts "officially" noted the plight of animals. In a valedictory publication in June 1945 the Poplar chief warden reflected: "Perhaps the most pitiful sight of this nightly scene of devastation was the behaviour of stray dogs and cats. . . . The joy displayed at the mere sight and presence of humans in these deserted place was affecting." [69] Routinely, professionally trained dogs and humans in the fire service searched destroyed houses for signs of human and animal life—and were photographed during the war doing this.[70]

The wartime press featured animals in its news coverage and accounts of the September 1939 massacre appeared in all major newspapers, including the *Times, Daily Telegraph, Daily Mirror,* and *News of the World,* and local press, such as the *East London Advertiser* or *Southern Daily Echo.* There were reports of animals in London and Whipsnade zoos or local rescues of bombed animals. As the *Hornsey Journal* reported a typical event: "As a group of people were comforting an old lady, telling her confidently 'he won't be dead,' a rescue worker appeared from a pile of debris with a cat, who proved the truth of the comforting story by the way he struggled and used his claws on the rescuer."[71]

Animals were (predictably) included in the written experience of vets and (less predictably) the discussion of civil servants. The National Archives have many files devoted to civil servants' memoranda about animals in wartime from dog breeding and feeding, evacuation of animals with humans, animals injured on farms, to Jumbo the cat employed as a "mouse eradicator" in the war cabinet.[72] Radio broadcasts on the BBC discussed what had happened to companion animals at the start of the war and after—and transcripts still exist. It is certainly not an absence of published "source" material that has caused an absence of historical writing on their presence during the war. More likely it is the sort of story that such materials might facilitate.

Personal diaries and letters demonstrate the daily life of animals and their role within a human family.[73] Both published and unpublished exist. Indeed some writers decided to write a diary during the war only because they felt it important to record such significant events. As one engineer wrote on 15 September 1939, "I don't know how far this good resolution [to keep a diary] will keep good, but, there being no harm in trying, let's try and keep it for the duration."[74] And he did. Another wartime diarist was Gwladys Cox, a middle-aged woman living in West Hampstead with her husband and Bob, a tabby cat with honey-colored eyes who was only 7 months old at the start of the war; Cox saw the writing of her diary as almost part of the war effort since she did this conscientiously, even when her home was destroyed. "I write up this war diary, which is more difficult than it sounds."[75] Gwladys Cox acutely observed the animal-human relationships inside her household, in the mansion block, and also in the wider locality. Materials about animals' lives can be found in such stories. While the observations at that time have been transmitted through the conduit of a human, there are traces of an animal's existence and their presence in the world. An example was an apparently trivial incident occurring in October 1940. Incendiary bombs had destroyed the top of the mansion block where the Coxes and Bob lived. They all (people and cat alike) went to stay with a neighbor. The human lives were disrupted but so was Bob's—in a different way. Gwladys took Bob outside, "hoping he would make use of the garden. Not he! Never before had he seen a garden, much less walked in soil, and was nervous of the unfamiliar surroundings so back to the dining room, where he squatted on the fine pile carpet. Fortunately Mary loves cats, and Mrs Snepps being blind, we mopped up and no one was any the wiser."[76] I am *not* suggesting that the toileting habits of Bob per se can help a rewriting of the history of the Second World War! However, as cultural theorist Walter Benjamin put it, "A chronicler who recites events without distinguishing between major and minor ones acts in accordance with the following truth: nothing that had ever happened should be regarded as lost for history."[77] This apparently trivial event indicates the way in which the war *did* disrupt the lives of actually existing animals: that Gwladys chose to document such incidents means that that event is not lost for those who wish to revisit the war from a new standpoint.

Gwladys Cox's diary is not unique. Many exist that describe individual and named animals and the different behavior noticed during the war. The collected (and published) early wartime letters to friends in America of criminologist and writer Fryniwyd Tennyson Jesse document the arrival of two new cats. Mice had overrun the flat so Fryn decided to "give an abandoned cat a good home and rang the RSPCA."[78] Unfortunately Muff, the re-homed cat, escaped during the first days in his new home but providentially was discovered by the daily help some two weeks later, in the course of which time he had had an accident that badly affected his hind legs. He was unable to catch mice: "Muff thereupon became a luxury cat — a pleasure cat — and we still had to look around for some way of dealing with the mice." A kitten, the size of a penny roll, named Perkin, was duly acquired for this purpose.[79] Tennyson Jesse describes the relationship between the two cats: they eat out of the same dish, sleep together, and hate being in a room without the other.[80] Perkin, the kitten, is put on the table when the humans eat dessert and tosses nuts out of the dish onto the floor, where Muff plays with them (not being able to jump onto the table because of his disability). The animals are present in their own right as well as acting as vehicles for Tennyson Jesse's emotions, as I shall later explore. These are small, "personal," stories but they are more than that. Such stories situate animals within more widely known public narratives of war but also start to show that animals too were affected by, and experienced, the war in particular ways. When a diarist wrote about attending a lecture on the need to wear gas masks and noted that Miss Corden's dog was "visibly shivering" during the lecture in which the humans "were all frozen stiff" we are not necessarily being presented with profound thoughts that challenge our idea of war but nevertheless *are* being reminded that animals and humans shared the same space and events.[81] We were there: they were there with us.

Sometimes animal traces were integrated into much wider war narratives. Chummy's paw print on the letter sent to Beryl Myatt evacuated to Canada was a small mark; but his mark was never received since Beryl was lost at sea on the famously torpedoed ship Benares. This enemy act against children received wide publicity and, inter alia, resulted in no further evacuations to northern America.[82] Similarly a pet canary became integrated into a wider war narrative of so-called enemy internment. This particular canary routinely had his nails cut by the local Italian pet shop owner, Mr. Azario. But the canary would need a new nail cutter. The published teenage diary of Colin Perry noted the death on the Arrandora Star[83] of the Italian owner of the local pet shop: "It was only a few short weeks ago that my brother, Alan, took our canary to him to have its nails cut; and only a few short weeks ago that we bought weed for the goldfish bowl from him." Azario had lived in Tooting for 42 years but once war was declared he was "immediately taken off in a police car for internment . . . it seems incredible that an old man who kept a pet store in Upper Tooting Road has suddenly been snatched away to forfeit his life in the Atlantic. I can see him now attending to his pets."[84] Obviously not all diaries describing animals have been published. However, even when they are, an animal presence is rarely noted in subsequent analyses and often do not even appear in an index. Although the Mass Observation diary of Nella Last has received much critical attention since its publication in 1981 and has even been adapted as a television film, Mr. Murphy the cat and Sol the dog have been resolutely ignored, even though they are prominent in the entries included in the standard published version.[85] In seeking to obtain details and observations of all aspects of daily life Mass Observation was providing a useful service for subsequent readers but, of course, also circumscribing the content of diarists' entries in the attempt to create "an anthropology of ourselves."[86] By refraining from analyzing the animal presence in such diaries an integral part of quotidian human experience is also being ignored.

MEMORIES AND CHILDREN'S FAMILY STORIES

However, often accounts of the animal-human relationship do remain in memories and stories transmitted down the years within families. If asked, people will often question their elderly relatives and elicit stories of animals within the wartime family. After interviewing her mother, Clare explained how Asta—whom we previously encountered "writing letters"—came into her mother's life and the family stories:

> During the war my mother's father was on a team firewatching at St Paul's. He returned home early one morning by way of Club Row, in the East End, where he was accosted by a ragged man selling a puppy. My grandfather said he only had a ten bob note, but he felt so sorry for the man and the puppy that he took it home. My grandmother was dismayed, having three children, her sick mother and a cat to cope with already, but being a kind soul she took on the puppy, a wire-haired Sealyham, who they called Asta, after the dog in William Powell & Mina Loy films.[87]

When the BBC initiated its website of war memories, companion animals were certainly present in public contributions. The role that Chum the cat played is a typical account as told by John Healey, who was 11 at the outbreak of war. John's daughter recorded his narrative. Tales of her own cat going to the vet for the "umpteenth time that year" had generated a childhood story not previously recorded. It was the juxtaposition of then and now—and of Chum, by way of contrast, only going twice to the vet in his entire life that prompted the memory.[88]

This specific time both of war and of a certain age was also a factor in the Mass Observation directive commissioned a few years ago on animal-human relationships. Because of the age of many of the respondents the time framework of the war did inevitably intrude. Animals were part not just of childhood but of a war childhood. Some of the recollections were humorous, such as the cat with a black smudge under his noise being called Hitler:

> This cat incidentally was the only one to be allowed into the living room during the day and I always found it asleep under Gran's chair when I came in from school in the afternoon. I think Gran favoured this one, because she often asked, "Does it want milk?" She laughed until she cried when patient Uncle B taught the animal to raise its right paw in some parody of a Hitler salute when it was given food.[89]

Such experiences were influential in later relationships. One respondent born in 1935 recalled:

> My Daddy gave me "The Photo book of pretty pets" for Christmas 1940 when I was six. I still have it. It features mainly dogs and cats, but also a budgerigar, mice, a rabbit, 2 young lambs, and young pig, a hen's chick, a small donkey, ponies naturally, and a monkey at London zoo's pet corner so there you have it. . . . The quality of my life has been enhanced by animals.[90]

If the life years between 18 and 21 are seen to be those usually embedded in the memory as one's own coming of political and emotional age,[91] then the ages between 5 and 15 might be characterized as those in which a defining animal-human relationship is created. Liberal Democrat politician Shirley Williams describes in her autobiography how as a teenager in 1944 she "notched up a resentment" towards her pacifist mother Vera Brittain, "conscientious but rather remote" for killing her little fox terrier puppy who would scream in panic during air raids.[92] Her mother's concern was not for the dog's emotional state: "My mother, sensible in most things, was convinced he might have convulsions and bite little Marian. In vain I begged, pleaded, shouted at her. She would not change her mind. So the terrified puppy was 'put to sleep' and I notched up a resentment I had never felt about being [evacuated] to the United States."[93] Such childhood memories are long-lasting even if sometimes not written down or verbally articulated until a researcher makes inquiries.

This book first explores the cat and dog massacre of September 1939 and then the animal and human relationship that followed as a shared and even common experience during a period of total war. Richard Overy's magisterial *The Bombing War* has persuasively analyzed the Second World War as a total war in which "all citizens had a part to play and encouraged the view that warrior identity was linked to new ideals of the civil warrior."[94] Total war involved a complete reorganization of the national economy, and necessitated incorporation of the civil population into the state's actions.[95] As King and Andrews have reminded us, the introduction of rationing of both food and clothing significantly extended the war into the domestic sphere. They argue that domestic activities that gave a sense of home and identity became problematic, particularly for women.[96] And although class differences were by no means eradicated, the lives of all people at work and at home were increasingly regulated from the availability of certain food to obstruction of light in windows to restrictions on travel. Unemployment fell, average earnings increased more than prices; conscription for women as well as men was introduced.[97] Sir Harold Scott, the commissioner of the Metropolitan Police from 1945 to 1953, declared, "Crime rose in wartime because there were quite simply, more laws to break."[98] Total war in practice certainly meant that thousands of people died: some 60,595 civilians were killed and 86,182 seriously injured by aerial bombing in Britain during the entire six years of the war.[99] It was not only humans who would die. Some 400,000 cats and dogs also lost their lives in the first week of the war—but not through "enemy" action but because of the decision of their individual owners.

A writing of histories of animals and the animal-human relationship on the Home Front is not a simple task. Any serious researcher is faced with a plethora of contradictions, counter explanations, and different accounts. Tom Harrisson, founder of Mass Observation, who was mindful of animals' role within the war, asserting that "cats play a remarkably large part in blitz memories,"[100] suggested in the 1970s that a "significant section of Britons, by the way, thought *first* [original emphasis] of their pets, canaries . . . included."[101] Although Harrisson chose to remember animals' importance in war he was aware that many readers would not think in the same way. It was incidental to a main story, it was "by the way" of the central narrative of the war. The usual Home Front story of the good "People's War" becomes disrupted when involving animals who are not there "by the way" but placed center stage. The 1939–45 war was—as with all wars—a time of rupture. This was evident in both negative *and* positive ways in the changing animal-human relationship. As this chapter has started to show, there exists material that can help new histories to be made. The war was a very particular moment that has never been repeated in the same way since in Britain.

But moments also have a context. The decision to go to war did not come out of thin air. And signs of a particular wartime animal-human relationship were seen before 1939. The next chapter discusses the animal-human relationship in the earlier decades of the twentieth century to explore the backdrop of the massacre and whether it could have been foreseen.

CHAPTER TWO

Being a Pet in the 1920s and 1930s: A Chronicle of a Massacre Foretold?

Let him come indoors . . . and associate with you, take him about with you whenever you go out, and you will discover what a surprising interest he can afford.[1]

HUMAN MEMORIES OF ANIMALS IN THE 1914–18 WAR AND THEIR RELEVANCE FOR THE 1939–45 WAR

People in the 1930s were different in many ways to their twenty-first century descendants—so too were the companion animals who lived with them. In writing about animal-human relationships in the nineteenth century Harriet Ritvo placed much emphasis on the role of class and gender in their construction. Thus cats, she argued, might be favored by those "who sneakingly sympathized with their desire for independence."[2] Indeed, if the nineteenth century witnessed animal protection campaigns initiated at least in part to "protect animals against the depredations of the lower classes," then the twentieth century saw an expansion of the role of animal charities to provide care for companion animals owned by such previously criticized working class people.[3] The growth of city clinics run by organizations such as the RSPCA or People's Dispensary for Sick Animals (PDSA) or the Our Dumb Friends League (now Blue Cross) demonstrate the growth not only in pet ownership amongst ordinary people but also in the willingness of people to seek veterinary care for their companions. While there may have been differences in the animal-human relationships between different classes and genders, the important factor in the 1920s and 1930s was that the sharing of domestic space between humans and certain animals *crossed* such divisions.

Of course, the 1939–45 war was not the first time in the twentieth century that war had problematized animal-human relationships. Recently, not least through fiction, the animal presence—particularly that of horses,

The . . .
People's .
Dispensary
for Sick .
Animals of
the Poor .

Head Dispensary :
542,
Commercial Road,
E. 1.

Head Office :
14, Clifford Street,
New Bond Street,
W. 1.

201,146
Sick Animals
treated in
ONE YEAR.

20 Branch Dispensaries.
2 Motor Caravans.

Our Caravan Dispensary at Work in the East End of London.

FIGURE 2.1 PDSA mobile clinic in East London c. 1920s (Libby Hall collection, Bishopsgate Institute)

mules, and donkeys—has been acknowledged during the 1914–18 war but less attention has been given to companion animals. Although humans alive in 1939 might well have remembered the events of a couple of previous decades this would not have been possible for animals, given their much shorter lifespans. No cat, dog, rabbit, or canary alive in the summer of 1939 would have experienced the First World War some twenty years before. What caused humans to act as they did towards a family pet was not related to the *existing* animal's previous wartime behavior as such. If experience of the previous war was relevant to behavior during the 1939–45 war it was because of human (and not specific animal) experience—as well as the general nature of the animal-human relationship that existed within a household during the '20 and '30s.

There were different human memories of the way animals had been treated during the 1914–18 war. Perhaps some people remembered the mood of Parliament when certain MPs vented their spleen against pets of all sorts. Sir Philip Magnus, a prominent promoter of vivisection, had encouraged (unsuccessfully) a dog ban in cities since such animals both consumed food and left London pavements unhygienic. "The undesirable," that is, stray dogs and mongrels rather than established breeds, he declared, "could be suppressed altogether."[4] In a similarly antipathetic spirit Ernest Pretyman, Conservative MP for Chelmsford in Essex, had declared of dogs, "Their usefulness varies greatly, and it is certainly desirable to reduce their numbers in urban districts, where many of them serve no useful purpose."[5] The eugenicism that had always underpinned Kennel Club canine differentiations was thus reasserted almost on human class lines. At that time the government had played on the fear—if not the reality—of wartime outbreaks of rabies to justify its concern about unregulated, mongrel, and "useless" dogs inhabiting cities.[6] In addition to categorizing dogs as either breeds or mongrels the government also attempted divisions between "utility" and "sentimentality," to some extent based on class and gender divisions. That is, the perceived canine relationship to humans would determine their treatment by the state. Thus dogs in the countryside were seen to provide a useful, economic, function. In this vein the National Sheep Breeders Association had called on the government to increase the dog tax: they believed that in the cities there were a "great many useless dogs" eating (human) food. [7] Even the guinea pig who, for decades, had been a pet and praised by Victorians as a clean, harmless creature now became treated as an item of consumption: "excellent as entrees in various stews with mushrooms cut up and stewed brown."[8]

Other people may also have remembered the fierce opposition by animal charities, and committed individual animal supporters, to any parliamentary attempt at suppression, the letters to the *Times*, and the way that people *had* carried on living with their animals, despite difficulties.[9] The National Canine Defence League (NCDL) had rebutted hostility towards dogs, arguing, "Dog haters are not punctuated by patriotism nor by the desire to safeguard the food of the people; they are attempting to take advantage of the country's position in order to attain their own selfish and vindictive ends."[10] People had made special efforts to feed their animals with what was available. Dog biscuits were not rationed as such but the Wheat, Rye and Rice Restriction Order of 1917 restricted their nutritional content. For some dogs, blood steamed until it solidified had sufficed as a meal.[11] For others there were fish trimmings and lights with a bit of carrot, parsnip, and potato from a man's own garden.[12] Dog owner John Sandeman explained that, apart from biscuits, his dog only ate waste gristle and skin that would otherwise go in the kitchen fire: "I feel that to sacrifice him would be a cruel injustice worthy of every resistance. The people who do not keep dogs are those who are raising the question but their cry is founded on ignorance."[13] However, although various MPs were hostile to dogs, there was never any directive either suggested—or passed—to kill owned pet dogs. In May 1918 the Chancellor of the Exchequer was forced to state in the Commons that "no order for the destruction of dogs, such as seems to have been anticipated in some quarters, is suggested."[14] As Philip Howell has carefully analyzed, campaigns never came close to wiping out either specific breeds or the dog community in general.[15]

Cats had also faced some hostility from those who saw them as an unnecessary expenditure. Thus the *Times* castigated an unspecified "cats' home" for taking in animals abandoned by Germans in London when the humans were interned or forced to flee. The cost was criticized: "when every penny is wanted for the Empire it is no time to maunder over cats."[16] Yet while some people saw cats as "wandering hoardes of carriers of disease,"[17] others recognized their value in preventing rodents eating stores or birds eating seeds in the fields. Of particular merit were "moggies" rather than felines bred for show. As one supporter explained, cats were preventing bubonic plague: rats destroyed £15,000,000 of food annually.[18] The very existence of cats created a focus for discussion about their utility and cost in the pages of the *Times*. Although taxing the alleged 15 million cats in the country was seen to be a possibility (albeit very difficult to implement), others suggested there should be an official department for the extermination of rats.[19] This would have the advantage of employing both wounded men as quasi cat supervisors and cats as rat catchers.[20] By way of contrast, the comfort of cats displayed in the Lambeth Cat Show of 1916 had brought forth hostile comments for their resting "on pink and blue silk cushions . . . all the cats were sleek and groomed. Several were fat."[21] To deflect such criticisms of the comfortable status of pedigree animals, profits were sent to the Star and Garter Home for wounded servicemen.[22] Contrasts were also drawn between the sleek and well-groomed dogs kept in obvious luxury and shown at the Lambeth pet dog show and the plight of men in dug-outs in winter: "After this, stories of people buying expensive dishes at restaurants for their dogs become credible."[23]

However, in a trope that would occur in later decades, defining benign treatment of animals as a civilized act, many individuals and animal charities had argued against hostility towards cats and dogs as a capitulation to "the enemy." As one diarist, deploring the "great deal of nonsense" about not feeding animals, wrote in April 1917, "Because we are fighting against brutes must we ourselves become brutes?"[24] The righteousness of the British imperial cause also entailed, it seems, behaving benignly towards companion animals. This was a theme that would reemerge in the 1939–45 war. Although some of the threads of arguments about the animal-human relationship would be started in the Great War, the ensuing decades were the time in which *patterns* of behavior for the interaction of humans and animals would be established. If humans changed—so did the animals who lived with us. As one historian has put it, "There have been massive shifts in the ways in which we live: the industrial revolution, urbanization, globalization—all have had and are having their impact on the lives of humans and animals. . . . Being a pet now is not the same as being a pet in 1800."[25] It was not only the relationship that was changed but the physical parameters of the space shared (or not) between humans and animals that in turn helped construct the relationship.[26]

BEING AN ANIMAL—AND DOMESTIC SPACE

According to the *Times* in 1939 the "only new domestic pet of the twentieth century" was the budgerigar, of whom three or four million were living in Britain by the Second World War.[27] Veterinary surgeon Brigadier John Clabby estimated that by 1939 in London alone there were some 2,000,000 dogs and cats, in addition to 50,000 horses and cattle and 24,000 sheep and pigs.[28] These figures may indicate the enduring nature of humans and animals living together in the same space but not the type of relationship or how that living took place.[29]

Dogs have been human companions for many thousands of years,[30] but their status, as defined by their physical place *within* (or outside) a house, was changing in the 1920s and 1930s.[31] Different animal charities and canine experts had different views about the appropriate location for a dog kept as a companion animal. The approach of Colonel Edwin Richardson, famous for training various dogs, especially Airedales, in the First World War, was significant. His book *British War Dogs, Their Training and Psychology* helped convey his approach and that of his wife, who also trained dogs. Mrs. Richardson had pleaded, for example, for the life of a bull mastiff offered to the War Dogs School, "so savage that it was feared nothing could be done with him," who had never been off a chain in four years. "She discerned that underneath the creature's savage behaviour there was a very highly-strung, sensitive nature, and that if confidence could be established the ferocity, which was really due to soreness of mind and fear, would vanish." She physically engaged with the dog over time: "her hand was laid on the large brown head, and permission was given for her to stroke the satin ears" and the chain was replaced by a lead.[32] Significantly, as Robert Kirk has recently discussed, Richardson believed that working with animals re-

FIGURE 2.2 RSPCA campaign for running chain c. 1930s (courtesy of RSPCA)

quired a special gift in the instructor, particularly choosing men who were fond of dogs and thus who would be able to relate productively towards them. The building of a relationship was key. Dogs needed to be trained: more importantly so did handlers working with them.[33]

Arthur Croxton-Smith, chairman of the Kennel Club, adapted some of this approach for peacetime, being highly critical of the practice of chaining dogs outdoors, "under conditions that are disgraceful, which approach very nearly to the borderland of actual cruelty. Have we no better recompense to offer for the service given so freely than a short length of chain with an old barrel at one end of it?" Like Mrs. Richardson, he concluded, "Is it surprising that he becomes morose and savage?"[34] More radically, against the norms of the day,[35] Croxton-Smith also seriously questioned the place where dogs should live: "When it is not convenient for the dog to live in the house, one should decide at once against any of the toys."[36] Even if a dog was primarily a "working dog" such as a Labrador, by changing the physical location of the dog a different animal-canine relationship could ensue: "Let him come indoors . . . and associate with you, take him about with you whenever you go out, and you will discover what a surprising interest he can afford."[37] That is, if the human acted empathetically by bringing a dog into her own space, she (as well as the dog) would be emotionally rewarded. This opposition to making a space outside the home for dogs was echoed by the NCDL that redefined the dog as "by nature a freedom loving animal," thereby arguing that the chaining of dogs was "not only cruel but injurious to the dog's health and tends to make a good-tempered dog savage."[38] When a pamphlet issued by the Tail-Waggers Club — that had enrolled some 400,000 dog owners (and their dogs) with the motto "I help my pals" — stated a dog may be a blessing in the home, this was not just a metaphor but a way of refiguring what was starting to happen in this space between human and dog.[39] What was being fostered here was a relationship based on different needs but also mutual benefits.

Designated spaces inside or outside the home were important too for other human-animal relationships.[40] Little attention was paid, however, to a designated place for a cat. Cats went into different parts of the house depending on their roles — mouse hunter, say, or affection giver — but cats were not expected to have a designated space in the same way that dogs were. This suggests not only human ideas of feline independence but also the feline *practice* of being wary of settling in one place for too long.

BREEDING AND THE NATURE OF EXISTENCE

The breeding (or not) of different types of companion animals meant that different physical and emotional characteristics were developed. Human intervention resulted in animals who were compatible with contemporary human requirements. Human choice specifically affected the types — and numbers — of dogs who were bred irrespective of the "mate choices" of an individual animal. The very physical form of a canine companion was often different to today.[41] Great Danes, declared one critic of excessive breeding, became "enlarged till they might almost be taken for donkeys."[42] After the

1914–18 war Alsatians were so popular that for a time they topped the breeds registered with the Kennel Club: "His fortunes were pushed by returning service men" who had encountered them on the battlefields of Europe.[43] Ironically, in order to "extend" the breeding base in the 1920s, dogs would be imported from Germany.[44] The popularity of the dachshund, also seen as a German dog, unsurprisingly declined in the 1914–18 war with a "catastrophic fall" in registrations with the Kennel Club.[45] Since Kennel Club dogs—unlike mongrels—were specifically bred at the whim of humans the human attitude had a specific effect on the very existence of particular types of animals—and genetic changes.[46]

Cats too were specifically bred both for appearance and intelligence. As Colonel Richardson wrote in 1929, "How much more intelligent cats have been since they have been cultivated by those persons of better education who are desirous of improving the different breeds of the species."[47] Siamese cats, for example, were rare.[48] When publisher Michael Joseph specifically chose to acquire a Siamese kitten, Charles, in August 1930 (in addition to his tortoiseshell tabby Minna),[49] he described the breed as at that time. "Today [1943] the Siamese cat is fairly well known by sight in most parts of England, but in 1930 there were many people who had never seen one." Thus an early story is told of the train ticket collector mistaking Charles for a marmoset.[50] Yet Joseph still found it necessary to describe for the wartime readers the distinctive features of Siamese in some detail, including the statement that the "Siamese voice is utterly unlike that of an ordinary cat."[51]

THE DIET AND MEDICAL TREATMENT EXPERIENCED BY COMPANION ANIMALS IN THE 1920S AND 1930S

Human food and leisure activities were more greatly influenced by the times of the year than today: so were animals' existences determined to a great extent by the seasons. According to Bob Martin, the dog supplies company, dogs' blood changed according to the season, overheating in the summer and needing to be pure in the autumn when dogs should be growing their winter coats.[52] The PDSA advised that March was the "month of winds. Never dawdle when exercising your dog, and encourage him to walk briskly."[53] The approach adopted by the NCDL was particularly benign in its approach: "Do give him a warm meal on winter days. He's not a faddy sort of fellow, but he likes to feel warm inside. . . . Do let him come in the house on cold and wet days. He does not really like lying in the mud and rain." This is undoubtedly an anthropomorphic approach but was also

aimed at changing people's behavior towards dogs (rather than just expect-
ing a dog to obey). Thus the rationale for not dragging a dog along forcibly
was not that it was injurious to the dog (which it clearly was) but "people
may think you are stealing them."[54]

Animals might have been sharing "human space" inside and outside the
home but there tended to be a distinction in the food that animals and humans ate. "Nonhuman" food had been specifically manufactured since the
mid-nineteenth century.[55] But pet animals were usually fed at the same time
as humans, whatever their class, thus effecting a sharing of some human
food—a habit even Queen Victoria practiced with her favorite dog, Islay.[56]
Thus Chum, an ordinary moggy adopted in the '30s primarily to catch mice,
was routinely treated to human food:

> We didn't buy any special food for it at the time, my mother used to more or
> less dish up a bit of meat and two veg., like we had for lunch. It might get an
> odd treat now and again. We used to have the Cats' Meat Man come round . . .
> but we never used to do that 'cause our cat had roast beef and Yorkshire pud.[57]

This practice was unusual: The food a cat was seen to need depended to
some extent on its particular feline status. [58] Cats bred for show required a
very specific diet.[59] Cats in a cattery were seen as almost different species
to a "moggy." While such cats were kept within a home they performed a
particular role: "In nearly every household there is a cat, kept either as a
pet or in order to destroy mice and rats." Linked to the idea of use value
was the notion of independence: a cat "can generally fend for itself."[60] In
addition to scraps, cats were fed raw or cooked horsemeat known as "cat's
meat" sold by street sellers, who also dropped skewers through letterboxes.

Dogs, however, were never expected to fend for themselves but were
routinely fed on types of offal. As one Mass Observation respondent has
recalled, there was "a constant supply of heavy saucepans all bubbling away
on the kitchen range, and containing a nauseous concoction of offal." Every
butcher's shop in the 1920s displayed cattle innards known as "guggles,"
the digestive tract from slaughtered cattle declared not fit for human consumption. The family Pekingese ate the stewed guggles tipped out onto
newspaper on the floor and the dogs seemed to thrive.[61]

Companion animals were not the medicalized animals of today—nor
were humans in Britain in the years before the establishment of the NHS
in 1948. Patent medicines from firms such as Sherley or Bob Martin were
available from the turn of the nineteenth / twentieth century but professional, veterinary, understanding of the ailments of companion animals

FIGURE 2.3 Cat's meat seller with feline customer c. 1920s (LHW 5-29, Bishopsgate Institute)

(and their suitable treatment) was at a rudimentary stage during the early decades of the twentieth century.[62] Fortuitously, veterinary surgeon Frederick Hobday had developed a small animal practice in upmarket Kensington, the experience of which would prove valuable in the development of the "Poor People's Clinic" at the Royal Veterinary College in Camden Town where he would become principal in the 1930s.[63] Generally, animals' lives were fragile since they could not necessarily be prolonged by veterinary intervention. Dogs were susceptible to distemper, a highly contagious and potentially fatal disease, that "carrie[d] off scores of dogs every year." Caused by a virus that affected the alimentary and respiratory tract and the nervous system, dogs were often dead within months of contracting the disease.[64] Thus a Newfoundland puppy, Bruce, died after a few months from distemper. Even at the age of 82 one man could recall very well his childhood reaction to Bruce's death at the time: "Again devastated!"[65] This prevalent disease was a common condition until it started to be prevented through vaccination in the 1930s,[66] affecting dogs irrespective of status or breed. In her account of dogs in the couple's lives, Ada Galsworthy wrote of six "enchanting" puppies, parented by Old English sheepdogs Biz and Joey, and named after characters in husband John's plays:

> Their babyhood was most joyous and healthy; but alas! All but one died at various times from that horrible form of distemper, or distemper's aftermath, meningitis. Fleur, who survived, was . . . of inferior size and quality . . . but she had brains in plenty.[67]

Although dogs (and cats) were not seen to be routinely subjected to veterinary treatment or management it was nevertheless expected that humans engaged with them to effect physical well-being. A 1930s manual for pet owners stated, "The ordinary individual is generally quite ignorant of the right way to care for his pet in health, or to treat it in disease."[68] Yet the sale of not only canine nail cutters but also tooth forceps for the use of dog owners indicates a hands-on approach—and the expectation that dogs would tolerate this, of course.[69]

The unqualified animal enthusiast was not necessarily less knowledgeable than one who had trained as a veterinary surgeon, which often proved threatening to qualified veterinary surgeons. Unusually one veterinary surgeon observed in a visit to the London headquarters of the PDSA where there were more than 100 animals waiting to be seen:

> The gentleman I saw alleviating the suffering of these animals was a "quack," but he had a better means of studying the sickness of animals than were ever accorded to me at the Royal Veterinary College. He had 30 years' experience attending small animals; the work he was doing was excellent; he handled his animals with a great deal more care and skill than many veterinary surgeons I have seen.[70]

This was a problem for the veterinary profession, if not impecunious animal owners, and there were lengthy disputes between vets and animal charities, particularly the PDSA, about the employment of nonqualified staff.[71]

Rudimentary "treatment" was provided within the family. Thus Blackie's kittens were first drowned and then her bad tooth was removed by pincers operated by the man of the household—inevitably without anesthetics.[72] Introducing his *Index of Diagnosis (Clinical and Radiological) for the Canine and Feline Surgeon* of 1939, experienced veterinary surgeon W. Hamilton Kirk commented on the lack of attention to cats and dogs during his own training. He had drawn on cases brought to the Royal Veterinary College clinic, rather than his own private practice, to develop diagnosis of small animal problems.[73] He emphasized that cats needed not just medication but a "kindly word and a soothing hand." Depending on their condition, barley water, milk with arrowroot, or aspirin could be effective.[74] This reinforces not only the general *absence* of benign human approaches to cats but also the lack of veterinary knowledge: Human empathy and comparable treatment almost substituted for clinical diagnosis and medication. Drawing on contemporary understandings of how to treat ill *humans* at a time when potions, pills, and self-diagnosed remedies for human conditions were the norm, much attention was paid to "nursing." Anthropomorphism in the proposed treatment of cats was more pronounced than in advice for dogs. Thus a cat showing any signs of a cold "should at once be put by itself in a sunny room, not too hot, but comfortably warm. It will be all the better if the room is not very large, so long as it is not draughty, as inhalations often do great good."[75] This approach was not necessarily against a cat's best interests: Here a cat was depicted as a sensitive being who could not tolerate pain for any length of time and who "seldom seem[s] to realise that what is being done is intended for their benefit."[76] Rather than dismiss this as a simple human projection this might also be read as an attempt to raise the status of cats, who tended to be treated dismissively. It was also a demonstration of the understanding of the "lay" role in creating a particular cross-species rapport.[77]

Since veterinary surgeons knew little of small animals' ailments and also considered such beings of less status than valuable horses or cattle, who provided most of their livelihood for those working in rural areas, many would not routinely visit homes to treat small animals.[78] But by 1938 Frederick Hobday, then former principal of the Royal Veterinary College, noted there was starting to be a change in big cities where a dog, cat, canary, or parrot, "whose value is almost entirely sentimental," would be treated either by privately paid vets or in the clinics of animal charities.[79] Thus the RSPCA clinic in Poplar in east London reported treating dogs and cats as well as goats, tortoises, parrots, a marmoset, and a duck during its second year of operation in 1937.[80] Reporting fewer animals being killed than in the previous year, its local Annual Report of 1937 optimistically interpreted this as indicating that "the public are taking a keener interest in the welfare of their animals for they are now brought to the clinic at the first signs of illness."[81]

COMPANION ANIMALS AND BEING, AGENCY, AND INDEPENDENCE BETWEEN THE WARS

Inevitably degrees of agency and independence that would prove to be so relevant during the war were also exhibited in different animals — with varying responses by humans — during the 1930s. Thus a 1934 manual, encouraging benign treatment of cats, described a cat as a "naturally independent creature" who "can generally fend for itself." The latter remark had implications, of course, for how and when the cat was fed.[82] But independence was not required, at least in the same way, in horses. Drawing on his lifetime experience working with horses, Pegasus emphasized the need for "balance" as the "sine qua non" of riding. This aspect of a relationship crosses time. A horse needed to move in a controlled way at the required pace but the rider had to adapt her own movement and adjust her own weight in reaction to the horse's behavior.[83] Acting both independently and in response to each other was what was required. Thus Trump may have bucked gloriously while moving through Hyde Park, but Laurance Holman, the human rider, needed to learn what to do: "He's a grand ride now, and we well understand one another."[84] The horse's movement was not inappropriate: The human needed to learn how to respond appropriately. What changed over time was the *way* such balance was to be effected: use the voice, said Pegasus, and the whip sparingly but when necessary don't tickle him but "give him a sharp cut or two he will remember."[85]

Dogs were more complex in what was required of their relationships with humans. Even if they roamed during the day they were nevertheless obliged to be with humans, rather than living autonomously, if they wished to be fed.[86] Walking alongside a human usually meant a dog being inhibited by being put on a lead. In addition dogs' defecation was controlled. Thus the Tail-Waggers explained the need to train a dog to defecate in a gutter: "Don't permit the dog to foul the public footpaths but train him to use the gutters." Such "fouling" was exacerbated by dogs who were not under the immediate control of a human being turned out first thing in the morning to "roam at will through market places" without supervision. Instead of roaming freely, explicitly a dog was a creature to be trained: Training would ensure that a dog behaved as a human required, and would lie down to order—and not seek a place in front of the fire in winter.[87] This suggests, of course, that dogs would not act in such ways, without training. Such notions of appropriate control were not being encouraged by an organization hostile to dogs but from a new group—the Tail-Waggers—seeking to promote a particular type of dog ownership and to create a community of like-minded people.[88]

Changing human attitudes towards dogs' autonomy meant the creation of the definition of a dog as a loyal friend who positively enjoyed a human's company. This idea had been strengthened during parts of the nineteenth century when dogs who were allowed to walk on their own throughout the city streets nevertheless consciously took a decision to return home. Most famously Greyfriars Bobby had become well known not simply for sleeping on his dead owner's grave but because he wandered on his own throughout the city of Edinburgh every day—and returned to the same place.[89] That dogs were so engaged with public space implied that they were free to create their own routes through the metropolitan landscape, unfettered by human restraint: affection—and obedience—brought them back to the human. [90] By the 1930s dogs were obliged to be trained as part of an ownership enshrined in law—through the wearing of a collar (and payment of tax).[91] The dog's role now was to be bound to a human family rather than walking independently. If the cat was seen as an independent free spirit about whom little care was needed, a dog was seen as needing human attention and direction.

ANIMAL-ANIMAL RELATIONSHIPS

Clearly dogs and cats could and did have relationships with other animals as well as humans, though this was not necessarily seen sympathetically by humans. As one early writer wrote dismissively, "Left to herself [a female cat] will either have constant families of mongrel kittens, growing poor, and, if a Persian, coatless and ugly after each litter, or she will wander about, bring in strange cats, and perhaps finally get stolen."[92] Neutering was less common than now. The reasons for this were varied—and had little to do with regard for animal agency or choice. Veterinary surgeons were not required by the Animals Anaesthetics Act of 1919 to use general anesthetics in performing castration on male kittens up to six months of age, although some veterinarians declared it to be more humane. Indeed the law did not change in this respect until the 1960s.[93] Neutering female cats was a more complicated procedure since it involved the use of chloroform that was difficult for a surgeon to administer accurately. Side effects could include hemorrhage, peritonitis, and shock.[94] Thus even cats of the wealthy, such as those living with film actor James Mason, were not neutered.[95]

Rather than existing just as an individual animal relating to a human, cats did also turn to their own kind for companionship: This could be seen negatively by campaigning organizations, as this was particularly observed when humans had abandoned them. Such cats performed the function subsequently acquired by urban foxes decades later by living either "largely on refuse" or pigeons, mice, and rats: "in most parts of London the rats have been driven underground into the sewers by the warfare of the cats."[96] Cats seeking refuge in the London Institution for Lost and Starving Cats and Dogs in Camden Town were relating to each other in the absence of humans. Outside a home they lived in space differently or, as the *Animal Pictorial* put it, "strays lurk out of sight in dark corners; some hundreds of thousands have to be destroyed every year." [97] Emotive language aside, this suggests that far from cats routinely living with discrete human family groups, thousands were living in almost "animal places" within the same city.[98] Some images were seen worthy of capturing as photographs as they were not of the "norm" of a feline relationship to humans—but to other cats. Yet despite such criticism, we can understand—as the Algers have more recently analyzed in their study of American cats placed in shelters—that cats in the past *did* relate to each other in groups rather than simply acting as individuals.[99] In contrast to human children, animal offspring who survived rarely lived with their parents. Cats and dogs who were bought from breeders were often not seen before purchase—even though this was discouraged by animal welfarists.[100]

ANIMAL DEATH IN THE 1930S

Despite the best efforts of animal charities and the veterinary profession, even at the end of their lives spent with a human family, animals were not necessarily killed humanely. A lifelong animal lover has vividly recalled the way that old, unwanted, or diseased animals were disposed of. He recalls dogs and cats taken to the fire station:

> While we watched and waited, cats were put into a cabinet then one of the fireman would turn on the gas while peering through the glass top. Dogs were attached to a special collar then made to stand on a metal plate before a switch was thrown. It was a cry often heard after some mongrel or feline misdemeanour: "It'll be the first station of you next time, me lad!"

He reflects, "It wasn't that there was more cruelty or callousness then but just the way things were."[101] Animal misdemeanors could indeed be punished with death. The 1930s story of Sprig, a Welsh sheep dog, is not unique. Here was a dog with brown and white markings and "lovely dark brown eyes." He was not chained outside the house but lived inside mainly in the kitchen or garden. He ate his own dog biscuits and also shared the same midday food as the humans. But one day the dog with the lovely eyes bit the little boy quite badly "and his fate was sealed":

> Before the time came for his departure for putting down I sat with him in the garage nursing his head with tears in my eyes. I blamed myself for telling Mother of what had happened. However the deed was done. I suppose he would be with us three or four years.[102]

Newly born "mongrel" cats and dogs were routinely killed. Kittens were drowned or, you would "take them by the hind legs and sling them against the wall—which was probably about comparable with drowning day olds. Spaying female cats was a new operation so kittens were very plentiful."[103] Thus ended Blackie's offspring in the 1930s: "her babies were drowned by grandad."[104] Sometimes killing did not go to plan: No doubt the reason that this particular drowning incident was recalled:

> I have never been able to forget the day when dad miscalculated the length of string between the kitten and the iron and how the little ball of fluff madly kicked its way back to the surface. The worst of all was in hearing dad whimpering as he pushed the kitten back down and held it under until it stopped its struggles.[105]

This suggests that although the practice was a norm it was not necessarily performed without mixed emotions. Another cat lover has recently explained: "I remember my grandmother saying, as we passed the canal bridge, that's where your grandfather used to drown kittens." It was presented as "a piece of historical information." It was not even just a family history but one that was a part of a wider landscape where an almost commonplace act routinely occurred.[106]

UNDERSTANDING THE PSYCHOLOGY OF ANIMALS—AND THEIR FUNCTION

The language of psychology employed by Richardson in his training would be increasingly used in dog "management" in the post–First World War period. (The term management did not appear in similar books on cat treat-ment). As one book put it, "Dogs may not be capable of reasoning, using the term in the exact sense in which it is employed by psychologists; but, at any rate, we must concede that they are altruistic."[107] A jocular work of 1939 quipped, "Psycho-analysis hasn't as yet hit the dog world, but in time we will undoubtedly have our Freuds and Jungs,"[108] but by that de-cade Frederick Cousens, the veterinary surgeon to King George V's dogs, could nevertheless include a new chapter on psychology in a standard dog management book, suggesting it was "the first time that the dog's character and nature have been approached from this point of view."[109] While not-ing that "we cannot . . . without becoming dogs, perfectly understand the dog mind," nevertheless Cousens encouraged the possibility of this since "common sense abundantly suffices to assure us that it really has certain affinities to our own."[110] He listed some 17 active canine powers, such as memory, imagination, and emotions, in which he suggested that the dog and humans were similar.[111] Cousens maintained that dogs communicated between themselves and had their own language. Dogs, he said, often "ex-celled man," namely in being a friend, and added the aphorism, "Friend-ship consists in being a friend, not in having a friend."[112] This approach, suggesting that it was indeed possible for humans to understand dogs with-out becoming dogs, is rather different to some of the more recent philo-sophical debates on the topic. It does, however, indicate the emphasis on the importance of a *relationship*: both dog *and* human are active participants in building this.[113] Although veterinary work at that time had not advanced to the sophisticated twenty-first-century analysis of emotional states, never-theless the first traces of such an approach were being developed and would be strengthened during the war.

In the mid war period—as today—companion animals were required to perform a particular function for humans.[114] Particularly in working class households a cat was being given houseroom in return for "services ren-dered." This relationship was not dissimilar to that of master and servant with the power clearly residing in the human running the family.[115] Seen in this way, a cat was almost an employee, rather than a focus of affection: "The house cat requires little in the way of food beyond scraps from the table, a saucer of milk and a pan of clean cold water, renewed daily."[116] As Dr. Mary Brancker, who started practicing as a veterinary surgeon in the 1930s, has explained, in harsh tones, "Many were just 'things' and they were taken for granted. They had cats for the rats, but not so much as pets." In one 1930s childhood home above a fish and chip shop, "It was always necessary to have a cat or cats about the place to keep away rodents."[117] Recalling his childhood cats, one elderly man has mused, "Indeed I must have appreciated at even that early age that they were, as you might say, on the payroll and had to earn their keep with no time for friendly overtures."[118] Another has commented, there was always a cat, "it was not so much a pet for us, more a deterrent to any mice who felt like taking up residence with us."[119]

A different narrative recounted of a memory of a child playing with both a cat and her kittens during the '30s childhood, however, reminds us that not all cats were treated so starkly:

> A particular delight was when our cat had four kittens, and no greater pleasure than to have them all jump on my lap and settle to sleep. I usually fed our cats, sometimes bought them tins of salmon out of my pocket money as a treat, and sometimes if there was no food for them, made minute Marmite sandwiches for them.[120]

Yet the human understanding of felines (and canines) was by no means intuitive: Manuals were needed for humans to understand animals. (They are still needed today.)[121] Many manuals of the early twentieth century had been devoted to discussing how to train a cat to kill mice, thereby challenging the idea that this was instinctive feline behavior. That is, *people* would have to perform in particular ways if they wished a cat to provide this service. Some manuals suggested that a cat needed encouragement — by not being fed for a day.[122] Others debunked this tactic.[123] Being desperately hungry, explained one manual, "is very likely to make a thief of puss, and draw him illicitly to the larder shelf or the kitchen table."[124] One might draw the conclusion from such contradictory comments that some cats did — and some didn't — kill mice and rats (and, perhaps more significantly, that people did not necessarily understand that this was an individual trait). However, while training cats to kill rodents was seen as possible, training to walk in particular routes was not.[125]

When Sir Robert Gower, chair of the national RSPCA, suggested in 1937 that there was a "general improvement abroad in the treatment of animals," he was not contradicted.[126] By 1938 its *Annual Report* noted that there were fewer cases of serious cruelty than in 1937. Animal suffering was caused, it suggested, more often through starvation and persistent neglect rather than sudden violence caused by anger, drink, or the like.[127] However, human ill treatment towards animals was still a persistent theme in the relationship. Some of this neglect had been tackled in different ways by various animal charities. These included membership of the Tail-Waggers Club, for which all dogs were eligible after their owners had paid 2 shillings and received an identity disc medallion for their dog and a manual of advice.[128] The Cats Protection League was also established in 1928, "to raise the status of cats generally" and to stress that cats "have hearts which feel, and suffer, as well as bodies which need our care."[129] In due course, imitating the Tail-Waggers, the League would also establish its own "tailwavers" scheme.[130] That an organization specifically aimed at feline welfare was not created until over a century after the RSPCA and decades after the NCDL indicates the lower standing of cats within civil society — and their lack of legal attention and protection.

So I am arguing that the animal-human relationships that existed in the prewar period were of their time when particular breeds of animals existed and when there was a defined role for a cat as, say, a mouser, or a dog as a trained walking companion. It was also a time in which women and men of all classes were starting to be more responsive towards companion animals. There seemed to be a growing understanding and human empathy towards such animals, albeit one somewhat less demonstrative or medicalized than today. It is true that work on animal emotions was not well developed but the references to psychology in relation to dogs indicated new ways of thinking. Importantly the word relationship can, I suggest, be used legitimately to characterize new developments.

STATE PROCRASTINATION AND VETERINARY LOBBYISTS

I have focused so far on the human-animal relationship as practiced in domestic spaces. But I am very conscious that state institutions would construct an explicit framework for people and animals during the war. This was also the case, of course, in earlier decades. Various attempts to introduce new legislation to protect animals were generally unsuccessful. In particular a move to exempt dogs from vivisection failed despite massive public support. MPs such as Thomas Groves, who represented West Ham in East London for over 20 years, regularly brought to light the number of experiments conducted annually on animals.[131] Those vivisected would include dogs unsold at the Sunday animal market at London's Club Row, who would be taken away by "the man with the van [who] soon became known as the 'knife man.'"[132] By 1926 a million people (four times the number needed today to get a motion debated in Parliament) had signed a petition, initiated by the NCDL, to promote a bill exempting dogs from vivisection.[133] More successful were some improvements in the welfare of animals who were not companion animals. By 1933—and after three previous attempts—obligatory pre-stunning of animals killed for food was enshrined in law.[134] After much campaigning for changes in the way animals were treated in circuses, rodeos, and music halls, the Performing Animals Defence League helped ensure that legislation restricted the number of foreign trainers allowed to work in Britain on the grounds that their methods were particularly cruel.[135]

However, the lack of attention paid to the status of companion animals and their welfare would prove significant in the (lack of) preparations in the buildup to war. While the state had been planning some protection of the civilian population in the event of aerial bombardment, primarily to prevent panic, nonhuman animals—of whatever kind—were excluded from such discussion.[136] In particular the government was reluctant to intervene in the treatment of animals kept as pets.[137] There were various reasons for this hesitation. Public disquiet over the government's attitude towards domestic animals in the 1914–18 war certainly played a part. As discussed earlier, Parliament had then discussed killing dogs (but not cats)—but this had met with public disapproval. The police too were mindful of their role during the previous war when the period in which stray animals were kept to be reclaimed (before being killed) was reduced from seven to three days. It was undoubtedly a potential problem area that the police wished to avoid in the forthcoming war.[138] The Commissioner of Metropolitan Police decided in March 1939 that the position of animals was not a priority: "In view of the many more important duties which the Police will be required to perform in the event of an air attack it will not be possible for them to extend, or even to maintain to the full, their peace time activities in connection with straying animals."[139]

The state's caution in considering domestic animals in wartime was also influenced by the contemporary low status of companion animals, especially cats. Pointedly, one of the aims of the Cats Protection League was to raise the status of cats as well as to create better understanding of these animals as highly intelligent and sensitive.[140]Another factor in the reluctance to make wartime provision was the status of the veterinary profession—a profession that seemed unable to exert sufficient influence on the government to act in good time.[141] Vets had previously lobbied for government action. Colonel Robert Stordy, a leading veterinarian, had directed missions to Spain during the Civil War in 1936 on behalf of the RSPCA. The absence of cats and dogs had been noted in Madrid as well as the eating of the flesh of killed mules.[142] Such knowledge had led the National Veterinary Medical Association (NVMA), the national voice of the veterinary profession, to approach the Home Office to urge it to establish an organization to protect animals in wartime.[143]

In the two years before the declaration of war in September 1939, the veterinary profession and the RSPCA did take initiatives to make preparations for animals in war—in the absence of state activity. A committee consisting of the NVMA and the Royal Army Veterinary Corps—but not animal welfare charities, the organizations that were more likely to deal, at that time, with the health of small companion animals—was established to advise the Home Secretary on "questions arising in connection with the protection of domestic and captive animals" in the event of air attacks.[144] As the Home Office gave scant attention to this,[145] the NVMA prepared papers on the effects of gas attacks on animals (and the possible knock-on effect on humans) and also the air raid measures that would need to be taken to protect animals.[146] For its part, the RSPCA, also concerned about ongoing delays in any official government response, held a conference in April 1939 on practical air raid precautions for horses in towns, with representatives of 19 organizations, including the NVMA and bodies responsible for horse welfare.[147] The emphasis was on working horses involved in the transport of goods (rather than those kept solely for leisure purposes) and also the consequences for humans if horses panicked in an air raid. In London alone some 40,000 such animals were still working. Subsequently, with the introduction of petrol rationing, constraints on horses for transport would be lifted and more would again work in the metropolis.[148] As the veterinary profession commented, "The horse is staging a come-back."[149] The conference considered the effect of gas on horses and ways of dealing with out-of-control horses but cats, dogs, and caged birds, "pet" animals, were not part of its remit.[150]

Despite behind the scenes lobbying, it was not until August 1939 that an umbrella organization was created in the form of the National Air Raid Precautions Animals' Committee (NARPAC),[151] established through the ARP department of the Home Office by the Lord Privy Seal, "to advise on all problems affecting animals in wartime."[152] Significantly there was no government money for the organization and, in due course, this would lead to internal friction and the collapse of the body into its constituent parts. The lack of government funding seems to have been influenced by the view of the Commissioner of Metropolitan Police, Commander Pulling, telling civil servants in April 1939:

One is well aware of Animal Societies' internecine politics, but I have been assured by the Secretaries of most of these Societies that they are anxious to offer their full resources and services *with no charge on public funds* . . . at a risk of being indiscreet, I may tell you that most of them are feeling considerably hurt that their offers made many months ago to the Home Office have, as yet, received little more than bare acknowledgement.[153] (my emphasis)

NARPAC was a unique organization. With H. E. Dale, a civil servant in the Home Office, as the chair, representatives of veterinary professional organizations held key positions. Colonel Robert Stordy—who also served on the RSPCA council—was the chief officer.[154] The deputy was Professor Woolridge, then honorary secretary of the NVMA. Others involved included Harry Steele-Bodger, president of the NVMA, who joined NARPAC as liaison officer and Mr. L. T. Foster, representing the Metropolitan Police.[155] But NARPAC also included representatives of animal welfare organizations such as the Battersea Dogs Home, PDSA, NCDL, ODFL/Blue Cross, RSPCA, and the Home of Rest for Horses.[156] (The Cats Protection League was not invited, again indicating the lowly status of both the organization and felines at that time.) The Battersea Dogs Home, PDSA, and NCDL were organizations focused totally upon pets, particularly in the poorer parts of cities, where the veterinary profession had few premises. But companion animals were not the main remit of NARPAC. Its official focus was on animals deemed to be of *economic* use, which tended to mean those living predominantly in rural areas. NARPAC's broad objects were utilitarian, namely to conserve animals of economic value—alive or dead; provide and protect food supplies for essential animals (transport and farm animals); protect human beings from panic-stricken or gas-contaminated animals; and prevent and alleviate animal suffering.[157] In practice, it was envisaged that the main task of the scheme would be to salvage animals, badly injured as a result of enemy action, as meat for human consumption in a regulated way thus preventing black market profiteering.[158] For the first time ever, however, professional veterinary surgeons, representatives of the police, and animal charities were brought together in one official body—each of whom had different relationships to a range of animals. What was being covered by the word "animal" organizationally was defined in particular, narrow, ways.[159] No specific attention was given to companion animals since, at this time, they were not deemed "essential" in upholding morale, finding bombed humans, or providing emotional support. These roles *would* be recognized officially in due course—but only once the war progressed.

Just a few days before war was declared, Colonel Stordy was asked to make arrangements "for the care of animals in the event of air raids."[160] Veterinary surgeons were asked to act without payment and were told they would be given only out-of-pocket expenses. Nevertheless initially 750 veterinary surgeons signed up to this "little-appreciated form of national service."[161] The lateness in setting up NARPAC would have deleterious consequences for many thousands of cats and dogs at the start of the war.[162] NARPAC estimated that there were between six and seven million dogs and cats in the country, more than fifty-six million poultry, and some thirty-seven million, five-hundred thousand farm animals: "That is to say there are nearly twice as many domestic animals as there are human beings."[163] It specifically encouraged people to take animals with them if they were moving to the country, and it argued explicitly *against* animal slaughter:

> Those who are staying at home should not have their animals destroyed. Animals are in no greater danger than human beings, and the NARPAC plans . . . will ensure that if your animal is hurt it will be quickly treated, or put out of its pain if it is too badly hurt to be cured. Another very strong point against destroying animals is that they play an extremely important part in keeping down rats and mice in our cities.[164]

However, NARPAC was late issuing advice: veterinary professionals themselves also left their own guidance to very late. Only in the last week of August 1939 did vets officially suggest that people send their animals into the country in advance of war, if possible, or have them placed in kennels.[165] Although these options would have applied to the more wealthy, there were also evacuation and informal schemes available to those without financial resources. However, it was not until September 16th—over a week after the killing of some 400,000 cats and dogs in London—that the *Veterinary Record* issued advice to veterinary surgeons listing arguments they might use to dissuade people from having their pets killed. These included the following: dogs and cats could not distinguish between gunfire and thunder; if an owner and animal shared a space there was no greater risk to the animal than to the human; animals could be evacuated— and this argument was paired with details of the scheme being organized by Nina, Duchess of Hamilton.[166]

As the war progressed there would be a belated recognition by all parties involved that the word animal did not just mean horses and cattle or something for humans to eat but the word embraced companion animals. This failure to acknowledge in timely fashion the presence of dogs, cats, budgerigars, and other companion animals would have severe repercussions for such animals, especially in London during the first week of September 1939. Although the state was not directly responsible for the decision of people to kill their pets, its lack of action made it easier for a positive animal-human relationship to be so drastically broken in September 1939.

CHAPTER THREE

September 1939: No Human Panic. 400,000 Animals Killed in Four Days

To destroy a faithful friend when there is not need to do so, is yet another way of letting war creep into your home.[1]

The declaration of war on September 3rd evoked "a sense of relief shot through with anxious expectation."[2] Many contemporary accounts analyzed the war, particularly on the Home Front, from a psychological and psychotherapeutic perspective. Psychology in warfare was "inextricably linked," as Mathew Thomson has elaborated, "to the defence of a democratic way of life."[3] The war served to promote and alter the practice of psychology, "producing new ways of calculating the relations between human subjectivity and administrative objectives."[4] Psychologists paid attention to the value of "people doing things." They had argued that civilians, unlike trained soldiers, would be unable to picture realistically what air raids would mean and thus would suffer "forced passivity without any means of escape or retaliation." This might result in directing emotions not towards the unseen enemy but towards "his own side."[5] But as the famous historian of social administration, Richard Titmuss, would later state, "fear of air attack was worse than the reality."[6] One solution to counter "isolationist individualism," particularly in London, was the creation of tasks to combat feelings of helplessness.[7] Wilfred Bion, the future psychoanalyst, who worked at the Tavistock clinic during the war, stressed it was important to feel involved not just at work but at home. Here the "head of a unit" needed to act the most responsibly.[8] On the first weekend of war people in the London area did indeed "do things." These included sending away children to the apparent safety of the country, making blackout curtains, digging up flower beds to create vegetable patches—and killing the family pet.

Psychologists had not anticipated that such acts of "doing" would involve killing animals on one's "own side." Despite the constant presence of Lun, the beloved Chow, in Freud's consulting rooms, animals did not come within the purview of physicians of the human psyche. Thus humans killing their own pets was not defined as a sign of panic. At the first air raid warning on 3 September, people apparently heeded the government's advice and they calmly did as they had been advised and went to the available shelters. The *Daily Telegraph* reported, "There was no panic and people responded calmly."[9] This was very different in practice to the earlier hysterical prediction of one military strategist who had declared in the 1920s, "London for several days will be as one vast raving bedlam, the hospitals will be stormed, traffic will cease, the homeless will shriek for help, the city will be in pandemonium."[10] While adhering to government advice about evacuating children and to the directive to black out light, people nevertheless ignored the advice of the government, veterinary surgeons, and animal charities about how to care for their companion animals on the outbreak of war.

In the first week of the war, as discussed in chapter 1, the press had used Baerchen, the abandoned Chow dog at the German embassy, to illustrate what Britain was fighting, "the inherent brutality of Nazi-ism."[11] In the same week as characterizing the British as benign animal lovers, the press would also cover the mass slaughter of some 400,000 dogs and cats in London alone. The figure of 400,000 was later corroborated both by the RSPCA and Brigadier Clabby, the author of the official history of the Royal Army Veterinary Corps.[12] This conservative figure is lower than the figure of 750,000 given by the president of the RSPCA, Sir Robert Gower.[13] The figure 400,000 seemed to represent around 26% of cats and dogs in London alone.[14] This animal death toll was more than six times the number of civilian deaths on the Home Front caused by enemy bombing during the entire war in the whole country.[15] It is important to emphasize that at this point no bombs had actually fallen and none would fall on London—or Britain—until April 1940.[16] Pet owners themselves took the decision to kill their animals: the British government had not issued a diktat or emergency measures requiring animals to be killed. The death toll was more than three times the number of pets killed routinely in a whole year by animal charities in the capital. (The routine killing of thousands of companion animals would include very ill animals as well as those who had become unwanted.)[17] Quite remarkably, this massacre had happened in just a few days. So shocking was this to animal loving individuals and charities that, amongst others, the NCDL referred to the killing as the "September Holocaust."[18] On 7 September 1939, the *Times* reported that thousands of cats and dogs had been destroyed and that centers run by animal welfare societies were "filled with the bodies of animals and thousands more are being brought in every day."[19] The RSPCA, the oldest animal welfare charity in the world, had doubled staff at its London clinics, employed night staff at its London HQ, and trebled facilities for euthanasia.[20] This was not a panic response by the organization but a situation that had been anticipated if there was bombing. Thus three months' extra supply of chloroform and human killer ammunition had been ordered for each of its clinics. As its emergency arrangements noted, "It is anticipated that for the first month or so very heavy demands will be made upon all Clinics and upon Headquarters for the euthanasia of small animals."[21]

The RPSCA magazine *Animal World* stressed (correctly) that "the clinics of other animal welfare societies were employed in the same way and so the work of destroying animals was continued, day and night, during the first week of the war."[22] The NCDL, set up in the 1890s to protect dogs at a time of rabies hysteria, said that so extensive was the slaughter that its supplies of chloroform had been exhausted.[23] The PDSA, the charity founded in east London in 1917 to provide veterinary treatment to animals of poor people, had a similar experience of killing. It claimed it was almost overwhelmed by the thousands of animals brought for destruction to its clinics. The day before war was declared the PDSA received information that "all destructors in London were working to full capacity."[24] It also meant that the "dust destructors could not in some instances burn the bodies fast enough as they had to damp down furnaces at night owing to the black-out."[25] The PDSA's policy was that animals should not be needlessly destroyed, but it reported that many hundreds of people "insisted" that their animals should be "put to sleep long before the threat of bombing materialised or even before the enemy's threat began to assume definite shape."[26] The small Wood Green Animal Shelter in north London witnessed a queue nearly half a mile long of people waiting to hand over their cats and dogs. On Sunday 3 and Monday 4 September the shelter killed 536 companion animals.[27] Later, many people would abandon their animals. As the shelter's treasurer appealing for funds poignantly asked:

> Do you know that scores of animals are left behind and are slowly starving to death? Do you know that cats jump upon women's shopping baskets in vain endeavour to find food? Do you know that dogs little more than skeletons, hunt the dustbins, hoping to find some scraps? Every hour of the day and night we hear their appeal for help: must we abandon them to their fate for lack of funds?[28]

Since 1860 the Dogs' Home had been taking in Londoners' stray dogs (and later cats too) to reunite them with their human companions.[29] But at this time the main premises in Battersea and the sub-branch in Bow in east London were approached directly by those wanting to kill their own pets. Commenting on this later, in the annual report for 1939, the charity estimated that it had killed few in comparison with "what one heard were destroyed in some places." The Home attributed this to the work of their secretary, Mr. Healey Tutt, who took time to persuade pet owners to take their animals home again. The *Annual Report* was pleased to record, "the number of grateful letters we have received from some of those who took his advice."[30] So numerous were the corpses of companion animals in those early September days that several councils, animal societies, and veterinary practices were unable to cope with their disposal. Accordingly the PDSA offered the use of a meadow in the grounds of its sanatorium where, the charity reported, half a million animals were buried.[31]

The mass killing at the start of the war *was* criticized at the time by animal charities and individual animal supporters. It was neither seen as an inevitable consequence of war nor construed as an example of the wartime propaganda of "Britain can take it." Rather this act undermined the propaganda notion of resolute behavior: it was seen as a lack of steadfastness and portrayed negatively in the media. Thus popular disc jockey Christopher Stone broadcast to the nation in November 1939, "To destroy a faithful friend when there is not need to do so, is yet another way of letting war creep into your home."[32] Appealing to a different demographic audience, Major Mitford Bruce, a dog breeder and writer on dogs—though no animal rights advocate—also criticized people killing their dogs. In the *Times* in November 1939 he wrote, "There is daily evidence that large numbers of pet dogs are still being destroyed for no better reason than that it is inconvenient to keep them alive—which, of course, is no reason at all, but merely shows an owner's inability to appreciate his obligations towards his animal." He rebuffed arguments about lack of food or shelter: horseflesh was available; gas-proof kennels were on the market and kennels existed in safety zones where pets could be evacuated.[33] Such examples indicate that although there is far more written material documenting the killing carried out by animal charities than by privately funded veterinary surgeons, perpetrators were not confined to any one class—or gender.

Although a minority of animal owners had companion animals killed the majority did not. And, as Nina, Duchess of Hamilton, noted, this majority specifically included working class people. Nina described the animals she

evacuated out of London to her sanctuary near Salisbury, who were "infi-
nitely precious to their owners, who are in very poor circumstances; sometimes it is their only friend, and whether they have children or not of their
own, these animals are like children to them." Her positive attitude towards
those who made arrangements for their pets contrasted with her castigation
of the thousands of cats and dogs killed in one slaughter-house [*sic*] with
three truck-loads of dead bodies going out from "a certain animal clinic
in London."[34] Contrasting this reality with propaganda she declared, "We
should be horrified if this had happened abroad. How can we explain such
a thing to our foreign friends in this so-called animal-loving England."[35]

NO PANIC BUT "DOING THINGS"

Civilization was maintained through certain practices: "On the morning
after the declaration of war many people returned their library books." [36]
These may—or may not—have been the same people who had taken their
cats and dogs to be killed. Suffice it to say that there are different explanations for what occurred at this time—and that animals are not usually
considered in this period of so-called Phony War, this time of "black bore-
dom" [37] or of "a dull acquiescence."[38] Even the sewing of blackout curtain
became derided, at least by Virginia Woolf, as an "anodyne, pleasant to
do something: but so tepid and insipid."[39] For some people the autumn
of 1939 was an anticlimax: "We have all the apparatus of war conditions
without war conditions. The result is disillusion and grumbling."[40] It was a
time of blackout but not, until January 1940, rationing. Coping with bore-
dom and bewilderment had not been foreseen by the government that had
concentrated instead upon measures for dealing with possible panic and a
breakdown of society—that did not materialize.[41] According to Tom Harrisson, of Mass Observation, by September 1939, 38% of homes studied had
done nothing at all about air raid precautions such as blackout curtains.[42]
Psychiatrists and political writers, such as Haldane or Langdon-Davies, had
warned about the need for people to "do something." Everyone needed to
have "useful work," a "hole into which to fit," said one.[43] They should feel
secure—thus erecting sandbags at windows was useful even if the protection was illusory. Walter Schmideberg, who had served as an officer in the
1914–18 war, exemplified this argument by a story in that war of "an old
maid." As a defense against the zeppelins she tied a dustpan to her head
and in her hand held a Bible. "We may smile, but," he continued, "from a
psychotherapeutic point of view it served this person well."[44] In some ways,

making curtains, digging a vegetable patch—and disposing of the family
pet—was a similar sort of "useful" work. It signified a change from "nor-
mality" to the demands of a total war situation, irrespective of the absence
of aerial bombardment.

A few months before the war, Mass Observation had published a survey
reporting on the actions people were contemplating carrying out if war was
declared. One 42-year-old woman said, "I have been collecting poisons for
some time with guile and cunning. I have sufficient to give self, husband
and all the children a lethal dose. I can remember the last war. I don't want
to live through another, or the children either. I shan't tell them, I shall just
do it." She was not unique. As a man of 45 explained, "I'd rather see my
two boys dead. I'd poison them if I thought it was coming," and a woman of
33 spoke of her two children, "I want to see my children dead before I am if
there is to be war, and I'll see that they are if they bomb here."[45] However,
people did not kill human members of the family either at the outbreak of
war or when aerial bombing commenced as they had threatened.[46] Indeed
psychiatrists would report on the *lack* of any outbreak of war neuroses.[47]
But no doubt in some instances such sentiments were displaced onto the
family pet.

A voluntary committee established in London to consider what wartime
emergency mental health services would be needed, concluded by 1941 that
"there has been no outbreak of war neuroses in the civilian population."[48]
This view has been endorsed decades later by the scholarly work of Nikolas
Rose declaring: "The air raids of 1940–1941 actually led to a decrease in at-
tendances at mental hospitals and clinics . . . There was no evidence of any
significant increase in neurotic illness or mental disorder in Britain during
the war."[49] Some professionals had anticipated that admissions to psychiat-
ric wards would increase in the few weeks after the declaration of war—but
this did not happen. Emergency stations for mental casualties folded up as
they were not needed: there was an "absence of bomb neurosis."[50] There
had been an expectation of panic if aerial bombardment had occurred but
this was ultimately defined by its absence. To suggest that the humans who
killed their animal companions in September 1939 were panicking is far
too easy an explanation and one not borne out by contemporary psychiat-
ric evidence. It suggests an inexplicable and unconsidered response rather
than a considered decision. Such a "theory" contradicts the contemporary
consensus that there was less "blind panic" than in September 1938 when
the Munich crisis had occurred.[51]

HUMAN PANIC IN 1938: THE MUNICH
CRISIS—AND THE KILLING OF PETS

I mentioned earlier how the RSPCA was well organized for the outbreak of war in September 1939. One reason for this was the experience that the society—and other animal charities— had had to face in September 1938 during the "Munich crisis" when Chamberlain had flown to speak to Hitler at the end of September and returned with a "piece of paper" that signified the postponement of war. At that time thousands of middle class people with cars had rushed from London. The distribution of gas masks and the digging of trenches in public parks described as "feverishly scratched open" had created, some said, "blind panic."[52] Although not a qualified vet, Buster Lloyd-Jones provided treatment for animals and remembered well the impact of the Munich crisis on animals:

> Nice friendly people who I knew to be devoted to their pets panicked and brought them in to be destroyed. I pleaded with them, argued with them, lost my temper but they insisted. Some I managed to find new homes for, but even that was becoming almost impossible. So many had to be put to sleep.[53]

Psychiatrist Wilfred Trotter described the mood at that time thus, "Anyone who was in London in September and October 1938 must have been aware of something new in the moral attitude of the people. Many of those who could afford it were openly running away, and people of whose nerves better might have been expected confessed to an uncontrollable alarm."[54] Tom Harrisson and Charles Madge of Mass Observation also observed that "fear . . . grew almost to a panic."[55] In poet Louis MacNeice's dramatic language the behavior of humans at that time was compared to the fear exhibited by animals in extremis, "The terror that seized London during the Munich crisis was that dumb, chattering terror of beasts in a forest fire."[56]

During the crisis Percy, a cat, had accompanied Mrs. Irene Byers to Bexhill while her civil servant husband Cyril stayed working in London at the Board of Education. Strict instructions were given to Irene: she should "destroy our pet cat, Percy." Intending to follow her husband's diktat despite her own misgivings, Irene felt "as if my heart will break" and saw the children's tears. Her mother-in-law intervened, Percy was saved, the crisis blew over, and the cat followed Cyril "like a dog." Ambiguously Irene wrote, "and all is quiet at nights"—whether this was due to the absence of bombing or the lack of tears and arguments is unclear.[57] In September 1938, within the space of 48 hours three thousand people had appealed to the headquarters of the RPSCA for help.[58] The NCDL had experienced a similar demand. Many people had brought their dogs to be killed, but the League had refused to do this, urging dog owners to wait to see the outcome of the Chamberlain / Hitler talks. Therefore, conscious of the ongoing threat of war, the NCDL had then established a register for safe addresses where Londoners could leave their animals away from the capital if war did come.[59] The Battersea Dogs Home reported that plans had been "hastily made for dealing with a state of emergency should it arise" but "happily the storm blew over for the time being."[60] "Innumerable" applicants had also sought help from the Our Dumb Friends League (ODFL) (now the Blue Cross), which had established its first clinic and animal hospital in London's Victoria in 1906: "Many having given way to a feeling of desperation, or panic, wished to have their pets put to sleep there and then, and so reduce at least some part of their [that is, human] anxieties." The ODFL had urged people "not to be stampeded into premature action, but often without success." The humans who had panicked in 1938 were not necessarily poor people without resources. As the League noted, "Many were hastening into the comparative safety of the country in cars piled high with their belongings, and only stopped long enough to hand over their dogs or cats to be kept until either the situation improved, or the worst had happened, in which case they were to be destroyed forthwith."[61] The League compared this behavior unfavorably with the actions of refugees from Nazi occupation who "even in the midst of their grievous troubles [were] trying to do what they could to save their pets."[62] The events of 1938 had taken many unawares, precipitating some panic and the unnecessary slaughter of companion animals. Thus the actual outbreak of war a year later was not altogether surprising (having been anticipated by politicians—and animal charities—alike).[63]

Significantly the calm apparently shown by the Battersea Dogs Home or the ODFL seems not to have been shared by the Cats Protection League. Since the organization's founding the League had been sharply aware of the low status of cats. Reflecting afterwards on the Munich crisis, the secretary A. A. Steward concluded that cat owners would need to rely on their own initiatives to protect felines, including preparing either a gas-proof room for humans and cats or a bomb-proof and gas-proof shelter for both in the garden for the future warfare. To even contemplate applying gas masks to cats—assuming that they would be available—would be an act of "gross cruelty." A gas-proof box simply for cat use, Steward concluded, would also be dangerous, leading to possible suffocation. Ominously the advice concluded that those who had had experience of the last war and of the suffering of homeless cats "on the Continent" "would not hesitate to avoid such a dreadful occurrence in this country by making the decision that would make their cats safe from the horrors of war."[64] The charity issued such advice since it believed that because of their low standing, cats would not be treated benignly during warfare. As shall be seen, the actual relationship between humans and cats would improve, often leading to strong emotional bonds during the war.

WAYS OF KILLING: ROUTINE KILLING, THE MUNICH CRISIS, AND THE OUTBREAK OF WAR

In the early 1930s, methods of killing unwanted animals even by veterinary professionals could cause animals physical pain. Although prussic acid was very rapid it nevertheless caused a "frightfully agonizing spasm of pain."[65] As one vet wrote, "An injection of morphia, with a quiet wait until it has taken effect, and then chloroform given slowly, is what I should choose for myself and for my dogs."[66] Killing her paying clients' animals at that time, Dr. Brancker has explained that animals would be given an injection, or a tablet down the dog's throat: both of which were "very quick," she said, but not "a very pleasant end" (and for the vet too "it would be horrible") and thus possibly gas "would be kinder."[67] The methods of killing unwanted animals had been highlighted at a conference organized by the Animal Defence Society chaired by Nina, Duchess of Hamilton, in June 1933. As Lind af Hageby, the president of the Society, had explained, "Death . . . is not such a simple affair as some people imagine . . . Even the best methods can be bungled and are bungled." Various veterinary practitioners explained their methods to a lay audience. Lt. Colonel Wakefield Rainer advocated the benefits of electricity, outlining the methods used by the NCDL in Croydon—stunning with between 200 and 350 volts followed by an intrathoracic injection of chloroform: "There is no fixed apparatus and therefore no terror," explained Rainey. He criticized the use of a chloroform spray or a carbon monoxide chamber then being used at the Battersea Dogs Home since animals did not go quickly to sleep, instead "they have a short but hard struggle against a powerful narcotic poison." Others disagreed: unconsciousness was swift. Mrs. Dubois from a shelter in East London explained they had destroyed no fewer than 13,000 dogs by chloroform. Plenty of air and an empty stomach were, she said, the secret to the system's success.[68]

The Battersea Dogs Home had first introduced lethal electrical chambers, similar to those used by the National Canine Defence League, in 1934.[69] These had been tested on animals by a number of eminent scientists, including members of the special NVMA veterinary committee that had explored methods of mass killing. The scientists had expressed themselves "eminently satisfied with this new method" being introduced at Battersea. In the normal course of events, animals were killed separately at the Dogs' Home to prevent distress caused by seeing other animals dying.[70] In 1937 the NVMA had furthered explored different forms of small animal euthanasia through a special committee that had included Professors Woolridge and Wright, who both taught at the Royal Veterinary College in London. It was established to "explore in all its bearings" the most efficient method of "humanely destroying" animals "en masse."[71] This exploration arose *not* from the demands of war but the routine killing of animals in peacetime. The veterinary surgeons were also keen to ensure that animals died with the "least possible pain or discomfort." From the animal point of view, they said, an intravenous injection was the most humane method.[72] There seemed to be "no valid reason, other perhaps that of economy for the adoption of mass destruction."[73] Concerned with the improbability that animals would become unconscious simultaneously, the scientists nevertheless concluded that if a large number of animals were "unwanted," then of the methods employed by animal welfare bodies, the use of an electrocution chamber would be the best and accordingly this method was "strongly recommended."[74] Although the committee's remit was the efficacy of killing large numbers of animals, nowhere in the report did the members refer to war: this was a response to the demands of "ordinary" peacetime killing.[75]

Therefore to understand why companion animals were killed in such high numbers and in such a short period of time—and why, I must stress, the majority of pets were not killed—we need to consider not only the "wartime" context of particular animals and humans but also the particular prior existing relationship within a household. Such relationships rather than any distinctions attributed to class or gender were the deciding factors in initial survival or death, as these four examples demonstrate.

FOUR STORIES: MANY LIVES

For Marx, living in Hertfordshire, late August 1939 had been fairly uneventful, albeit hot. The French poodle's attempt to attack young partridges had been prevented by their mother leading him away from them by flying slowly and squawking. Although a healthy dog,[76] Marx seemed to be affected by the heat: in the last week of the month he was very "lousy" with his ears full of nits. Antiseptic soap, flea powder and vinegar, and combing of his black and white hair by Eileen, the woman of the household, gave him relief.[77] If this dog had reacted in any way to the declaration of war at the start of September his human companion, George Orwell, did not record it in his diary. The war at this time seems to have played no part in their relationship. That Orwell noted a pet animal in his diary at all is surprising since the author was known for his hostility to those humans who campaigned for animals: "The animal cult runs right through the nation and is probably bound up with the decay of agriculture and the dwindled birth rate."[78]

The end of August was more significant for Angus, a black retriever dog. His owner, a shy doctor, had been called up into the armed services. His family was not fond of dogs and the doctor was reluctant to leave until he could find a place where Angus would be well looked after. Angus was lucky.[79] Nina, Duchess of Hamilton, had remembered what had happened to animals the previous September during the Munich crisis when the country had stood fearful on the brink of war and thousands of people had panicked.[80] Determined that this ill-considered killing of animals should not happen again, Nina had broadcast on the radio that animals should be brought to Animal Defence House in St. James off Piccadilly in central London and they would then be taken to the sanctuary created at her country home at Ferne near Salisbury.[81] Some dogs were also tied to the railings of her home in St. Johns Wood where she set up temporary kennels. Here too were both moggies and pedigree cats.[82] They would be successfully evacuated alongside Angus with his label, like those worn by evacuated children, declaring "I am Angus." The animals would live out the war far from the bombing of London.

Lulu had been used to disruption in his [sic] life. The black and white half-Persian cat was about two years old in 1930 when he had made himself known to the humans who would take him in near Marble Arch in central London. In an underfed condition with watery eyes and uncombed coat, he had arrived one day declaring his presence by sleeping on the bed. A neutered cat, Lulu had previously sojourned in a restaurant but there he had not been well looked after, surviving on a pennyworth of so-called cat's meat (or rather horseflesh from worn-out horses brought to a knackers' yard) every day except Sunday, "when he had to make what he could of whatever scraps were going." He was then "like tens of thousands of London cats: he got just enough food to sustain life, but not enough to reach his full development."[83] Like Marx he too was flea-ridden: 69 being counted

FIGURE 3.1 Dogs being evacuated to Ferne animal sanctuary, September 1939 (from Nina, Duchess of Hamilton, *Chronicles of Ferne* [Ernest Bell Library])

by his new human companions when a comb was first applied. Humans and animals in the neighborhood had known Lulu: the landlady advised that he had been kicked in the head as a kitten, creating the weakness in his eyes, and, in turn, he suffered from ingrowing eyelashes that needed to be routinely plucked.[84] A sociable fellow, Lulu ran to the rescue of a feline companion attacked by a large dog or shared his bed by the fire with an ill cat or played hide and seek. And although an excellent mouser, he did not attack birds.[85]

Such details are found in the cat's extended obituary, or perhaps more appropriately eulogy, published in successive issues of the *Cat*, the newsletter of the Cats Protection League. His owner was clearly fond of the cat, saying, "If with Lulu in mind I said of any human being that he was catlike, I would be bestowing the highest praise, and that judged by human standards."[86] Yet the reason we possess such a full account of this fairly ordinary cat is because of his death caused by the owner who had written of him so fondly: "War came, with a distant posting." It was, he said, impossible to take Lulu or "to think of him in other hands or exposed to the risks of war." Lulu was killed, leaving his keeper "a sense of loss and grief deeper than words can tell."[87] The implication here was that there was a unique understanding between the two that no "other hands" could replicate and thus death was preferable.

Minnie, a white rabbit, was also killed. The grandson of Mr. Mayne, the man who caused her demise, knows the story even though he had not even been born at that time. Minnie exists in memory: Her story had been passed down by Mr. Mayne's daughter to her own son. Minnie lived in a hutch on the roof of the Southall bank, then on the outskirts of west London, where Mr. Mayne was the manager. She was the pet of Alison and Madeleine, two little girls who used to wheel the rabbit about in a doll's pram. Once war was declared their father decided to evacuate his family to the coast where they had a seaside property. Although they were going in their own car and to a familiar destination, Mr. Mayne decided not to take Minnie. She was shot by one of his friends and taken away to be skinned, jointed, and returned to be cooked in a pie by Mrs. Mayne. The children were told who was in the pie. Alison was slightly upset but still ate the former family member with pleasure, saying, "If someone had to eat her it was nice that it was us." Her sister Madeleine spent the meal in floods of tears and refused to eat any of Minnie.[88] Such transformation from family member to discarded thing was not unique, but it was sufficiently important within the family not only to be remembered but to be transmitted to a future generation.

Here we have four different stories of the fate of animals at the start of war—and different outcomes. One, Lulu, was killed by a distressed human who thought no one else could provide the same care for the cat as he did. Another, Minnie, was killed in almost cold-blooded fashion but not by the head of household himself. Angus, a dog, was evacuated. The start of the war seemed to have no impact on Marx. These accounts help to illustrate that although hundreds of thousands of animals were killed there was no single reason why humans at the start of the war chose to kill—or not kill—their nonhuman companions. Describing the work of the Blue Cross in those early September days, Phyllis Brook has noted some animal killers were "broken-hearted." She also noted that many people abandoned animals "to fend for themselves."[89] Interestingly she observed the attitude of older people, "We've seen one war through and we'll stay to see this one out."[90] The written accounts in diaries of keeping or evacuating an animal tend to be more numerous than those including accounts of killings. This can, of course, be interpreted in various ways—including the lack of significance of such an event for the diarist.

CRITERIA FOR LIVING AND DYING
DURING THE SEPTEMBER MASSACRE

Although, as discussed earlier, Ribbentrop was seen to be "uncivilized" by abandoning the Chow Baerchen in the London German embassy and in due course the German nation would be castigated for the alleged mass killing of dogs, inevitably those who killed their own cats and dogs in London in September did not see their own actions in this way. I stress there is no single explanation for whether specific companion animals lived or died. One correspondent wrote to me, "My granny had her cat put down at the beginning of World War Two because she remembered the bombing of the First War and didn't want to think about the cat wandering about homeless and scared." This story told to a granddaughter may be true even if the details are vague but it is, of course, a story of human emotion—and experience.[91] It was not necessarily the circumstances of the animal per se, such as age, monetary value, or type, or even the material circumstances of the human, such as being called up, that determined life or death. Rather, the nature of the preexisting relationship between animal and human was key. As Penny Green has recounted:

> My father then twelve years old, and my Grandmother encountered a queue of people standing on the pavement carrying pets of all kinds. Father asked Gran what was happening and she told him that pets were being killed so they would not suffer if bombs started falling. In the line was a woman carrying a beautiful ginger cat. My Father was upset and Gran tried to hurry him along. To cut the story short, Dad and Gran returned home with the ginger cat, renamed him Charlie, and kept him throughout the Blitz! Charlie lived to a good age despite the efforts of the Luftwaffe.[92]

This family story is worth unpacking for it gives us different insights into the animal massacre. First, it is a story passed down through generations but primarily through someone who was a child at the time. Thus the explanation for [other] people killing animals ("My Grandmother . . . doted on my Dad and loved animals") is one given to a child and it is this story that is passed on. Those who did the killing (or rescuing) are themselves likely to be long dead but the germ of the idea that animals were killed "so they would not suffer" lingers on through their descendants. Secondly, this story is not just about transmission of a benign explanation for animal death. The rescuing mother was living in the same location as those in the queue but prior to the incident was clearly defined as an "animal lover." It was the relationship of earlier years that influenced her stance at this time — and saved Charlie the cat.

Such a story is not unique. Repeatedly the stories we now have of animals during the war are also stories of children, albeit remembered as adults. Now in his 80s, Paul Plumley has recently recalled the death of the family dog:

> At the outbreak of war I was five years old and my Mother told me to take our young Welsh collie to the vets to be put to sleep. It was quite a long walk for a five year old! Not that I thought too much about that at the time.[93]

The matter-of-factness of the act is in sharp contrast to the emotional recollection of art critic Brian Sewell, a well-known dog lover. In different places he has written about his first relationship with a dog, Prince, a Labrador. In the first volume of his autobiography Sewell has described how his stepfather, Robert, killed Prince as the family evacuated from Whitstable on the outbreak of war:

> Robert shot him and left his body on the beach for the tide to sweep away. Packed among the suitcases in the car I saw Prince led toward the sea and heard the shot. I did not cry, as I would now, but a cold, hard, vengeful aversion lodged in my memory.[94]

It was Brian rather than Robert who had had a close relationship with the dog and his adult sentiments combined with those of the child in remembering the event. The stepfather was not being called up to fight, and evacuation of this coastal town was not mooted at this time. It was not external material factors that determined the canine death but ones within the human-animal family.

A contemporary account of an adult places the killing in a wider context. Returning to London in the second week of September, diarist and animal lover Gwladys Cox described a conversation with her neighbor, Miss Fox, whose friend Dr. Dobbin "might be" called up: "She smilingly informed us that Dr Dobbin, who thought she might be called up at any time, had had her cat and two kittens destroyed." At pains to provide for her own cat, Bob, throughout the war, she continued her entry with the following observation:

> There has been a perfect holocaust [sic] of cats in London, and, as a result, some districts, according to the papers are threatened with a plague of vermin. So now, the authorities are begging people to keep their pets, if possible.[95]

Gwen Brown, a teenager rather than a small child, was living in Chiswick in west London during the war and has recently described the neighbor who killed his two Borzoi dogs:

> I think they were the first Borzois I'd seen . . . They were beautiful. I thought they were lovely. We were shocked, the whole road was shocked. They'd all got cats and dogs and things, and nothing had happened at that stage. The air raid siren went almost the moment that war was declared, which was just a mistake, and everyone was riveted by this hideous sound . . . The war broke out on Sunday and I think he'd had it done by Tuesday or Wednesday, maybe even Monday, I don't know, very very soon, anyway, and the entire road was agog.

Her own dog, Spady, an Irish Setter, would continue to live with them until his death in 1943. Refuting the idea of a contagious panic, Gwen has continued, "Dogs used to sit outside at the gate or wander around on their own. Some of them might have been evacuated, but I didn't hear of any others being killed locally, which is why we were so shocked about the Borzois."[96] This is an unusual account for various reasons. It is a recently told story, unlike the contemporaneous diary account of Gwladys Cox, and it is not only about the family's dog but those of the neighbors. Several family stories have been told by those who were too young at the time to be aware of other families' circumstances outside the home. Thus stories are often of pets within the family rather than those living with neighbors. Here the rare nature of the breed seems to have played a factor in the memory of the then teenager. Although children were seemingly often shielded from the killing within the family, this was a distinctive story of a dog-loving family witnessing needless deaths within the street—from which the young woman was not protected.

By way of contrast, Bonny, a little dog from Euston in central London, survived seemingly against the odds. His human companion, a forty-year-old female shop worker, explained the circumstances to a Mass Observation interviewer during the war. She had originally taken in Bonny, albeit reluctantly, as she did not want a customer killing him:

> I haven't had this dog long. I didn't really want to have him in the first place because I didn't think dogs are right in London, but he had no home. A customer of mine kept talking about him. She had to go away because of her health, and one day she came into the shop and showed him to me and he was such a dear thing I couldn't think of him being killed (she said she'd have to do that) so I said I'd take car [*sic*] of him.

"Although," she continued, "he was rather a nuisance at first because he cried so much but then he settled down and he's never been any trouble.

He's so sweet! I wouldn't be without him now, he carries my papers and any little thing I ask him to about [sic] don't you Bonny?" She interpreted her empathy as being rewarded by the engaging behavior of the dog.[97] Such an account is not simply about the dog (or the human) but the way in which they had *both* related to each other. In so doing a particular relationship had been constructed that had affected them both.

KILLING ANIMALS OUTSIDE THE HOME

Animals outside the supposed protection of "the home" were also affected adversely in the first days of war. Animals previously kept as a source of spectacle and education in zoological gardens were often destroyed. In Bristol the polar bears were killed and their enclosure converted into entrances and exits into the air raid shelter. The Bristol Rhesus monkeys were offered to the scientist Solly Zuckerman for experiments—on condition that the government would pay for their food.[98] All the lions at the Kursaal zoo in Southend were killed; subsequently all the remaining animals and birds held there were "disposed of" and the zoo closed.[99]

London Zoo had prided itself as a showpiece of empire and an impetus for encouraging "civilized" behavior. Previously the zoo authorities had suggested that by observing particular animals with guidance from a gazetteer, people would change their own behavior and act in civilized ways.[100] Such an approach changed in the first days of the war. All the poisonous and some of the constrictor snakes were destroyed—and a black widow spider was beheaded—although big pythons were reprieved (placed for safekeeping in big wooden boxes).[101] The release of certain birds was justified on the grounds of them being "a few birds of a kind which could safely be trusted to look after themselves" (which might raise the question of why couldn't they do this normally). Such birds included kestrels and herons and kites, subsequently observed flying over Regents Park.[102] Freshwater fish were released into a pond: saltwater fish in the aquaria were killed.[103] Pandas and elephants were transferred to Whipsnade. Here a young African bull elephant was killed in order to make room for the transferred animals.[104] People had raised their concerns about the plight of the zoo animals. Thus the destruction at the London Zoo was explained as the killing of a "few redundant" and "mostly elderly" animals[105]: "an ordinary visitor to the Gardens to-day would scarcely notice any difference in its stock of animal inhabitants."[106] The important factor here was the emotional impact of the cull on humans rather than the destruction of living animals, as such. The killing of the animals in the zoo would prove as impulsive and unnecessary as the killing of companion animals. The ban on places of entertainment and assembly would be lifted within two weeks—and the London zoo reopened.[107] By the end of the year in a new initiative some 135 animals were financially adopted: "A dormouse cost 1/- board per week."[108]

Animals' status, function, and relationship to humans would change drastically during the war. Initially some animals did thrive. "Domestic" rabbits, instead of being kept for petting, were still being bred but now their function was as human food. As one woman remembering her childhood in the war has recalled, "my parents kept rabbits and chickens to exchange or sell for other food. I grew fond of one rabbit, a beautiful white angora with pink ears and eyes. But like all the others, once it was fat enough, it was killed and strung up to eat. I have never been able to eat meat since those days and have been a vegetarian ever since."[109] Wild rabbits in the countryside were also killed: "Wild, crop destroying rabbits were the country's enemy; tame, fat rabbits were likely to be the country's salvation."[110] Such rabbits were potentially subject to killing when injuring crops or trees or "wasting" pasture. By May 1940 people were legally required to destroy wild rabbits, irrespective of their specific behavior. In due course rooks, rats, and wood pigeons—including their nests and eggs—would be subject to similar eradication.[111]

While various animals would be threatened with death, some thoroughbred animals were in a privileged position. Continuity with the breeding of particular types of animals was maintained. To obviate the need for dogs to be imported in due course from Germany, as happened after the 1914-18 war, the *Scottish Daily Express* announced that "the aristocrats of Scotland's dog kingdom had been evacuated to the United States and the colonies. Not wanting to run the risk of rare strains being wiped out in air raids, many famous prize winners and most of the older pedigree stock left 'for the duration of hostilities.' "[112] Breeders of other creatures also paid specific attention to the maintenance of good breeds. These included mice fanciers in the National Mouse Club and breeders of guinea pigs.[113] Teenage diarist Hazel Frost, who declared her adult ambitions to be a great singer, piano player, nurse, and breeder of guinea pigs when she left school, belonged to the Fur and Feather Club, breeding and selling them and recording their, often short, lives alongside other members of the family:[114]

> Grandad died at 3 pm. Dorothy found him nearly dressed and dying on the floor. Jinny [one of the guinea pigs] died about 9 p.m. after going unconscious. Both passed of old age.[115]

FIGURE 3.2 Graves of former resident animals, Hillside Animal Sanctuary, Norfolk, c. 2003

ANIMAL MASSACRES IN CONTEXT

The animal killing during the first week of the war happened on an individual household basis. But individual deaths became part of a mass slaughter. Of course it was not the first slaughter of animals in war (or peace). The Animals Studies Group has argued that the killing of animals is a "structural feature of all animal-human relationships."[116] In a discussion at the end of their collection *Killing Animals*, Diana Donald noted that "perhaps the absolute basic distinction is between those kinds of killing that are wilfully invisible, removed from the consciousness of the perpetrators and excluded from the sight of anyone else, and those that are in some way commemorated or represented?"[117] Yet there is a taboo on the visual imagery of animal death. The modern graves of cows and other large "farm" animals at the Hillside Animal Sanctuary in Norfolk are unusual exceptions. The rescued animals are not killed but live out their days safely. They have then been buried in a small graveyard in the center of the sanctuary adjacent to the fields where cows graze. The graves are simple, but large, and adorned with modest wooden crosses.[118] What is striking about the Hillside example is that the type of animal usually killed in a slaughterhouse and whose corpse is eaten has taken on the status of a companion animal or human being very visibly in a cemetery form.[119] Significantly, although memorials commemorating the 1939–45 war remain popular, the animals killed in the cat and dog massacre are still invisible and are not even commemorated through a formal plaque at the PDSA animal cemetery that contains their remains.

The word massacre is not applied to animal deaths in a slaughterhouse— nor to deaths of thousands of people who die routinely in times of war— though it was used *at the time* to describe the September 1939 killing.[120] The word has been applied to exceptional circumstances even in war. Thus the My Lai killings of more than 500 innocent civilians in the Vietnam war in 1968 (that led in due course to the prosecution of soldiers who had carried out this killing) are called a massacre (while the thousands of deaths from bombardment of napalm and Agent Orange in both Vietnam and Cambodia are not).[121]

The huge loss of life of horses and mules in the Boer Wars was one of the first mass deaths of animals in war that aroused human concern. Many animals had been transported from South America to South Africa to aid in the war effort but over 16,000 had died on the arduous sea voyage before even reaching the site of battle. In the course of military engagement more than 400,000 animals had died; however, this mostly through neglect and lack of food.[122] What caused outrage was the way in which animals had died. The Army Veterinary Service estimated that in two and a half years of warfare only 163 animals died through bullets and a mere three from shellfire.[123] Brigadier Clabby, an army veterinarian, described it thus: "It has been said that never in the history of any British war has there been such a deliberate sacrifice of animal life and public money."[124] At the time animal campaigners erected various memorials both in Britain and South Africa, at Port Elizabeth where animals were disembarked. The neglect led to some better treatment during the 1914–18 war, including the creation of specialist-staffed veterinary units and animal hospitals.[125] But it was not described either by contemporary observers or by historians as a massacre since the killing of horses, donkeys, and mules was neither deliberate nor intentional.

In the past few decades various animal "massacres" have received critical attention. Nancy Jacobs researched the donkey massacre of 1983 that happened in Bophuthatswana in South Africa. In summary, an indigenous elite class in the "independent" Tswana "homeland" of Bophuthatswana argued that cattle were more deserving of the available grass than the donkeys owned by the poor and disenfranchised. Accordingly, 20,000 donkeys were killed and became, Jacobs has argued, "thoroughly politicized" and a cause against apartheid.[126] She adopted an oral history approach partly because there was "virtually no mention of the donkey massacre in published sources."[127] While noting that to their owners donkeys were fellow living beings they were also, she argues, dominated and represented by humans. In the course of seeking to make the donkeys historical subjects and not "material objects," Jacobs has emphasized how the relationship between people and other species are reflective of "relations between people."[128] She, inevitably, refers to the famous work of Robert Darnton of the 1970s entitled "Workers Revolt: The Great Cat Massacre of Rue Saint Severin." Darnton analyzed an event that apparently took place in Paris in the late 1730s.[129] Apprentices in the printing workshop of Jacques Vincent, a master printer, were suffering from poor food and conditions, and were also kept awake at night by alley cats howling outside their bedroom. To get back at the master and mistress, the apprentices howled at night outside their bedroom as if they were cats. The master and the mistress then ordered the apprentices to kill the alley cats. The apprentices murdered every cat they could find, including the prize gray pet cat of the mistress. The apprentices responded to the master's rage with "joy, disorder, and laughter."[130] In Darnton's analysis this story became a good example of workers' revolt, as indicated by the title. As a cultural historian he referred to the narratives constructed around the event. Darnton acknowledged that real cats were killed and explained their cultural representation and treatment in different Western cultures. His interest, however, was primarily in the joke the apprentices played on the bosses, their skillful use of ceremonies and symbols, rather than in the killing of the animals. It was, he wrote, "a metonymic insult, delivered by actions, not words, and it struck home because cats occupied a soft spot in the bourgeois way of life."[131] Within his essay, as his title shows, cats were subsumed within a human story. They became a device to explore people's activities. Cats here were analyzed symbolically: how they were represented culturally. The cats' fate was caused by their cosseted and loved place within the boss's household: These cats were no mere mice eradicators. If they had not occupied particular roles in relation to wealthy women then their lives would probably not have been destroyed. Nor would they have been discussed in this way. A third, lesser known, example is a prize-winning cartoon film of 2010, *Chiennes D' Histoire* (confusingly titled *Barking Island* in the English version rather than the more accurate translation *Bitches of History*). The film, by French Armenian director Serge Avedikian, depicts a moment in which stray street dogs were rounded up in Constantinople in 1910 and placed on a deserted island en masse to starve and die a slow death. This event did happen (and in reality, as Avedikian acknowledges, some humans did intervene to try to prevent the destruction). However, both the director and subsequent commentators have seen the dogs' death representationally presaging the Armenian human genocide. Thus Avedikian draws the attention of people outside Turkey or the Armenian diaspora to the canine slaughter. But simultaneously the dogs are being obliterated as dogs and being seen as mere metaphors for human death.[132]

However, the cat and dog massacre in London in 1939 is different to these examples. It does not function merely as a metaphor for the start of the war—although it certainly acts in this way. It was an event that was not initiated by a state institution (as had happened in Constantinople or Bophuthatswana).[133] Nor did the massacre happen as a result of a "trick," as happened in eighteenth-century Paris. Rather, it occurred against the advice of animal charities and the state-sponsored body, NARPAC, that argued, "Those who are staying at home should not have their animals destroyed. Animals are in no greater danger than human beings."[134]

It was individual humans from a range of backgrounds, with individual relationships of varying strengths with their animals, who chose whether their pets would die or live. The destruction of the September days certainly marked a rupture in some relationships. However, during the next six years of war, as the next chapters explore, the relationship between companion owners and their keepers would grow stronger.

CHAPTER FOUR

Disrupting Previous Stories:
A Phony War for Whom?

The black out made him very uneasy . . . Since then he has stayed at home more than usual and has shown every symptom of puzzlement and disquiet.[1]

There was no bombing in Britain in the autumn and winter of 1939 but it is still appropriate to include this period within the framework of total war. This time may have been called a "Phony War" but it was war nonetheless, affecting both humans and animals—and the relationship between the two started to change in different ways. Physical environments altered: Previous routines started to be disrupted. For example, many horses who during the first months of the war had been used to trotting in fashionable Rotten Row in London's Hyde Park, alongside the horse of Joseph Kennedy, the American ambassador, soon found themselves moved outside London. Some horses were then employed by the government on transport duties; 300 others were bought by the French government in the first months of the war.[2] Horse dealers were approached to register their horses with the War Office. Cavalry troopers between the ages of 5 and 10, "deep bodied, with short back, well sprung ribs, with substance, quality, and true action," as well as light draught horses "capable of pulling a big weight over rough or broken ground" were particularly in demand.[3] For horses such as Mariana and Trump, who continued to canter daily in Hyde Park carrying Laurance Holman on their backs, their exercise would continue but with different food to nourish them. In due course, with shortages of corn, only "dusty, inferior hay" was available. As a result many horses would contract lung problems and chronic coughs.[4]

Even without the imminent threat of bombing, the blackout regime—dramatically changing movement through urban landscapes—was rigorously enforced. Convincingly, Angus Calder has argued that that the initial effect of the blackout "transformed conditions of life more thoroughly than any other single feature of the war."[5] The very landscape of cities was altered, resulting in people losing their way and, inter alia, by December 1939 eight times as many fatal accidents involving humans as had happened in prewar London had occurred.[6] But, of course, it was not only people who lived in London—and the nature of the population changed. The glitter of London street signs and advertisements had been replaced with a "pall of black velvet."[7] Then the city became a location for birds hitherto residing in the suburbs or countryside. The blackout noticeably encouraged the return of owls into central London.[8] As one American journalist observed, "A yellow moon was shining, and out of the depths of Hyde Park an owl began to hoot. The owl was too much for me."[9] One woman mused on the outbreak of war, "I wonder how the moths will get on with so few lights to fly to."[10]

The changed and restricted light also affected the daily habits of companion animals. Cats who lived in flats were no longer permitted to sit at the window or on the balcony at dusk, as was their previous custom, since the windows needed covering. As a result, "There is reason to believe that the lack of air and greater stuffiness of living rooms has tended to impair appetite, upset digestions and cause skin troubles."[11] The Cats Protection League gave specific advice about feline welfare, such as "Feed it [sic] regularly. Provide it with an elastic collar and some form of identification, above all *keep it in at night*"[12] (original emphasis).That the instruction to keep cats in at night is emphasized suggests that earlier requests had been ignored when Albert Steward had then exhorted: "Don't turn your cat out at night. Don't expect to take it into a public shelter. Don't experiment with drugs to keep your cat quiet."[13]

Inevitably, animals (as well as people) were killed in road accidents due to lack of light—and people ignoring advice about restricting animal movement. Thus Nigger [sic], a "beautiful black kitten," was not kept in at his southeast London home at night. He was run over and killed in the black out.[14] A consequence of more responsible humans restricting the external nighttime excursions of cats meant not only that cats were safer but, of course, that there was a longer period of time which cats and humans spent together. Writing about her rural cat, one contributor to the *Cat*, the CPL magazine, noted:

> The black out made him very uneasy. He has been accustomed to seeing the reflection of the lighted rooms on the garden, which he has learned to understand as a sign that the family was in. On the first night of a "black out" re-

hearsal he did not come in at the usual time. Search was made for him all over the garden: he was found sitting on the steps under the French window which was half open but from which, of course, no light showed. Since then he has stayed at home more than usual and has shown every symptom of puzzlement and disquiet.[15]

Here the human was not only noticing where the cat was — since his behavior was different to the norm — but also trying to understand how the cat was thinking. The new circumstances, as in the case of caution in the dark, changed for them both *and* in relation to each other. The physically changed circumstances accentuated different species' abilities. Readers of the *Cat* were reminded that although cats could see in dimmer light than humans they could not see in total darkness.[16] This was borne out by the observations of another contributor who noted that during the night the cat changed his sleeping place onto the human's bed. Nervous about the pitch darkness, the cat fumbled his way through the house, and "I then hit upon the simple device of a nightlight on the floor where it cannot show outside." The writer concluded, "Provide enough light to enable him to move about with confidence, and let him see any changes made in his surroundings so that he may adapt himself to them."[17]

Despite NCDL discouragement, dogs had been allowed out on their own during the 1930s.[18] However, this became less likely since in the event of bombing, for example, surviving humans would need to be able to direct emergency services to retrieving family pets. Dogs were also affected during the night hours and blackout. Bob Martin, the dog supplies firm, advised: "Dog owners are being requested not to take their dogs out after dark, as a safety measure to all concerned."[19] The NCDL advised fitting a luminous lead or collar so dogs would be safer in the blackout.[20] Not everyone, of course adhered to this advice. Mouche, a large poodle, for example, had a specific role in his blackout walks, carrying a small torch so that light shone where needed on the pavement and he then waited at the curb for humans to catch up.[21] Ingenious advertisers promoted the possibilities afforded by the blackout. As one advertisement in the *Times* personal column declared, "Black Out. Carry a white Pekinese. Lovely puppies from 2 guineas."[22]

In addition to putting up blackout curtains that altered the relationship between inside and outside the house, people filled receptacles with water — or sand — as emergency precautions in the case of bombing and fires. These changes to internal space also affected the animals of the house in different ways to humans. In one instance Perkin, the kitten living with Fryn

Tennyson Jesse, "misunderstood the purpose" of buckets of sand on every landing. The buckets were duly emptied and refilled with pieces of cardboard laid over the top, "so that the kitten can't make the same mistake."[23]

Outside the home, the blackout also disrupted the practice of racing greyhounds during the evening. Initially, racing was forbidden on the grounds that a site of *people* gathering together would be vulnerable to bombing. Within weeks, however, tracks were reopened but racing was not permitted in the conventional evening time as illumination was forbidden during the blackout—and no meeting could be held if there was a threat of air raids, which occurred at nighttime. Greyhounds would continue to race but now this would take place on a Saturday afternoon or on public holidays.[24]

EVACUATED CHILDREN—AND ANIMALS:
THE ABSENT RELATIONSHIP

The autumn of 1939 on the Home Front has generally attracted little attention from historians apart from the plight of the four million mothers and children evacuated nationally at the start of the war.[25] In this grand narrative of mass human movement it is often overlooked that no more than half the eligible schoolchildren were sent away from London (with many "only" children staying at home or being evacuated privately).[26] This was some 30% fewer than had previously been estimated by the authorities, having based their own calculations on feedback from parents.[27] Clearly many parents had changed their minds even before the evacuation process started, suggesting that the disadvantages of leaving children with strangers outweighed either the possibility of death or the mutual comfort provided within the family home. It is also suggests that many adults were in fact sanguine about the outbreak of war rather than giving way to so-called panic. Many adults took this decision: Many more would quickly reverse their action. Thousands of children were quickly brought back to London. Virginia Woolf recorded quarrelling amongst the eight women from Battersea and their children who had been evacuated to her home in Sussex. By Tuesday 5 September, a mere two days after war had been declared, some of these evacuees had already returned to London.[28] Animals, however, are routinely overlooked in analysis of this process though they played an important role.

If the decision to bring back children to London was triggered, in some way, by regret or anxiety at their absence, this homecoming obviously was not possible for destroyed cats and dogs. The plight of companion animals and children *was* closely intertwined in these autumn days. Initially the press urged parents to write to their evacuated children to explain what had happened to the family animal. In the *Daily Mirror* of 4 September women were encouraged to write to their children thus:

> If they have left pets behind them, write to them and tell them what you have done with them, whether they have been sent to friends in the country or sent away to places of safety. Many children feel a great responsibility towards their animals and they may be worrying about them.[29]

In the *Daily Express* of 2 September an image was printed of evacuated children with their "temporary parents." Suggesting that the children were getting "settled down" this notion was enhanced by the image of one of the girls cosseting a large black cat.[30]

In Devon Mrs. Hill took in a child evacuee from London—but also a lovely Samoyed dog called Olaf, named after the King of Norway, as his female owner had been conscripted. The dog, little boy, and Mrs. Hill appear together posing for a photograph, in the style of a family image.[31] Although the relationship between children and animals has been subsequently ignored by historians, it was seen as important at the time, as a significant survey of London children evacuated to Cambridge indicated. Susan Isaacs commented in the introduction, "Love for the members of one's own family and joy in their bodily presence alone makes life worth living." So deeply rooted was this need, she continued in her explanation for why children had returned home so quickly, that it had "defied even the law of self-preservation as well as urgent public appeals and the wishes of authority."[32] Although pets were not explicitly included here within Isaacs' definition of family, the feedback from children within the survey itself certainly indicated this. The children studied were evacuees from Islington and Tottenham, then both working class areas, in North London. They were asked to write an essay in half an hour on their own—and were told not to write to please the teachers—on what they liked in Cambridge and what they missed from home.[33] For boys the 12th most popular "like" in Cambridge was farm animals, and 15th was pets. Girls did not mention farm animals or pets in their "likes." Instead, animals featured highly in what was missed from their London homes. For girls the third most mentioned "miss"—and the eighth for boys—was their family pets. Thus this elision of pets with home was not just a figment of the popular press representations of the first days of September. The experience of being with a pet *and* the routines of daily life were elided in children's memories. As one boy of 13 wrote, "I miss my dog and cat and I miss going to the pictures on a Friday, Saturday and Monday."[34] A younger boy of six, consciously aware of animals in his new location, dictated his essay to a scribe who noted:

> He likes to go and watch the ducks on the river. He doesn't like to see the bulls going into the slaughterhouse, which is next door to where he is living and he can hear the gun go off plainly when they are slaughtering cattle. He may return to Tottenham soon, but he likes Cambridge better.[35]

This little boy's ambivalent relationship with "farm animals" was also reflected in the writing of Alice Griffin, now an animal rights' campaigner. When she was evacuated from Deptford, then a dockland area of south London, to Cilmanharen farm in Wales, her main companions were the animals. She learnt early on of their status, asking "Uncle Tom," who had been out with his gun, what had happened:

> He explained that Nelly, our lovely very old sheepdog was ill and had to be shot to save her further suffering. He left the room to put the gun back in the cupboard it was quite some time before he came back. If animals were not "pulling their weight" they were of no use. Pets were unheard of.[36]

Animals were an integral part of the evacuee story—and memory. The London teachers who had accompanied the interviewed children in the Isaacs' study were themselves interviewed, and one argued that children should be kept together in camps or hostels rather than private homes so that, amongst other things, there might be facilities for the keeping of pets. Every evacuee, one teacher declared, had missed his or her pet animal, and there was no chance of having any in a school shared by so many people.[37] If the animals seen on the farm or in the houses of "substitute parents" were definitely "real," the cats and dogs left behind were simultaneously real but also *symbols* of another time and place before war had disrupted family life. Evacuated from working class Bermondsey in inner London to her grandparents (rather than strangers) in Teddington, to these "orphans from the storm," as Jill Watts has described herself and her brother, the animals living there were important:

> There was the dog, Tinker, a big Grey English Sheepdog with his great tatty bed under the dresser and the canary Joey. My grandad always gave my Gran a canary bird, always called Joey, which hung outside in the yard in the sun in the summer, and sang, and indoors in the winter scattering his seed about. Grandad said it reminded him of his sailor days abroad.

In such narratives animals formed part of everyday positive and negative experience. Significantly the experience of the death of different animals also formed part of the children's stories. Another boy in the Isaacs' survey, an eight-year-old carpenter's son who was defined as "not too bright," wrote as his entire essay, "I like my dog I like my cat I like my Granny dog it is dead my granny did not cry I made the grave the other dog run and he nock the grave down [sic]."[38] The simultaneous inclusion of pets within the notion of family—but also separation and rupture—was also found in the wartime work of psychoanalysts Dorothy Burlingham and Anna Freud. In 1942 they analyzed evacuees from London (and children of refugees from mainland Europe) living in a residential nursery near Chelmsford in Essex.[39] Their work was significant in that their studies constructed "the fragile emotional life of normal children."[40] It was only the wartime circumstances that had deprived the children of "normal" family life. Burlingham and Freud stated, "'Home' is the place to which all children are destined to return irrespective of the fact that in most cases they are aware of its destruction,"[41] and within this "home" noted by these psychoanalysts, animals were present as creatures who had suffered bombing alongside other members of the family. As one small child later explained human and animal death, "My mummy and I were under the table and my poor little sister was in bed all by herself covered with stones, and my pussycat was thrown away."[42] Animals, then, featured in different ways in the lives of evacuated children, but animals too were specifically evacuated.

Given the understanding by some people of animals and children as integral parts of a family, it is not surprising to discover that families who evacuated often took their animals with them, rather than killing them. Thus Blackie, a cat who lived with the working class Kirsch family in Stepney, went with the parents on a train to High Wycombe. Although the cat survived the journey she jumped out of the train when they arrived and was never seen again, much to the concern of Sylvia, the daughter of the family.[43] More fortunate was the cat evacuated with her family to the Midlands. Although a billet was not ready when they arrived the family—mother, children, and cat safe in a basket—trooped off to the local cinema until arrangements were sorted.[44] In Hillingdon the local RSPCA inspector was asked by one family to keep their dog "for the duration" when the dog was evacuated alongside people from Kennington in working class south London.[45] One exhausted woman was even noticed standing for six hours journeying on a train to Bideford in Devon and "had held the large and restless black family cat all the way."[46]

Companion animals—like children—experienced dislocation being moved to new places, including to the care of "new" humans. There were various "official schemes" organized by charities such as the previously mentioned Animal Defence Society and the redoubtable Nina, Duchess of Hamilton. Hackbridge Kennels, which had been established by Colonel Richardson for training dogs during the 1914–18 war, reinvented itself as a site of dog evacuation for "the duration."[47] The PDSA had compiled a list of available accommodation for animals and, as Commander Pulling of Scotland Yard confidently explained, all the animal welfare societies "are willing to undertake work of registering, collecting, labelling, conveyance and arranging for accommodation out of London for animals in good condition."[48] The Cats Protection League also agreed to convey cats to temporary or "duration-of-war homes" if their members could take in cats.[49] In Lancashire Mr. Bernard of the Lido cinema in Bolton organized 900 homes for evacuated animals.[50] The Tail-Waggers Club that had so enthusiastically signed up nearly half a million of the nation's dogs in the early 1930s was "inundated" with letters from people offering good homes to unwanted dogs.[51] It also gave special mention to Miss Barnett of North London, who was a feline rather than a canine enthusiast. She had found a home for 22 evacuated cats and issued each of them a free collar and identity discs that made them, slightly oddly, members of the Tail-Waggers Club.[52] Unofficially animals were also evacuated to strangers. Thus Joey, a budgerigar, was taken in by Annie Blackwood in Wallingford in Oxfordshire, as a London evacuee. Apparently a resourceful bird, he opened his own cage and flew off never to be seen again. Undeterred Annie took in a second London evacuee, a Yorkshire terrier dog, Pickles, who survived the war—and was never reclaimed by his owners.[53] Rapunzel, a cat, arrived at the local station of unofficial vet Bruce Lloyd-Jones with her label, "Please keep me alive. My name is Rapunzel." Due to shortage of space in Lloyd-Jones' premises, the cat was going to be killed but as she went to sleep in the lethal box before the process started Lloyd-Jones did not have the heart to kill her. She lived for a further 14 years more and followed him everywhere, including trips on public transport.[54] Temporary homes existed throughout the country for companion animals who could not be kept by owners, but who were nevertheless concerned about their welfare. While some arrangements were commercial ventures many were facilities offered free of charge by fellow animal lovers. Animals living in the households of different classes had an opportunity for evacuation. There *was* an alternative to killing. It was not inevitable.

However, although I have shown the way that animals, like humans, were affected by the blackout and that animals, like children, were evacuated, as I stated in the introduction, I am not arguing that animals should be added in merely to boost the *existing* story of the "People's War." By way of analogy, in the 1980s some well-meaning historians were inclined to "add in" women to existing Labour Movement histories, a sort of "me too" approach. (Others, however, realized that gender challenged and disrupted the existing accounts.)[55] In similar ways I am suggesting that the animal presence does not only show that animals experienced the war alongside humans, more importantly it disrupts the existing accounts we have of *human* activity. The way animals responded to total war was significant. They were not mere adjuncts to human activity but they behaved in different ways that also *changed* human behavior. In the conventional story of the Blitz people went to shelters; grumbled about, but got by on, rationed food and "dug for victory"; and generally proved to be resilient. Acknowledging animals as active agents alters such stories of individual humans acting alone. As was reported later in the war, "cats seem to know when bombs are coming. I'm told cats take cover when a bomb is coming down and that many cats wriggle their way to safety."[56]

For some historians animal agency is "the problem with animals and history." Dorothee Brantz, for instance, has chosen to define agency as the ability to directly transform *human* structures, which she suggests would thus apparently exclude animals. However, this, of course, begs the question of the nature of the historical question being discussed. Analysis of domesticity, for example, could certainly easily embrace particular animals as historical agents.[57] This might include the very structure of the family, quotidian routines, the arrangements for social events, the human relations constructed around friendships created by dogs' own canine relationships. In many of their actions during bombardment animals would be effecting change for both themselves and their human companions, for example, through their response to the sound of air raids. Animals did not necessarily run away from the house but through running within sight of humans also influenced how they in turn responded to the raids. Others working in the Animal Studies field have been less cautious about animal agency. Thus Sue Donaldson and Will Kymlicka have demonstrated that animals exhibit various forms of agency: "Animals can choose to avoid human settlement, but they can also choose to seek it out for the opportunities it offers. . . . Humans either choose to leave animals alone to get on with their lives, or choose to hunt, capture, or breed them in order to serve human wants and desires. If we stopped interfering with animals, relationships between humans and animals would largely cease."[58] In different ways humans were being trained by their animals to both observe their actions and to interpret their behavior to facilitate their own—as well as the animal's—safety. Previously some humans had recognized particular attributes in animals. Thus the notion that a dog possessed "human" qualities was viewed positively. The admiration of a dog as "a true comrade, and a companion nearly human in its feelings" was high praise indeed.[59] But the capacity of pet dogs and cats to also use their *distinctive* capacity for smelling to construct and navigate routes or to hear particular sounds (other than a dog whistle to which a dog was obliged to obey) had not been commonly acknowledged. The war did not change the particular skills enjoyed by cats and dogs but enhanced their importance both to themselves—and to humans. People started to notice—and value—different animal characteristics. Animals used them to ensure their *own* survival—but in turn these skills assisted human and animal companions.

THE START OF THE BACKLASH AGAINST THE SEPTEMBER MASSACRE

The events of September 1939: the cat and dog massacre, evacuation, the effect of the blackout, and changed daily routines, were all indications of the way in which the words "phony" are inaccurate when applied to animals. In the weeks that followed the needless September killing citizens, politicians, and state functionaries responded in different ways to that moment. One animal magazine had noted, "A number of people who have regretted their hasty decision, have since acquired new pets"[60]; another publication reported the numbers of people "who were sorry they had been so easily influenced to kill their faithful friends."[61] By the middle of September 1939 the authorities were "begging people to keep their pets, if possible" because of the threat of "vermin."[62] For author Tennyson Jesse the acquisition of a new cat at the start of the war was circumscribed by the wider circumstances of the mass pet killing. Her flat was overrun with mice so she decided to:

> . . . give an abandoned cat a good home and rang the RSPCA.
> I said: " I want to talk about a cat."
> And a very weary voice answered: "Oh yes, you wish to have a cat destroyed."
> "Not at all," I cried, "I want to get a cat."
> The voice said: "What! You want to adopt a cat? Hold on, don't ring off whatever you do.[63]

And thus Muff came into her life. By December 1939 there was "an out-cry" for kittens in London and their cost had risen accordingly. Not alto-gether seriously, Gwladys Cox's husband suggested "hiring out our Bob as a mouse-disposer."[64]

A veterinary surgeon writing in the *Eastern Daily Press* expressed the view of many of his colleagues, " all that is necessary is that the animals should be prevented from running wild about the street . . . in my opinion it is ghastly that people should sacrifice their pets without reason."[65] Colo-nel Robert Stordy, the CEO of NARPAC, the state body established to pre-vent "unnecessary animal suffering,"[66] had described that September time as one when "notwithstanding every endeavour to prevent such slaughter, tens of thousands of animals, many of them valuable, were prematurely put to sleep. It was not only the poor that took advantage of the facilities of the clinics, but many well-to-do persons that had their animals destroyed." Added to the words in the margin of Stordy's report held in a Home Of-fice file, an anonymous civil servant had penciled in ¾ of a million.[67] This first phase of reflection of the September days ended in the first months of 1940. Thus historian Philip Ziegler has neatly concluded, "By the Spring of 1940 many owners were regretting the holocaust of pets that occurred at the outbreak of war."[68] Words such as slaughter, sacrifice, and needless are certainly more in keeping with a recognition of the early months as a "real" or total war—rather than a phony one. Expressions of regret may also help explain why people did not want to remember *this* wartime event. By the spring of 1940 the relationship between animals and humans would start to enter a new phase.

A DISRUPTED DUNKIRK STORY

What is seen generally to mark an end of this first period of the war is not the death of a rabbit in the Shetlands, due to isolated bombing, as the first casualty of enemy action on the Home Front in November 1939.[69] Although bombing started in earnest on mainland Britain during May 1940[70] the mili-tary defeat of the British Expeditionary Forces at Dunkirk is usually seen to mark the end of any "Phony" war. In summary, with France subject to Nazi invasion in May 1940, the British troops were pushed to the coast in Dunkirk. By 26 May some 28,000 nonfighting British personnel had been evacuated to Dover—but more than 300,000 were left stranded in Dunkirk.[71] However, despite the odds, and aerial bombardment from the Nazis, hundreds of thousands of troops were evacuated in very difficult circumstances. This military defeat, however, was refigured and mythologized, partly through the journalist skills of "Cato," as a victory for the "common man" against an alien force. In particular, in terms of propaganda, much attention was paid to the "little ships," rather than naval vessels, that went across from England to France in assist in the evacuation of the defeated army. Although the new Prime Minister Churchill had realized that "Wars are not won by evacuations" and saw Dunkirk as a military disaster,[72] at the time (and subsequently in popular memory) it was seen to be a moment of resilience, steadfastness, and overcoming odds. The story of "getting on with it" and "muddling through" was reconfigured as a typical and laudable

FIGURE 4.1 The last dog evacuated from Dunkirk

"British" trait.[73] This would become another aspect of the "People's War." However, this was—and is—resolutely presented as a human story. In practice, this was not the case. Animals, particularly dogs, feature prominently in Dunkirk memories and diaries.

Men were accompanied by stray dogs who gathered with them awaiting rescue while the French beaches were being strafed. Although largely written out of modern accounts and public memory the dogs were an integral part of the events. Many soldiers were keen to repatriate dogs who had followed them through France (dogs who had often been abandoned by the fleeing French or who had left the Nazis). Thus Frances Partridge recorded the story of Colonel Dick Rendel, who had been on the English south coast beaches. He was receiving evacuated men and needed to make provision to differentiate the dead from the living humans:

> In the midst of all of this horror . . . Dick saw men making a cage on the beach.
> "What's that for?" he asked.
> "The dogs."
> "What dogs?"
> "Why the ones from France, the strays the soldiers are bringing back."
> "What will happen to them?"
> "They'll be sent to quarantine, after being carefully marked with that rescuer's name and number."[74]

A similar story of apparent human compassion, of civilized behavior against barbarism, amidst the horror of war was also recounted by the RSPCA. The organization saw the canine attachment to the retreating troops as "testimony to the humanity of our men that in such circumstances dogs should seek refuge from them."[75] In this instance the nature of humanity—and its division from animality—has been expressed differently in more recent memories:

> They [the Nazis] were trying to kill these poor refugees. We saw people and horses and carts blown sky high, it was terrible. I remember seeing people mutilated, blown to pieces. We saw people going up in the air in pieces. We could do something about the animals. We saw a horse that had its guts blown open, and we could shoot it. But there was nothing we could do about the human beings. We couldn't stop and give first aid . . . It was just murder.[76]

Other soldiers in the Royal Army Medical Corps "managed to persuade the doctors to let us have some stitching material, and we tried to stitch these cows up . . . one or two mooing in pain . . . It was something to do [sic]."[77] In such extreme circumstances the condition of being an animal meant, ironically, that there could be increased amelioration from pain—even if this meant death.

But—as had been evident in September 1939—human relationships with companion animals even in crises are never homogenous or straightforward.[78] Thus the little dog "Blackie" yapping to alert his human companion to another's presence was shot—by a comrade: "The bloody stupid thing! The enemy's here, and he's giving the game away!" The soldier who accompanied Blackie later explained, "It broke my heart because I'd become very familiar with Blackie."[79] Certainly some stories of rescued dogs endorse the compassionate story the RSPCA and Dick Rendel conveyed. Thus a terrier-type mongrel who understood only French was "taken on the staff of the parish" where a sub-lieutenant's father was vicar.[80] One of the Royal Naval rescuers who had taken some six trips to rescue the troops was permitted ashore on one of the occasions and, "he evacuated a very special person—a stray cat that he found hiding amongst the rubble and wreckage of Dunkirk." He tucked the cat under his coat and smuggled it home to Britain where it lived contentedly," a much-loved family pet," for several years to come."[81] But other stories give a very different impression of the animal-human relationship in Dunkirk. A sailor in the Royal Navy remembered the stance of military police:

> When the troops arrived alongside us it was very sad—a lot of them had got dogs with them that they'd picked up. But as the men arrived with their dogs, the military police were shooting them and throwing them in the harbour. Every time they did this, there was a great 'Boo!' from the sailors on the ships loading up the men. We couldn't see any reason why these dogs shouldn't be taken back to Britain.[82]

And when the dogs did arrive not all were taken into a vicarage. Rodney Foster of the Kent coastal Home Guard noted the "trains dashing through every few minutes with troops" and, ambiguously, "The [RSPCA] Inspector has been busy killing scores of dogs which have come over with the troops."[83]

In the book that largely created the "good" Dunkirk story, *Guilty Men*, there is a distinct absence of any animal presence. But animals *were* there. Their presence certainly disrupts the popular memory of this event and, I suggest, leads us to question whether the treatment of dogs—at least by the military police—was indeed part of the good "People's War." By adding in animals there is not a more complete account of what happened at Dunkirk per se but an *undermining* of the way this military disaster was constructed as an achievement.

Historian Amy Helen Bell has confidently declared that, "The Blitz provided the first tests of civilian morale."[84] I am not convinced by her dates. Before September 1940 there were many occasions—if we acknowledge an animal presence—when people's "morale" was tested. Certainly the rhetoric of civilization being observed through a nation's attitude towards animals had been sorely tested in those first months of war. But as war progressed, instead of just regret (or shock) at the earlier massacres, new cross-species relationships would be forged on the basis of a common experience of total war.

CHAPTER FIVE

Building Cross-Species Experience: Eating and Food in the War

It was snowing. They were loaded with heavy shopping bags, and then came a long wait for the cat! But they seemed amazingly cheerful. They waited for Pussy's dinner with the same good humour they had waited for their own.[1]

The last chapter concluded with an example of the separation of human and animal at Dunkirk, but it also started to explore the conditions in the physical landscape of war that began to bring animals and humans closer together. I now want to discuss some of the common characteristics crossing animal-human species that came to the forefront in the war. Fairly obviously humans and companion animals both need food in order to survive for any length of time but this basic requirement of life was changed by the war. As noted, previously, there had been food products specifically created for dogs and cats but there had also been the sharing of human scraps with animals. However, the diet of *both* animals and humans started to change during the war: such practices resulted in shared cross-species experiences.

WARTIME CHANGES TO ANIMAL AND HUMAN DIETS

There was a plethora of advice on what to feed humans and animals during the war, especially when rationing for humans (but not companion animals) was introduced from January 1940.[2] After the introduction of rationing of meat for human consumption, Parliament then discussed specific provision for dogs. In response to a parliamentary question William Morrison, then Minister of Food, advised that supplies of "offals," unsuitable for human consumption, could be obtained by butchers from wholesale distribution depots for selling to pet owners. Other "by-products" mainly used in livestock feeding-stuffs would also be available. Major-General Sir Alfred Knox, however, voiced his concern that such foodstuffs were very difficult to obtain in country districts and that the Minister was "really condemning [dogs] to death." In reply Morrison confidently asserted, "I do not think that any dogs are being condemned to death."[3] Dogs could indeed "get by." Biscuits produced specifically for dogs continued to be produced, albeit using fewer cereals and low grade flour.[4] And even when Spratts, the dog biscuit maker, was bombed, a Mass Observation survey reported that no dealer was unable to provide for his customers.[5] Tinned and packet food for cats also continued to be produced, albeit in different containers.[6] The yearly manufacture of some 15,000,000 "portions" of cat and dog food in tins were replaced by such food now being sold in glass bottles at the rate of some 300,000 a week.[7] That is, although war circumstances altered the format of the food, the legal provision of discrete animal food as such was not in doubt. Although the RSPCA realized that such food would still be available for dogs and cats it cautioned against its overuse as starchy, unhealthy, food. Instead, cooked bought food should be mixed with soups or gravies made from bones or household meat scraps. But soup could be dangerous using bones from poultry or rabbits: "unless the bones are crushed with a hammer almost to a powder, they should not be fed to dogs, or cats."[8] NARPAC too devised recipes for dogs and cats. These included boiled rice, mashed butter beans, and vegetable tops for dogs; or sardine oil, kipper trimmings, and tails of white fish for cats. It recommended baking a sort of cake for dogs from potato peel with parings of carrot and turnips.[9] Scraps moistened with Marmite liquid baked for an hour then cut into slices once cold were suggested for cats. Conditioning powders would also be useful.[10] The RSPCA encouraged dogs to eat congealed ox blood and "residual carcass substances" such as (boiled) windpipe or lungs.[11] For its part the NCDL reminded people that offal and horseflesh and bones from the butcher could be used for canine feeding.[12] "Cat's meat," that is meat from worn-out horses, was still available as was "dog's meat" from the same equine source.[13] As Vere Hodgson noted, "The cat meat shop is the joy of Notting Hill Gate. All the ladies go up to get the favorite 'steak' of their favorite cat. They nearly drive the man crazy suiting all these animals. He sells out every day."[14] Baked liver and cat's meat were available from various dealers and Harrison Barber, the horse slaughterers and carter firm, would deliver horsemeat at 6d a pound but with "no guarantee of freshness on arrival."[15] The euphemistically named Continental Butchers, newly opened in Chelsea's Manor Street, was scarcely patronized when it first opened. In due course, queues would form outside to buy the linguistically disguised horsemeat.[16] Theodora FitzGibbon's dog also took her dietary needs into

FIGURE 5.1 Keeping a cat in condition (London Collection Magazines, Bishopsgate Institute)

her own paws by visiting pig bins in the Chelsea area, and the local work-house where an old man fed her crusts; "I think she was probably his only friend." In pubs the dog was given arrowroot biscuits that she enjoyed with a drop of Guinness served in an ashtray.[17]

Needless to say, advice from charities—and innovative recipes—do not tell us what animals actually ate: to know this we need to look elsewhere. What emerges from diaries and memoirs is, unsurprisingly, that—like humans—individual cats and dogs had individual tastes. Little Doodle, for example, a marmalade kitten, had been bombed out of his previous home and when found seemed unable to meow: "just opens his mouth and no sound comes" through the trauma he had experienced.[18] At one point he was offered "some black sausage, cut up into the most attractive morsels—but it was no good. He gazed [up] with the-'You'd be far better off in a Home' expression. Very common on his face these days."[19] Plans to bring up Little Doodle "as a vegetarian, is failing dismally."[20] On one occasion, however, when "Kitcat" [sic] was obtained "he wolfed it down as if it were a banquet."[21] The cats living with the Sladen family in wartime Swindon were fed mainly on trimmings from meat, fish, and poultry eaten by the people of the family. Chris Sladen, then a child, has attributed the cats' wartime existence both to a family tradition that children liked pets and to keep down the mice, although "neither cat was any use at the latter." Unrationed rabbit was popular with the cats as well as fish, probably coley, bought from Macfisheries specifically for the cat: "My mother, a keen RSPCA flag seller, continued to buy coley (and other fish etc) even after catching the Macfisheries manager plucking live fowl at the back of the shop—not much choice, really."[22] To illustrate the difficulty, on occasion, of getting fish and thus returning home just with poor stale whiting and a small bit of cod, Gwladys Cox wrote that Billingsgate wholesale fish market declared it was the worse day for fish "ever known."[23] To emphasize the point the next day all that was available was "rock eel"—(still a favorite fried fish of Londoners even though it is dogfish)—but Bob in disgust refused to eat this so survived the day on evaporated milk.[24] Despite eating a variety of fish—whiting, cod, herrings—Bob seemed to prefer the weekly purchase of rabbit, getting bored with fish.[25] Similarly in the Landen household the cats preferred rabbit to fish; "cats are tired of fish."[26] One of them, Peckle, also disdained other foods: "Bought half a pound of 'pet food' from the butchers at 6d a pound but 'Peckle' won't touch it. Fussy animal!"[27]

QUEUING FOR FOOD: FOR WHOM?

The painting by Evelyn Dunbar, an artist working for the War Artists' Advisory Committee, titled "The Queue at the Fish-Shop"[28] and apparently based on an observation at Strood near Rochester in Kent, is worth considering here. Commentators have noted the depiction of her husband, Roger Folley, in RAF uniform and her sister crossing the road. Some have ignored the dog but, no doubt copying the catalogue entry of the Imperial War Museum where the painting is held, have observed the cat, suggesting he "has joined in, rather hopefully."[29] But there is wide evidence to suggest that such a cat's expectation of food from the fishmongers was not merely hopeful but *would* have been met. People, usually women, would spend as much time queuing for food for their animal companions as for the human members of the family. Vere Hodgson observed the patience of such women in the cat food queue: "It was snowing. They were loaded with heavy shopping bags, and then came a long wait for the cat! But they seemed amazingly cheerful. They waited for Pussy's dinner with the same good humor they had waited for their own."[30] People "queued for hours" to help Buster Lloyd-Jones look after his wartime "evacuation sanctuary" of around 200 cats and dogs, and monkeys, goats, two donkeys, and a horse. They would bring biscuits, Oxo cubes, dog meat, and kitchen scraps.[31]

The system of acquiring—and queuing for—nonrationed food epitomized not only a blurring of class divisions but also the way in which the divisions between animal and human became broken down. Although civil servants observed that horsemeat graded as fit for human food was available in some shops—and therefore for human and not animal use—nevertheless dog owners purchased it for their animals.[32] Novelist Theodora FitzGibbon observed that the horsemeat and whale meat she bought sometimes was for herself—and sometimes for the dog.[33] Gwladys Cox recorded queuing for 45 minutes outside the fishmonger although she was told there was no fish but her efforts were rewarded with a small tail of cod and four herrings.[34] She noted in detail her search on one particular day for suitable food for Bob, the cat. Declaring "nothing in the larder for Bob or for our own supper," Gwladys Cox did what any resourceful middle class housewife in northwest London would do in the circumstances. First she rang Macfisheries but the firm was hazy about deliveries. Jones, the fishmonger in West End Lane, was closed. So having met her husband for lunch in Oxford Circus she proceeded to Selfridges, buying conger eel for the human supper. Meanwhile her husband tracked down a small tail of cod in

Hampstead. Although the eel was intended for the humans, "Bob took such a liking to it that he got most of it."[35]

BLURRING THE DISTINCTIVENESS OF
ANIMAL AND HUMAN FOOD

The time apportioned on waiting for food for animals or humans could be similar and not distinctly determined given that the food consumed was "cross-species." What had been defined separately as either human or animal food became somewhat interchangeable.[36] Unofficial barters and gifts profited human and animal alike. For example in the Landen household, Spratts cat food was swapped for a quarter pound of tea; an aunt arrived with rabbit for the cats — and cake for the humans.[37] Gyp, a south London dog, liked to eat the whale meat sold off ration from a butcher's in the Elephant and Castle. The comment of the daughter of his household, "it was like steak . . . you'd really think it was steak," suggests, however, that it was not only Gyp who ate this food. But the dog did not get bones from the butcher, despite being given them, for these were diverted to the woman of the household: "You'd ask for a bone for the dog but Gyp didn't often get the bone, because Mum used to make stews with that."[38] The practices in this household were not distinctive. Both working class and middle class people and their animals were the beneficiaries of "swapping food." For example, Nella Last was given the remains of dried-up turkey wings by a friend who had thought they would be good for her dog. But as a dog owner, Last realized that splintering bones would be unsuitable so used them in a stew as stock for her own meals.[39] Her elderly dog, Sol, usually ate "bits off the table" and dried scone and bread and butter. But when he collapsed in a coughing fit, Nella gave him some tinned salmon, "As soon as he smelled it, he took notice, and I shared it with him- only keeping back a little for tomorrow, when I'll fix it up with beaten egg and breadcrumbs to make another tea as a steamed mould."[40] In another instance a friend invited to lunch asked Gwladys Cox if she might take home the bones of the oxtail the humans had eaten for a "hungry dog friend." In addition to consenting, Gwladys also donated a "bottle of soup for the poor creature."[41] More extravagantly Dandy, a Glaswegian dog, enjoyed — apart from liver and dog biscuits spread with butter — a bar of Cadbury's milk chocolate every day. As a colleague of his human keeper, weary of hearing such daily accounts, declared, "Catering for Dandy's needs is becoming an issue."[42]

Sometimes this cross-species practice caused difficulties, at least for humans. Thus the story of "some poor old dear in the queue in front of me . . . [at the horsemeat shop in Mornington Crescent], and because she had too much pride to admit that she was going to eat it herself, instead of keeping her mouth closed, she said 'It's not for me you know, it's for the cat,' and the butcher wouldn't let her have any. We just took it and went, don't care what people think, and the cat got a bit of horsemeat to eat."[43] The practice of continuing to give "human" food to cats was recognized opportunistically by advertisers. Although rationing for people was not yet implemented, albeit being discussed, on the occasion of this particular advert, Kit-e-Kat depicted a cat's exhortation "Keep all your rations—and give me Kit-e-Kat!" The sentiment appealed to human selfishness to "give puss her due without short-rationing the family" and, of course, viewing the cat as simultaneously inside and outside the family.[44] The "new bread" for humans, described by one unimpressed diarist as "pale, grey-brown, mealy in consistency and smells of barns," found unintended enthusiasts; "the cats adore it."[45] Such cross-species sharing of food and even "treats," such as chocolate, may not seem surprising to those of us who live in the twenty-first century with other animals, but it is nevertheless a rather different narrative to the usual presentation of the British nation at war. Quotidian practices, such as queuing or using food that was available rather than what was necessarily desired, were changing—providing for a companion animal was part of this process. In some ways the very process of obtaining food seemed to actually strengthen the animal-human bond. Material shortages and the time and ingenuity involved in humans obtaining food for animals seemed to strengthen the relationship.

However, although the animal-human bond was being forged more closely, there were still differentiations within species that determined diet. Thus for humans with money, food off ration, such as salmon, crab, or oysters, became almost a regular diet. Businessman Laurance Holman, the horse rider, would record at the height of the Blitz in autumn 1940 such meals.[46] Within animal species, diet was not differentiated by money per se but the particular function performed, as had been the case before the war. From November 1941 milk was rationed for humans and every adult was permitted two pints a week (plus evaporated and dried or tinned milk).[47] It was not permitted for cats and dogs, outside those in vivisection laboratories or animal hospitals. One exasperated diarist wrote in response, "This has driven me nearly demented . . . The cat is being initiated into a water and milk diet. He thinks we have gone feeble minded. But he must live on the fat of his earlier days for the time being."[48] However, "warehouse cats," living outside a family structure, and who were seen to be performing a

FIGURE 5.2 In anticipation of rationing

valuable task in protecting foodstuffs from mice and rats, were still allowed milk.[49] A differentiated diet was thus more determined by criteria of a narrow "usefulness in war" than by difference between animal and human species. This process of differentiation would create problems for horses who were stabled, rather than being put out to grass, when former grazing land was prioritized for cattle or crops. Hay and chaff was not rationed for horses; however, oats, beans, and bran was for those living or working in towns. (It was assumed that certain nonrationed feeding stuff was available on farms.) Both "working" horses as well as those kept for riding were initially included within the rationing—with higher quotas being allocated for animals working used in transport and haulage.[50] This was later amended so that horses who were not "performing useful work" were expected to be fed on food grown by their owners.[51] "Too much hay and too little corn" resulted in a horse such as Mariana being "all springs."[52] As part of his daily riding routine in Hyde Park Laurance Holman would walk "with a bag of greens" to the stables where Mariana was based.[53] Given that "warehouse cats" would also be found in stables they too needed to be fed: "went to the stable for fresh air and to feed the cats."[54] This, of course, included milk as these were "working" cats. As Holman noted, "This feeding of the cats takes up a lot of time!"[55]

CROSS-SPECIES FEEDING—AND CIVIL SERVANTS

Slaughter of animals for food was strictly regulated to prevent trade on the black market. However, there was provision for offal "by-products" to be used in producing livestock feeding-stuff and to be available to butchers to sell as dog food.[56] Nevertheless, "fiddling" inevitably took place. Once a ginger tom's sores and thinness were attributed by a vet to lack of appropriate food with a "prescription" of raw, red meat, his owner "wheedled some pieces from the butcher but he told me we were liable to two years' imprisonment! I wonder what Lady A does for her Alsatian. He used to be given 1lb of meat a day."[57] Such cross-species "arrangements" were discussed by civil servants in the Ministry of Agriculture and Food. Apparently dogs were consuming c. 280,000 tons of food per annum, practically the whole of which was defined as "human" food that should not have been wasted or food that might have been better used by more "economically useful" animals.[58] Civil servants were working—with some difficulty—to the remit of their Minister that "dogs are not to be interfered with." Accordingly "they must be fed."[59] But there was a dilemma. Either there needed to be sufficient specialized and patent foods or "there is no doubt that the owner will use bread, oatmeal, and, to some extent, milk—all of which are subsidised food—notwithstanding the provisions of Orders . . . which prohibit the use of flour and oats products for purposes other than human food."[60] Pragmatism won the day. The civil servants concluded that if they further restricted materials for manufacturers of dog biscuits "people would probably substitute for them other forms of human food."[61] It was agreed that

> to depict the ravages of dogs into our food supplies will create exasperation amongst the non-dog owners against dog owners, and resentment in dog owners who will deny that their own pets do more that eat a few scraps unfit for human consumption.[62]

Cats too came under civil service scrutiny. If dogs were eating 280,000 tons of "human" food then cats were apparently still consuming at least 18,000,000 gallons of milk a year even though this was against the regulations. However, the issue of enforcement was the problem: "It is thought to be quite impracticable, even if it were desirable, to attempt to prevent the owner of a cat from sharing, if he wishes to do so, his milk with his cat . . . it is not thought that the Waste of Food Order could be applied to the use of milk for feeding to cats."[63] And people did, of course, share milk. Jean Lucey Pratt recorded, "We are to be rationed to ½ pint of milk per adult per day. I can manage with this but with 3 cats it will be a watery ½ pint and there will be no milk puddings."[64] Jean rather than the cats would go without. To intervene too closely into families' domestic arrangements would smack of Nazi behavior—and undermine morale. Interestingly, by engaging in such discussions civil servants were recognizing the role that animals were starting to play in the war, particularly in the maintenance of human morale—and the growing strength of animal-human relationships.

In a recently well-received book on the operation of the black market, Mark Roodhouse has argued that people obeyed the law selectively "not because of coercion or fear of coercion . . . but because they thought the regulations both necessary and fair."[65] Although he does not consider animals in his analysis, the practice of people ignoring regulations and civil servants being aware of this but turning a blind eye supports the general argument that such restrictions on animal feeding were not felt to be "fair."[66] There seemed to be a blurring between animal and human forms of eating because of the joint experiences of total warfare. The restrictions affected both of them: a response in those people who continued to live with companion animals was to share more expansively what little did exist—whether this was legally permitted or not.

BUDGERIGARS, WILD BIRDS, AND HUMAN UNDERSTANDING

The companion animals most affected by dietary changes and food shortages in the war were not cats and dogs but budgerigars and canaries. Despite the efforts of the RSPCA, substitutes for "normal" food that had worked for cats and dogs were generally seen not to be suitable for caged birds, who were perceived to have a highly specialized diet. The prestigious British Small Animal Veterinary Association has recently compiled extensive advice on the treatment of psittacine birds such as budgerigars. It has cautioned against high-fat seeds such as sunflower and noted the value of a pulse diet.[67] Twenty-first century advice from the PDSA and the Budgerigar Society on the feeding of caged birds such as budgerigars is also clear. It emphasizes root vegetables, green leaves, and fruit, with care taken to avoid pesticides. The idea that millet or seeds should be a staple is debunked since such a high-fat diet causes obesity.[68]

Unfortunately, this way of thinking was not prevalent during the war. Frank Finn, the all-round expert on " exotic" pets, declared that "the budgerigar comes near being the ideal pet bird."[69] Certainly it was an extremely popular one, with the *Times* surmising in December 1939 that there were three or four million alive "in this country today."[70] Although attention was paid to green food, "common wayside flowering grass, pulled up by the roots if possible, but watch it has not been fouled by animals," Finn also recommended making canary seed the staple food during the winter, and "only" giving millet three times a week.[71] Other experts of the time also mentioned greens while advocating Spanish canary seed and white millet.[72]

U-boat attacks would have a direct effect on the welfare of budgerigars. The attacks on food conveys in the Atlantic had reduced the availability of seeds, including millet. In due course the government specifically decided to suspend the import of bird seed. Bird lovers were highly critical.[73] They were particularly incensed because provisions (including fodder) for race horses owned by the wealthy were permitted but, as one parliamentarian argued:

> It is put to me that this is providing for the rich man's pets, sport and enjoy-ment, whereas no provision is made for the pets which the poor man enjoys keeping . . . It seems a small thing, but these pets are greatly prized by their owners, and they think there is something wrong in the way in which this matter is being looked at by the Government, that race-horses can still be pro-vided for while their pets, which consume far less, cannot be provided for and maintained.[74]

The RSPCA suggested alternatives, encouraging people to grow their own seeds while recognizing that "the prospect of a satisfactory crop of seed would depend largely on the weather in any particular season." A sat-isfactory crop needed "the warmest and most sheltered sunny positions available with rather light, well drained soils . . . they will only produce a satisfactory crop of seed in a hot, dry summer." These endeavors sug-gest, however, the availability of sufficient land to grow crops (as well as unusually good weather). Inner-city dwellers did not necessarily have ac-cess to such an environment. This was also hinted at in RSPCA literature that encouraged people "to take every opportunity of visits to the country to collect and store the seeds of . . . plantains, dandelions, groundsel and chickweed."[75] The exhortation to grow seeds seems not to have been taken up since the charity issued a further leaflet focusing solely on the collec-tion of weeds, arguing, "It is quite possible to collect a sufficient quantity of such seeds during one's daily constitutional to keep several canaries or budgerigars in health throughout the year, even in more or less built-up areas, proving the seeds are collected when they are mature and during dry weather."[76] But the caveats here suggest that even at the time of writing the Society recognized it would be a difficult task to carry through with success.

For many birds the government decision not to import bird seed would prove fatal. Although Ian Coleman is not old enough to remember the birds living there, he has recalled the abandoned and derelict aviary in which his parents, in rural Surrey, had previously kept budgerigars:

> My parents had started with a single pair, but, by the start of the war, had a dozen or so. The first cock was a striking blue one called Joey. My mother would mention him sometimes. My father never talked of them at all.
>
> As the war progressed, it became impossible to get millet to feed the birds. My father went into the RAF and my mother, aunt and grandparents scoured the countryside to find wild seeds for feed, but could not get enough. My father took the decision to get a neighbour, skilled in the dispatch of chickens, to come round and kill the birds. The aviary remained like a shrine. My parents could not bring themselves to have birds again after the war.[77]

This story of death and mourning for killed caged birds is not rare. As another child of the war has written, "I had the impression that it was in anticipation of [my father's] inability to get food that he had to kill [the birds]. I think he wrung their necks themselves. It was . . . very upsetting for him as he was both proud and very fond of them—so much so that he could never be persuaded to have any more after the war when he could have done."[78]

At the time such deaths were deemed unavoidable since such caged birds were thought to only eat seeds such as millet. Yet even specialist veterinarians in the twenty-first century have been unable to satisfactorily ascertain the appropriate nutrition for certain birds today because of the lack of scientifically controlled studies.[79] Arguably food grown for *humans* in allotments and gardens—root vegetables and those with green leaves—may well have been able to support caged birds, albeit not fulfilling all nutritional requirements—if people and welfarists at the time had realized this. Here human lack of understanding of animal dietary requirements contributed to birds' deaths—which bird owners certainly did not wish to happen.

London Zoo, however, managed to keep its own collection of 600 parrots, parakeets, macaws, and cockatoos "the finest collection of living parrots in the British Empire and probably in the world," according to the *Times*.[80] And some stalwart budgerigar fanciers did continue to breed birds during the war. Les Martin, a breeder since the 1940s, has offered an explanation largely reliant on ways and means of obtaining millet:

> We couldn't get the seed during the war. It was basically just keeping the bloodline going. We were feeding them on gleanings from the threshing machines and any seed that we could get brought into the country. We used to have soldiers who were in the war and brought seed back from places like Morocco in their kit bags.[81]

Another early member of the Budgerigar Society who possessed a large garden turned this over to "the cultivation of millet, which he sold to regular
customers in Blackpool on an improvised rationing system."[82] And George
Orwell, in his customary critical public stance towards animals, noted that
for those who could afford it, "even in poor quarters of big towns the bird-
fanciers' shops display canary seed at prices ranging up to twenty-five shillings a pint."[83]

Birds kept for their eggs or flesh fared somewhat better when specialized food for poultry became rationed.[84] Thus Diana Cooper fed her hens
on boiled scraps mixed with rationed meal. In turn their eggs were sold
to those who passed on their eggshell coupons and their scraps.[85] Others
collected cockle-shells from the coast for their hens[86] or made a "corn" of
mixed carrots and crumbs "and they dash madly for it if I take green stuff,
as if they were starving for it!"[87] Such birds lived in both country and town.
Thus Cocky, a Rhode Island Red cockerel living in a Stepney back yard with
various hens, was proudly displayed to Harold Scott, then a civil servant in
London's Civil Defence Administration, on an official visit.[88] Nevertheless
chickens could be killed "because it was hard to find food for them," suggesting that chicken's eggs (rather than the widely available dried substitutes) were more valued than their flesh.[89]

THE IMPLICATIONS OF THE WASTE OF FOOD ORDER

Later in the war, there would be some prosecutions for feeding wild birds.
This arose from the Waste of Food Order enacted by August 1940. Quite
specifically, as noted earlier in civil servants' deliberations, the feeding (or
not) of companion animals was excluded. That the RSPCA felt obliged to
issue a leaflet of explanation refuting alarmist and inaccurate reports in the
press, suggests that there was at least consternation amongst some animal
carers. As the charity sensibly argued, "It does not seem possible that any
court would hold that the moderate feeding of a *pet* upon food suitable for
human beings would be waste" (my emphasis). While suggesting that people use available substitutes for human food, the RSPCA argued, "But certainly do not deny your pets your table scraps because some well meaning
person chooses to tell you that you are liable to a penalty thus disposing of
your leavings."[90] It is significant here that the advice—which included legal
advice—was focused on the feeding of "pet" animals, that is, animals living
within a family and animals who would be fed behind "closed doors." But
the RSPCA interpretation did not extend to wild or " non-owned" animals.

Many did not take enforcement of this regulation entirely seriously. Thus Vere Hodgson wrote, "[Going to the café in Hyde Park near the Albert Memorial the] sparrows came to my hand to be fed. I feared Lord Woolton* would suddenly appear from behind the bushes but, fortunately, he did not. Who can resist a sparrow on your hand?" *(Lord Woolton Minister of Food).[91] Nevertheless in Barnet in north London Miss Mary Bridget O'Sullivan was fined £10 for permitting bread to be wasted. Her servant, Miss Persi, was also fined 3/11d [nearly 20p] for "wasting bread." The servant had twice been seen throwing bread to birds in the garden. Miss O'Sullivan admitted that bread was put out daily. "I cannot let the birds starve," she said.[92] Here the status of the animal—rather than the act itself of feeding another species—was key to prosecution. More bizarrely, the caterers Jo Lyons were prosecuted for "allowing mice," who had infested their kitchens in their Hammersmith headquarters, to eat scraps they found.[93] This differentiation between "owned" and "wild" animals was also seen in the countryside treatment of sparrows, where sparrow clubs were formed to kill the birds. A reward of ½d or 1d (halfpenny or 1 penny) was given for every sparrow killed whose dead body was produced as evidence.[94] This initiative seemed to have forgotten the plague of caterpillars that had apparently continued without constraint in 1918 when sparrow clubs had flourished then and killed off insects' natural predators.[95] In a leaflet aimed at children the Royal Society for the Protection of Birds argued against this approach, stating that it was "entirely wrong" to suppose that because birds were seen amongst crops "they are necessarily doing mischief." In one such observation birds were, in fact, killing caterpillars. Birds were thus doing their bit for the "Dig for Victory" campaign. People who interfered with this war effort of birds were acting as a sort of fifth columnist. They were aligning themselves with the "ranks of the Hitlers of the Brute Kingdom, who delight to attack the weak and helpless." They were hampering "our War Effort, or rather the War Effort of the Birds."[96]

Diets of humans and animals did change because of the shortages created by warfare but it was never the case that nonhuman animal species, particularly cats and dogs, were sharply differentiated because of this. This is partly due to the relatively adequate food supply. Pragmatically Jean Lucey Pratt wrote in her diary in January 1942,

We have been, and are, promised to be the best-fed nation in Europe . . . A regular supply of butter, marg, cooking fat, cheese, bacon, sugar and tea arrives every week. As much bread and flour as I need . . . There are still plenty of tinned beans, carrots and soups . . . Meat is more difficult than it was, but there is often sausage meat and corned beef as substitutes and makeweights. Fresh and salt fish can be bought at controlled prices in fairly good supply.[97]

After a specific area was bombarded, people would also feed animals displaced from bombed houses. As one rescue worker declared, "I find most of these poor people will give their last crust to their cat or dog. Old women of seventy or more have called me into their rooms where they have had several stray cats they had been feeding."[98] Such cats would also be routinely fed by animal charities. As one RSPCA officer reported after a raid in Canterbury, "There are still a number of cats around the debris. These I am feeding each day until such time as I can contact the owners."[99] Rather than usual diets being merely restricted, total war meant that human and animal alike would routinely eat "new" food that was usually eaten by another species. The animal-human divide was being eroded.

CHAPTER SIX

Blurring the Boundaries: Who Is Going to Ground? Who Is Protecting Whom?

"I've had this old fellow six years, I wouldn't think of life without him . . . I don't like shelters because of my asthma so I never go to one, so he's not alone ever."[1]

In the previous chapter I considered the cross-species practice of eating that blurred the distinction between animal and human. In this chapter, I explore the effect of entirely new built structures upon animal and human alike. In anticipation of aerial bombardment the state had made, albeit limited, various provisions for shelters. This included Anderson shelters consisting of embedded arched sheets of corrugated iron for back gardens; and for inside use for houses without gardens, Morrison shelters that comprised essentially a large caged box to be placed on the floor in which the household would shelter from falling masonry.[2] There were also communal shelters often in the middle of a street made of brick walls erected above ground to cater for a number of people in a small locality, as seen on page 103. Later, in London, underground tube stations would be taken over as shelters in the evenings: expensive hotels would turn over basements to their guests for night-time sheltering during air raids.[3]

People were not permitted to take animals with them into communal shelters outside their own home. Given that most communal shelters initially had neither toilets nor washing facilities, it is not surprising that the Home Secretary, Sir John Anderson, refused to allocate a part of the shelters for humans with their dogs.[4] Some people — much to the consternation of the NCDL — tied dogs up outside while they sheltered. But, the charity also noted, other "people used to stay outside with their dogs."[5] A well-publicized example of such abandonment was in the heart of London in Kensington Gardens, frequented by the well-heeled, and there was an unsuccessful campaign to allow dogs inside the shelter. The authorities had even provided tethering places outside, "their owners being presumed to

FIGURE 6.1 Surviving back garden Anderson shelter, south London, 2013

be sufficiently callous to desert them whilst they themselves go to earth."[6] In due course the RPSCA and NCDL would jointly finance a specific—separate—shelter to cater for 36 dogs in the Kensington Gardens. At the stone laying ceremony Sir Robert Gower called it the first such shelter, implying that more would follow. That this didn't happen, suggests that the separation of human and dog was not mutually satisfactory. Indeed as Gower stated, "It is, I believe, true that the majority of dog owners would decline to avail themselves of an air-raid shelter while their pets were exposed to grave peril outside."[7] Although canine and human would be—discretely—safe, they would not be together. The decision to save oneself (but not a companion animal) or risk death and injury (for human and animal alike) was influenced by the nature of a relationship with an animal that was not static but evolving. The NCDL, as noted earlier, suggested that people place notices in their windows to offer shelter to humans and dogs caught out walking when the air raid warning went.[8] Specially printed posters were available from the League: "If caught far from home look for Red-White-and-Blue notices on private premises, 'Dogs and Owners welcome during Air-Raids.'"[9] People would welcome strangers—human and canine alike—to shelter in their personal space. In this way both human and animal were safe—and engaged with other beings in a time of stress. An alternative approach was to restrict the parameters of the dog's walk so that both human and animals were never far from home: "Home is best for both of you during air-raids."[10] Those who were wealthy still needed protection from air raids. Thus horses and riders were offered common shelter. At the suggestion of Lady Churchill, members of her local branch of the RSPCA on the western outskirts of London agreed to follow her example and put placards outside their stables in which, in the event of air raids, horses and their riders could shelter.[11] The King too offered part of the Royal Mews for an emergency horse hospital. And horses who were on the London streets were offered shelter during a raid in the Knightsbridge and Whitehall barracks of the Household Cavalry.[12] Although "civilians," on several occasions Mariana or Trump, who would daily traverse Hyde Park with Laurance Holman, their businessman rider, would be offered shelter in the Horse Guards' barracks—that housed soldiers and horses alike. As Holman noted in his diary on 30 September 1940, "Said a little prayer of thanks for another night of safety: midday ride with raid shelter in L[ife]. G[uard]. Barracks on the way back. Mariana went home so walked her from the Victoria Gate."[13] Here the horse's usual routine and riding route (as well as that of Holman) was changed because of aerial bombardment.

How communal shelters operated seemed to depend in part on the discretion of the warden or marshal. One particularly hostile warden certainly recognized the value of the canine-human relationship: "For childless couples & single people their dog was often their child." But such understanding did not prevent her turning away people with their dogs. She observed, families "were heartbroken . . . But it could not be allowed. Apart from hygienic reasons, an animal's reactions to a nearby bomb burst are unpredictable, and it was not safe."[14] This suggests that although the value of the relationship was recognized, assumptions were being made about how that relationship would function if a bomb were to land. (I have yet to find accounts of any dog attacking a human in such circumstances.)The existence of regulations did not necessarily imply, of course, that they were always implemented. Thus one woman in central London used to take her dog to a small communal shelter nearby, "He's so small no-one makes a fuss he curls up under the eiderdown to get away from the noise, but he never makes a noise himself he just shivers all the time."[15] A more striking example is that of an old costermonger who during a raid remembered that he had not released his donkey from his shafts and returned to lead the donkey into the street shelter; "it went in docilely enough." The man, meanwhile, went outside again amidst the heavy bombing to protect his barrow against looters.[16] The reason one woman appeared before the Westminster magistrates was, it seems, not primarily for attempting to take her pet monkey into a communal shelter but because of the subsequent physical fighting with the marshal who refused entry.[17] However, as the *Animals' Defender*, the journal of the National Anti-Vivisection Society (NAVS), reported in October 1940, "Dogs are still not officially admitted to public shelters, though a humane-minded marshal will employ his blind eye."[18] Certainly in propaganda images Rip, the dog taken in by an air raid warden in Poplar who would assist in rescuing living beings from bombed buildings, was seen visiting communal brick shelters and being welcomed by those sheltering.[19] The material circumstances of particular moments of total war would also play a part in decisions to allow (or ban) dogs from sheltering with humans, as this story from South London recounted some years later suggests. The physical presence of the dog together with the dramatic plea of a young woman during an actual raid seems to have been key here:

> We had an Anderson shelter in the front garden, so we were all in there. Then another bomb dropped but it didn't explode . . . So we had to go down the *public* shelter, through the street with eiderdowns round our shoulders, pillows on our heads and there was shrapnel flying everywhere. We got to the public shelter and my sister's got our little dog; and they wouldn't let her in. So she's standing at the top of the stairs with all this lightning flashing and she's screaming, "If my dog dies, I die with it." So they had to let her in.[20] (my emphasis)

A similar story was reported in the New Street area of central Birmingham. During one particular raid people were shaking with shock as they approached the entrance of the communal shelter. An old man was carrying his dog and an old woman "crying for her cat and kittens she had left in the kitchen." The wardens explained that the woman could not have all the animals in the shelter, but another shelterer said she would go and find them: "With this the old soul went into the shelter, where she was well looked after. The cat and kittens were fetched."[21] Cat owners were encouraged to place a harness on the cat to also take her (with them) into the shelter. Those who followed such advice did not always have successful outcomes. Ellen Potter recalled being woken by sirens at 1 am, taking cushions to the Anderson shelter, and putting the harness on the cat to also take him there. The cat struggled out of the harness and was let back in the house and, for some protection, shut up on the ground floor.[22]

Animal charities debated whether it was safer for animals and humans to stay together or for there to be discrete provision within a house. Thus the PDSA advocated a gas-proof shelter for dogs.[23] And this was certainly

FIGURE 6.2 People and dog after bombing, Watson Street, New Cross, 1944 (LHW 17/87, Bishopsgate Institute)

popular at the outbreak of war. By 6 September 1939 the shelter designed for the animal charity had already sold out, with a 3-4 week wait for new supplies.[24] Such shelters were small, round, metal contraptions. At least one dog was found to like this as a measure against the noise of a thunderstorm, or to keep cool in the summer heat.[25] The NCDL, however, was much less enthusiastic about a canine-specific shelter. There were practical reasons: Dogs would consume much air—but be confined in a tiny space. More importantly, being together was advocated for both animals and humans: "Allow the animals to share their gas proof or other shelter that they themselves occupy."[26] This would enable humans to know precisely where their dogs were—and allow for the provision of mutual support.

SHELTERS AND SHELTERING:
HUMAN AND ANIMAL SPACES

Companion animals would shelter together with their keepers; and the animals are remembered as part of the recall of time spent in such structures.

Then a child of six, one Londoner recently explained that her family had shared their Anderson shelter with two women from next door "and their fat old brown and white mongrel."[27] Other animals (and humans) were seen to be "too independent," like the cat living with Doris Pierce who declined to go into the Anderson shelter—as did Doris's brother.[28] Significantly, shelters of whatever type were "war structures" that were new for human and animal alike in Britain. In practice, of course, taking shelter involved "going to ground," a practice routinely undertaken by various domestic and wild mammals: Humans now imitated this behavior in order to survive bombardment. Far from it being the case that air raid sirens alerted people to pending bombing, it was animals who often ensured that the humans (as well as themselves) went to the Anderson or Morrison shelter speedily. Dogs' hearing is significantly more sensitive than that of humans. They can hear high-pitched sounds that humans cannot hear at all. And, as anthrozoologist John Bradshaw has put it, "Cats, which can hear even higher-pitched sounds than dogs can, would presumably describe dogs as having high-frequency deafness."[29] Such distinctive animal skills helped animal and human alike. But it was not just that pets heard sounds and reacted to them. Animals were exhibiting agency—and in so doing saved themselves and their human companions. As Erica Fudge has recently argued, "To say that animals are agents, when agency is understood as not automatically requiring 'self-reflexive intentionality' is to recognise what has been known by anyone who has ever worked with or lived with an animal: they are not simply objects to be shunted and counted, but subjects to be negotiated with."[30] Thus their carers would read such behavior as meaningful actions. Dogs and cats would be actively observed as reliable indicators of forthcoming bombing (rather than simply being watched by humans to ascertain the location of the animals to take them to safety). One particular story of a bombing in Bermondsey in June 1944 has paid tribute to the cat's sensitive hearing, "Suddenly my mother notice our cat behaving strangely, in the way animals used to do when a raid was imminent." The family was got into the Anderson shelter and the neighbors also woken up. "When we emerged we found the house blasted inside-out." The humans were taken to a rest center but the cat remained. "Before we left for the Rest Centre, mum tried hard to feed him. He refused all food. We think, in his little cat head, he suspected all the damage to his home was my mother's fault and refused to have anything to do with her. He wouldn't even come inside the house. He must have been traumatised. But my father found him a home with a nearby neighbour whose undamaged house allowed her to stay put. And there the cat stayed until years after the war, when he died." Years later

FIGURE 6.3 Rest center: men, women and a dog, East End, September 1940 (LHW 20/11, Bishopsgate Institute)

the neighbors expressed their immense gratitude towards the woman of the household for alerting them. But, says her now adult daughter, "She did of course, but we all know it was the cat who was responsible for alerting my mother to danger. God bless our pets—and observant owners."[31] It was joint animal-human action that saved lives.

By unpacking the story of the kindly human compassionately taking a companion animal into a shelter I am suggesting both that animals were proactive but that—although they may have been compassionate—humans were using animals' skills to also save themselves. Animals would often literally lead the way to shelter. As one Londoner described it, "The dog's ears used to go up and it used to run and was in the dug-out before us."[32] The skills of Jack, a dog living under the German flight path for Swansea in South Wales, would alert the family. "If the air raid was at night, which was usually the case apparently, Jack would get them from their beds. It seems Jack was never wrong in his predictions. They were all under the stairs by the time the sirens went off. Jack soon realised that it was a bit of a squeeze under those stairs and it seems he always went under after everyone else had gone in, manoeuvring himself in backwards to that he could see out and be first out."[33] In Barrow-in-Furness, the cat and dog in the Last family would beat the humans to the shelter "and were comfortably settled by the time we had slipped our shoes off to get on to the bed. My wild, free cat does not care tuppence for planes—he is very much the captain of his soul, and can take his chance."[34] This suggests that the cat was running to the shelter to be with the people rather than hiding from the noise: he did not want to be left alone in the house. The "being together" of, in another instance, man and dog, was eloquently explained by a wartime Mass Observation interviewee thus: "I've had this old fellow six years, I wouldn't think of life without him . . . I don't like shelters because of my asthma so I never go to one, so he's not alone ever."[35] The dog was not alone: but nor, of course, was the man.

War changed public and personal space, most obviously through the destruction of buildings, streets, and even entire localities, but also through the new spaces created to protect people from bombardment. As new spaces they required cross-species "negotiation." Thus the Chislehurst caves in the southeast London suburbs, originally constructed by digging out chalk used in lime burning and brick making, became one of the largest deep air-raid shelters in the country (in the late 1960s they would be a venue for a Jimi Hendrix concert).[36] Initially one family would feed their dog, Gyp, and leave him in a relative's house, their own house having been bombed out. They would say, "Now be a good boy, Gyp. You stay here tonight," before going to the caves. But the dog kept running back to the bombed house, having "put his foot through the anti-blast paper on the windows, climb(ed) out and run back home again." Eventually Gyp was also taken down to the caves although "he didn't really like it down there. He was like me, he couldn't wait to get out."[37] Animal geographers have questioned whether spaces should be viewed anthropocentrically, as solely the result of human intentional actions, and also whether there are ever spaces that can be designated as nonhuman space.[38] War circumstances highlighted the relevance of such thinking. Thus diarist and horse rider Laurance Holman often configured the topography of the previous night's bombing in relation to where he lived—and where his horse Mariana was stabled. While horses may not be conventionally seen as "pets" in that they live outside the perimeters of a human's geographic home, certainly the horses featuring in Holman's life fulfilled the function of "creating stability for a human."[39] Mariana and Trump possessed names and by being named were, as Nik Taylor puts it, "[brought] into our human worlds."[40] Thus: "last night my M.G. was within 100 yards of a house demolished in Woburn Sq and Mariana was about the same distance from a crater made in Wimpole Street."[41] The war itself had not made him aware of where Mariana lived—he obviously knew that very well. However, the nature of topography in a war context, identifying places by the falling of bombs in this example, served to highlight the different spaces inhabited by man and horse and the way they were united by the experience of war. Further, on various occasions, the daily ride would often include a visit to see the previous night's damage, thus witnessed by man and horse, Mariana, alike. "An easy night for us, last night, but Whitehall got it: 2 in Birdcage Walk, 1 behind F[oreign]O[ffice], 1 . . . in St James' Park: 3 in Whitehall: 2 in Trafalgar Sq[uare] . . . Mariana passed all these spots in my ride."[42]

What had been hidden places for material goods in the home, such as cupboards under the stairs or basements, became cross-species spaces to be shared as shelters. Beatrix Lehmann, for example, wrote about her flat in Charlotte Street in central London where "she and her old dog crept down to the basement and lay there wondering if anyone knew they were there."[43] Similarly, over in the Isle of Dogs in east London, Dodger, the dog, would shelter under the stairs with Margaret, the woman of the house, while her husband, Arthur, would go upstairs to watch the bombs fall.[44] In a moment of apparent sudden bombing near the offices of the Greater World Association Trust (that also included living accommodation) in Notting Hill, two women and Scamp, the little cat who had just been let in, improvised some joint air raid cover:

> He was just warming his paws before the warm hearth when the bombs fell and he streaked under the desk beside me. So we spent the next two hours laughing at ourselves and the cat. The Old Lady [of 80] and I dived under the

desk hand in hand. The little creature was there also, looking at us and saying clearly, "What you do, I do. When you go under, I go under."

After the bombing finished the cat came paddling round and "jumped straight at me . . . and settled down on my feet and ankles. I lay like a medieval statue on a tombstone."[45] Other spaces previously designated simply for human use also became shared animal-human spaces. Thus in the Dorchester hotel, the Turkish bath acted as an underground shelter for hundreds of wealthy humans and their canine companions, barking as people went past.[46] More modestly, Jerry, an Airedale puppy, was "allowed" on a small landing near the top of the stairs on which he had "his carpet." There he would sleep with his head "overhanging the next steps. If we went upstairs he would open one eye and watch." However, when bombing occurred—which Jerry did not like—"we were all together in the kitchen in those times."[47]

STRESS: A SHARED CONDITION

Both animals and humans—depending on their individual personalities— suffered from stress due to aerial bombardment. Although professional veterinarians had claimed that the sound of bombs would be perceived by animals no differently to that of fireworks released on Bonfire night on 5th November, many animals, like their human companions, were anxious. Mick, a mutt, in normal times was an independent sort of dog living with the Townsend family in Queen's Park in northwest London. "When allowed Mick would sit on the corner outside the sweet shop and woe be tide any dog who wanted to walk by, they soon learned that they had to pass on the other side of the road. He also had a real hate for motorcycles and would chase after them as they turned the corner. He was only a little thing but had a big heart and lick for all the neighbourhood kids." But this tiny dog was not impervious to all dangers. "Mick had one fear, he hated fireworks, and two years in a row the day after Guy Fawkes night we had to fetch him from the dogs home where he ended up terrified." There had been no discussion about killing Mick at the start of the war but the first raids on London terrified the dog and he had cried all night. Consequently the dog was destroyed. In this instance the decision to kill was based on a knowledge of Mick's earlier behavior and his actual reaction to bombardment, rather than anticipated projections.[48] Similarly, a middle class young woman in Mill Hill explained that her dog had to be "put to sleep eventually" since the air raids drove the dog mad, "we did all we could—we spent no end of money on vets. But it all did no good."[49]

Other animals suffered less acutely. The French poodle Marx, whom we encountered being groomed in the week before war was declared, seemed to have had an ambivalent relationship with the Blairs. As Eileen Blair had written, "We called him Marx to remind us that we never read Marx and now we have read a little and taken so strong a dislike to the man that we can't look the dog in the face when we speak to him."[50] His stance during raids was "subdued and uneasy."[51] Other dogs reacted differently. Rex, for example, would become excitable: "When he started barking for no apparent reason we knew an air raid was on the way and the guns starting up make [sic] him even more excited. If he got out in the street when a raid was in progress we couldn't get him back indoors until it was all quiet again." The barking unsettled the woman of the household. Unsympathetically, she forbade Rex from coming into the Anderson shelter "barking all night" and he would stay in the house with the son of the family, "who slept through anything." The dog's anxious barking irritated the woman, who interpreted it as a sign of the dog "enjoying himself" while others were terrified—but quiet.[52]

The Mass Observation overview of the survey conducted in London in July 1941, stated that "the average person seemed to think their dogs had not been seriously affected by [the air raids], unless it had made them *more* hysterical"[53] (my emphasis). The insertion of the comparative adverb implies, as veterinary surgeons had posited, that the raids exaggerated existing tendencies. As the *Times'* special correspondent noted, Billy, a badger in the zoo, had escaped from his cage before any air raid warning and had dived straight into one of the tunnels converted into a shelter. He continued, "Certainly there is no evidence that wild or captive creatures in London have noticed the Blitzkrieg to any more significant extent that its human inhabitants have."[54] A later article compared the behavior of parrots "who dislike the noise [of bombing] and scream loudly and hysterically" with "human counterparts . . . in every shelter and every block of flats. They always explain that they are so highly strung and sensitive."[55]

Animal charities gave advice on dealing with anxiety in animals: Anxiety in humans was often ameliorated by an animal presence.[56] Animal specialists observed that if a human was calm this could positively influence their animal's mood. Thus "Bob Martin" reminded people that dogs and cats reacted very quickly to the "emotions of their owners" and advised that if people wanted to minimize animals' "possible fear, it is important that in handling them in times of emergency you do so without fuss or undue agitation." To emphasize the point, the following instruction was given in capital letters: "KEEP CALM!"[57] Certainly it was not just animals who were "driven mad" by air raids. Expanding on the effect of war on people as well as dogs, one man explained to Mass Observation interviewers, "I know the raids for instance drove many dogs mad. The war's done the same thing to everything and everybody. I suppose it just can't be helped. Only it does seem rough on the animals—after all they didn't make the war, yet they have to suffer the most."[58] The analogies between humans and animals under the stress of air raids were also explored in the work of psychoanalyst Melitta Schmideberg. Discussing "non-neurotic" children she concluded that they were little affected by raids (unless injured or lost) so long as the adults in the immediate environment remained unafraid. Rather they reacted more to underlying anxiety: "This applied equally to infant children

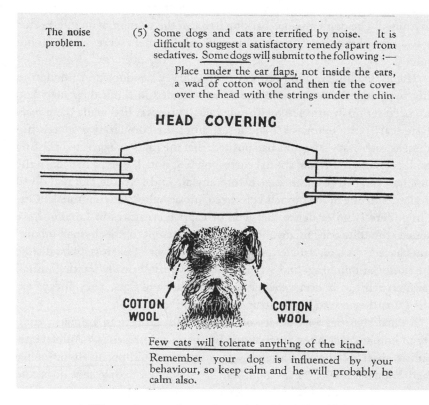

The noise problem.

(5) Some dogs and cats are terrified by noise. It is difficult to suggest a satisfactory remedy apart from sedatives. Some dogs will submit to the following :—

Place under the ear flaps, not inside the ears, a wad of cotton wool and then tie the cover over the head with the strings under the chin.

HEAD COVERING

COTTON WOOL   COTTON WOOL

Few cats will tolerate anything of the kind.

Remember your dog is influenced by your behaviour, so keep calm and he will probably be calm also.

FIGURE 6.4 A difference between dogs and cats, *Animals and Air Raids* (courtesy of RSPCA)

and to domestic animals." In a departure from standard psychoanalytic approaches Schmideberg introduced the reactions of her own cat "normalising" the air-raid warning: "my cat seems, to judge by her behaviour, to have mistaken the sirens for the call of a tomcat."[59]

To diminish sounds that might worry some animals, the RPSCA had suggested that "some" dogs might permit the addition of cotton wool "under the ear flaps, not inside the ears" tied down with strings tied to a head covering. Sensibly the charity cautioned, "Few cats will tolerate anything of this kind."[60] The CPL evaluated the efficacy of bromides on calming cats. Too frequent a dose would cause depression. Luminal was "unreliable" and Choletone was difficult to administer and ineffective. The CPL writer concluded, "We have concerned ourselves with sedatives with exotic names and have completely overlooked the common Aspirin which, as we all know, is a sedative and which can be given quite easily in a little sweetened water or milk. A five-grain table would be equally as nerve soothing as any of the other preparation." It cautioned against routinely giving cats sedatives, advising people to check the specific reactions of their own cat: "there is no need to give what is not required."[61] Nella Last, who used her Mass Observation diary to record her own anxieties and unhappiness as well as the mood and condition of her animals, resorted to aspirin for both Mr. Murphy, the cat, and Sol, the dog, as some sort of tranquilizer during an air raid:

> I fell back on an aspirin for old Sol and half a one in milk for poor little Mr Murphy. Sol paced the hearthrug and swayed from side to side like a lion—I did not know my old dog. They are such odd, sensible animals. They took their aspirins as if they knew it was for their own good, and they lay down where I pointed, in the "well" of the strong, oak gateleg table, and were no more trouble.[62]

More dramatically, Nick, a cat hiding in a London Anderson shelter near an unexploded bomb, was eventually enticed onto a wall and grabbed. "He was in a terrified condition, but bromide powders soon sent him to sleep."[63] A memorable advertisement for "Admin" vitamins for "nervous dogs" pictured a bulldog puppy asking an older dog if it was true that Nazis ate dogs.[64] But, oddly, the advertisement suggested that anxiety was not caused by bombardment, stating "Nervous dogs are usually the victims of wrong feeding." This particular problem (unlike bombing, of course) was soluble with Admin vitamins.[65]

In reality not all animals became anxious: nor did all humans. Pat, the dog, for example, would sleep on Dorothy Bartin's feet or on her lap all

FIGURE 6.5 Canine fear solved by Admin powders

night in the Anderson shelter. Dorothy herself would also occasionally doze off with her head resting on the dog, even on the night in which two land-mines fell in the road nearby.[66] Elsewhere in southeast London the family's black dog would be left alone with Babs, then a young girl, and her baby sister in the Anderson shelter while their mother went fire-watching. "He was a black Pomeranian, and he was always down the shelter before the siren went."[67] And there are accounts of deaf cats, aware of danger but not overly worried, and kittens born during a raid, who would later demonstrate lack of concern about bombardment and would possess a "placid disposition."[68]

MUTUAL SUPPORT IN AIR RAIDS

But if the human stance was perceived to affect animal mood, the very presence of an animal could also profoundly influence human behavior. In this detailed account from Hastings on the south coast a young woman found hidden capacity for calm and responsible action because of the presence of Dale, the family dog. Dale was being walked by two teenagers of the household in the large Alexandra Park less than a mile from the coast. Initially ignoring the sirens, but then taken unawares by the speed of the raid, the young women put Dale on his lead and tried to shelter "under a scanty little bay tree." Unknown to them at the time, this would be the worst raid on the town with much loss of life.[69] The tree offered a slight protection:

> We were exposed Dale [*sic*] to bullets, machine-guns, shrapnel, from blast . . . that was flying around. I have never seriously been scared in a raid—not even that London blitz—I'd only been worried where the bombs had fallen. But . . . this morning I *was* scared. It was so hideous having to stand there under that scanty little bay with the plane roaring over so low . . . The worst part of it was Dale was howling and struggling to get away—in despair I sat on him with his little head pressed to my chest—he didn't even snarl but stared into my eyes, terrified . . . all I could think was I mustn't let go of Dale, who all the time I was expecting (is the only word)—the thought of being killed! . . . But I think also that having Dale was both a good and a bad thing—good because I was too preoccupied with him to worry what Mummy and all the others were doing. But it was bad because with him I had to struggle and stay with him under a silly bit of cover, exposed to fire because we could easily be seen from the air . . . and if we hadn't had Dale with us, we could have run to more secure cover. But my one thought was I mustn't let go, I must calm Dale. I don't know whether I spoke to him or not . . . Rita said I didn't, but I thought I said "all right, boy" like I generally do.

However, Dale's collar was too loose for him and he slipped it and dashed home during, as the writer put it, "the most savage attack on a south east coast town."[70] The account is interesting on a number of levels. The presence of the terrified dog ensured the young woman did not run in the open to more secure cover and that she focused on staying calm to reassure the dog. Abandoning the dog was not an option: this was a predicament they jointly shared and which she sought to mitigate. As she suggested, the dog both added to her fear—having to be responsible for him—as well as help-ing her get through a terrifying moment. There was later relief that the dog had decided to rush straight home and was safe. "I thought he might run wild and we would never see him again." Dale's experience of a severe raid was, of course, not unique. Esther Rowley described the effect of the worst raid in Exmouth—when 25 people died—and her fears for her dogs and cat[71]:

> I heard the unmistakable sound of machine-gun fire, rather deep-throated but it came nearer—nearer still. Domino rushed out in the garden before I could stop him. The noise now was terrific. Four German fighter-bombers raced across our lawn at tree top height, machine-guns rattling as hard as they could. Domino rushing madly round the lawn below them barking furiously. I thought he would be killed for certain. I had Rusty in my arms and little Sammy frightened, crouching at my feet. Then before one had time to think the bombs had begun to rain down as well. The house swayed, the windows shook, the German guns spattered and roared.[72]

Here we witness the different reactions of the individual animals to the same event: Sam, a usually boisterous poodle,[73] now cowering; Rusty will-ing to be held; and Domino highly agitated. The diarist's recollection, writ-ten down later in the same day, was not about her own possible death—but that of one of the dogs. This account illustrates a human's role in protect-ing her animal companions—as best she could. But, importantly, animals could also act reciprocally. For example, when planes were flying overhead, Rover, a black Labrador Retriever living in Speldhurst in Kent, would push the evacuated children with whom he lived into a hedge for protection.[74]

Such material is, of course, written by humans seeking shelter from bombardment. But animals were there too and were also responding to the situation. The plethora of extant material on sheltering from bombardment refutes the idea that there was *only* a human response, that animals merely reacted to humans or that the process of sheltering was one inevitably led by humans. Here animals came to the fore as protagonists in the survival of the nation on the Home Front. Increasingly the term *People's* War becomes a misnomer—experiencing bombardment was clearly a joint animal-human activity. Such joint activity was not just taking place on an almost personal level: the state started to take notice of animals in the war in ways in which it had failed adequately to do before the war. This changing relationship became a focus of discussion and planning during a period of war that was increasingly explicitly encompassing in its totality both humans of all ages, classes, and genders—and nonhuman animals.

CHAPTER SEVEN

The Growing Strength of Animal-Human Families and the Wartime State

The steps we take cannot always be logical . . . We have to take into account psychological factors.[1]

TO-ING AND FRO-ING AND STATE EVACUATION

Although the first weeks of September 1939 had seen a significant internal movement of people and animals within wartime Britain, there continued to be such to-ing and fro-ing particularly around the capital during subsequent years. While sometimes homes would be evacuated quickly, resulting in animals not only being abandoned but shut up inside the house, translocation as a result of a particular bombing incident was often a joint animal-human activity for people and families of all classes.[2] Thus following the bombing and looting of their West Hampstead flat, Bob the tabby cat and Gwladys Cox went to stay with relatives in Barrow-in-Furness, traveling by train. While waiting for her husband to collect a car for the last part of their journey, Gwladys and Bob waited in Carnforth station. (Carnforth station—and refreshment room—would be a future important location in the romantic film *Brief Encounter* . . . .) In the bar café the barmaid asked what was in the basket: "She said she loved cats so Bob was invited out for a run along the counter among the beer bottles and tea cups, we were glad to have him stretch his legs."[3] Bob was certainly not the only animal to leave London. Tired of bombardment in Bermondsey, then a thriving dock area, one family moved to Watford in north London. As the daughter explained, "Mum put her bits and pieces of china and glass in a tin boiler and tied the lid on it and put it behind a chair in the front room. We took the dog and what we could carry and left." This was a fortuitous exit for their own house was bombed shortly afterwards—and the looters would take even the tinned food, jam, and sugar.[4] Other animals (and humans) who had left London returned during the war even though bombing continued. Thus Robbie, a Cairn Terrier who lived with Mrs. Snepp in northwest London and was frequently noticed around the streets by diarist Gwladys Cox, had stayed in the autumn of 1939 in the country but after a couple of months both Robbie and Mrs. Snepp returned. "She'd rather chance a bomb in London, than be safe outside." [5]

Individual families initiated such comings and goings. But in the aftermath of the military defeat at Dunkirk in spring 1940 there had been widespread fear of invasion that would affect entire communities—and this fear continued for several years. Perhaps the most well-known wartime speech of Prime Minister Winston Churchill occurred after this defeat and was about the real possibility of invasion—coupled with resistance. And although his oratory, on this occasion, is remembered for its intransigence, it was also explicitly preparing the British for the prospect of invasion: "We shall fight on the beaches, we shall fight on the landing grounds, we shall fight in the fields and in the streets, we shall fight in the hills; we shall never surrender." [6] Unsurprisingly the Dunkirk military defeat coupled with the later speech affected people's physical and mental behavior—and the plans of civil servants.[7] Such anticipation of invasion continued for months turning into *years*.[8]

In some instances people resident in southeastern coastal towns, thought to be under likelihood of invasion, were not just advised but ordered to leave their homes. Residents of Shoreham Beach Bungalow Town were so instructed and were considerably distressed as the elderly occupants had built them as an investment and no provision had been made to protect them (from looting, etc.).[9] This was no mere panic: Bungalow Town was subsequently demolished to ensure a field of fire for the army's guns.[10] Under the Defence (Evacuation Areas) Regulations 1940 access to coastal towns such as the Sussex resorts of Eastbourne, Bexhill, and Hastings, was restricted to residents. All retired adults and those not in essential occupations were encouraged—though not instructed—to leave.[11] By the middle of July 1940 some 80,000 people from the coastal towns of nearby Kent alone had been "evacuated inland (or had evacuated themselves)." The majority, however, were told to stay put. Schoolchildren were evacuated from the coast and although this was *not* compulsory, schools were closed in the attempt to make such a move more persuasive. Sheep too who grazed on the Romney marshes were evacuated; some 125,000 were transferred to the Home Counties.[12]

WHY NOT ANOTHER MASSACRE?

Initially some of the response of individuals suggested that a repetition of the massacre of September 1939 might happen. One resident of Hastings, further east on this coast, remembered those weeks in summer 1940: "The German invasion was expected at any time. Every household received instructions about what to do if it actually happened . . . Everyone, not needed for defence, was to have a small bag ready packed and go to the nearest railway station and await further orders."[13] In this particular household there was no longer a family cat: the mother, a nervous individual, had already had him killed at the start of the war: "because she remembered the bombing of the first war and didn't want to think about the cat wandering about homeless and scared."[14] One local history of the town suggests that "not everyone could take their pets with them and the saddest of scenes were the queues of people outside the veterinary surgeons with pets under their arms or in boxes weeping to have them put down. Any pond was eagerly sought by parents to put their child's goldfish into."[15]

However, generally the response of individual animal carers—and the state—was rather different to the first week of the war. It is true that the notices prepared for individual households by the Ministry of Home Security instructed people to "turn off the gas, electricity and water supplies at the main and make provision for your animals and birds."[16] In this respect the advice was similar to that of summer 1939, placing responsibility for their animals on individual citizens, rather than the state.[17] But physical and material circumstances had changed: The day-to-day experience of living together in new ways had strengthened the animal-human bond. Although the state still did not wish to intervene too closely into family lives, including the animal-human relationships therein, the animal deaths of September 1939 (and reaction to them) *had* been seen to undermine war morale. The unprecedented attention civil servants gave, not just to the position of humans but also to animals in the event of enemy invasion, was contextualized by the earlier—unanticipated—massacre of September 1939. In the Home Office files are detailed accounts of the civil servants' expectations of people's attitudes towards their companion animals if invasion occurred. These indicate ways of thinking different to the start of the war. Both administrators and politicians discussed animals accompanying people *if* coastal populations needed to be compulsorily evacuated by train. Initially the civil servants considered a directive that "no dogs or cats would be allowed to accompany owners compulsorily evacuated" and thus provision would be needed for the "humane destruction" of animals and notification to the public "so as not to create any panic."[18] Despite well-laid behind-the-scene plans, NARPAC, the civil servants had declared, had jumped the gun and "have made a thorough mess of things" advising people that they should take advance action for their pets—thus in effect publicizing that invasion and compulsory evacuation was imminent and affecting morale.[19] (The organization had, of course, also alerted any lurking fifth columnists.)

However, discussion continued at length because the civil servants anticipated that people *would* want to take animals with them—rather than killing them. Reports mentioned lapdogs, cats in baskets, a Great Dane or Alsatian. The former—small animal companions—would be allowed on a train journey: the latter would not.[20] It was, however, realized that, irrespective of what specific official instructions were drawn up to make provision for animals, people *would* go to stations with their cats and dogs. (Accordingly it was determined that a yard for housing dogs before their killing and a room for cats with empty baskets or boxes would be appropriate.)[21] The invasion scare of the summer of 1940 did pass but nevertheless NARPAC and civil servants continued to make plans influenced by assumptions that pet owners would *ignore* state directives—and any law. Thus by June 1941 a draft leaflet had been prepared for south coast households. It was careful to use the conditional tense, advising people what would happen if there were to be an invasion. Instructions included going to the station with just one item of luggage. It also stated, "All domestic animals would be put down."[22] I must emphasize, however, this was not put into action. Nevertheless the bureaucrats busied themselves writing memoranda about future possibilities. Bizarrely, by November 1941 civil servants finally realized that was there "nothing in law to prevent evacuees taking animals with them."[23] Yet a whole year later in October 1942 evacuation was *still* being discussed but by now it was realized that it would also be "impossible" to prevent small animals being taken on trains.[24] Clearly such memoranda and discussions were part of the routine work of state policymakers but it is significant that animals were now playing a large part in their deliberations. They concluded that it would not be desirable to stop the transport of animals forcibly: "Although a certain amount of inconvenience to other passengers would result, the police would not be expected to take forcible action to prevent people from bringing small lapdogs with them."[25] This suggests that both animal owners and the state *had* reflected critically on the September 1939 events. The animals, who by now had shared food, shelter, bombing, and adversity with humans for several years, seemed more closely entwined with human existence than previously may have been the case (and vice versa, of course). People who lived alongside their pets knew that: Now so did those who implemented the government's decisions.

Although the Home Office files discussing compulsory evacuation—and rationing of animal food and pet ownership—do not explicitly refer to the work of Mass Observation, it seems more than coincidental that many of their conclusions are similar. The Mass Observation survey conducted in central and northwest London in the summer of 1941 recorded hostile views towards the government's perceived stance on dogs. Asked whether he thought the government approved of people keeping dogs or not, one 40-year-old man in Neasden replied, "I don't think it does, otherwise it would do something to help."[26] Another respondent replying to the same question said, "It certainly does not—but then like all things they haven't given it much thought and won't give it any thought till they've killed every dog in the country and wonder what's gone wrong."[27] Another interviewee saw dog ownership in war as proof of how "fond" people were of dogs. "The people who really couldn't be bothered gave them up as soon as it became a little expensive or a little more difficult to keep them."[28] It is scarcely surprising that after interviewing many people in London about their attitudes towards dogs in wartime, the Mass Observation report concluded: "It appears that men and women of all classes most certainly do not want to lose their dogs, and that if they *were made to*, would be very upset"[29] (my emphasis).

In due course the selfsame civil servants who, as discussed in chapter 5, had contemplated—and finally given up on—attempts to regulate cats and dogs eating "human" food also explored restricting dog ownership. The consideration of controlling breeding establishments was problematic: "Public opinion would be extremely sensitive about any drastic step to reduce the number of dogs" and there was also the dilemma of allowing "genuine pedigree breeding" while leaving "the general breeding of dogs uncontrolled."[30] Nevertheless there was debate continuing over months dragging into years about restricting dog ownership. One suggestion was to allow a dog to be licensed in 1943 only if it had been licensed in 1942 (thus restricting breeding and sales of puppies, who were not licensed until 6 months old). But this would result, they concluded, in hardship. Thus women "now living alone, for the first time" who would want dogs for protection or company should be able to appeal and obtain a certificate.[31] Another civil servant who had lived in Berlin in the 1930s suggested following the "progressive" dog taxation policy of that city, namely, £5 for the first dog, £6 for the second, and £12 for the third. But this was rejected: the British were less law abiding than Germans—and would give the second dog to a neighbor.[32] These various suggestions were finally all rejected. A senior civil servant pragmatically concluded that heavy increases in dog tax would "entail a great deal of work and still greater unpopularity and in the end have achieved no real saving." The Minister concurred: "The steps we take cannot always be logical . . . We have to take into account psychological factors." It would depress public morale: Would it assist the war effort? Concurring with the sentiments of the Mass Observation survey of the previous year, the politician answered his own question: "I think not."[33]

PROPAGANDA: NAZI DOG EATERS AND BRITISH ANIMAL LOVERS

One of the reasons for the decision not to regulate dog ownership or feeding was the part played in propaganda by the notion that Britain—as opposed to Germany—was a nation of animal lovers.[34] As Philip Howell has wisely argued, historically such an epithet "seems to have been mobilized largely to discredit complacency." The humane treatment of animals has typically been "honored more in the breach than in the observance."[35] Although not all of the population was a dog or cat lover or lived with such animals as companions, the idea of this characteristic of benevolence uniting the whole nation at war could be employed for propaganda purposes.[36] While there were still sharp class divisions in wartime Britain, human feeling towards animals crossed these lines and became appropriated within the nation. As previously noted, the somewhat crude juxtaposition of Hippy the supposed dachshund returning to Britain with the British ambassador to Germany being unfavorably contrasted with the plight of Baerchen the chow apparently abandoned at the German ambassador's residence in London was an early wartime example of the promotion of these "national" characteristics.[37] Early on in the war, various dog supporters had urged a benign treatment of dachshunds and a suspension of their use as symbols of Germany or Nazism.[38] The dog breed, it was argued, was English.[39] Indeed Queen Victoria had had dachshunds within her household.[40] Nevertheless there was some hostility. For example, the secretary of a local NCDL branch acquired a dachshund as the previous owner was tired of people remonstrating with her for keeping a "horrid" German and Nazi dog.[41]

Reports of the malign treatment of animals in Nazi Germany were widespread—and widely published. Thus the *Animals and Zoo* magazine reported how the Nazis "conscripted" the dog population for the war effort. Dogs over a certain height were appropriated for training for military purposes.[42] Carrie, an Airedale bitch living in Berlin in 1942, was obliged—like other dogs—to be taken to be tested for her suitability for war work on the Russian front. On this occasion a sympathetic vet gave the dog a sleeping tablet of some sort so Carrie did not stir or obey commands. The military assessor "gave up in disgust, telling us that our dog was the most useless he had ever seen and telling us to go and not waste his time anymore."[43] Those under 21 inches were issued with ration cards for a daily allowance of oat or barley meal—but no meat or bone allowance. "All such food must be provided by the owners. Butchers' scraps and bones are intended for human consumption in Nazi Germany."[44] This emphasis on food suitable for human consumption to be eaten by humans alone was not that different, of course, from the British position.[45] Importantly British propaganda encouraged dog owners to remain supportive of the war effort because of the threat to pets if the Nazis were victorious: Both British humans and animals would starve, it was argued. Moreover, Nazism would not be a good state for animals since one needed military victory, peace, and moral law.[46] There was practical evidence to support this claim, particularly in the Channel Islands invaded and occupied by the Nazis. People queued in their hundreds to have their animals killed at the Jersey Animal Shelter. About 2,000 dogs and 3,000 cats were destroyed in five days. Pet tortoises were collected in tomato baskets and released daily in the Beaulieu Convent: "It could be seen where they had made traces, disappearing into the undergrowth after having a good feed at the nuns' expense." The shelter discovered that meat and offal unsuitable for human consumption was being destroyed. With the agreement of the authorities the shelter issued some 2,000 ration cards to distribute meat for the island's animals.[47] Cats, however, survived with difficulty. Thus Winston Churchill, a Siamese cat born on Jersey in 1941, was fed on limpets and evaded the troops since he scarcely left the house.[48] After D-Day in 1944 (and the impossibility of German ships delivering supplies), occupying soldiers raided gardens for vegetables and killed cats and dogs for food.[49] When the Jersey Animal Shelter made representations to Von Aufsess, the Nazi Chief of Administration, he agreed to make this a punishable offence. "One of the worst facets of this nastiness was that often the animals were shot and not killed and those not picked up left to suffer."[50]

Probably the most significant anti-Nazi propaganda involving dogs concerned their alleged mass killing in 1940.[51] This was widely publicized and noted in diaries of animal lovers.[52] It is worth discussing the various analy-

FIGURE 7.1 Different versions of NARPAC disks for cats and dogs (Ernest Bell Library)

ses given for this. The veterinary profession, who had continued professional links with German colleagues throughout the 1930s,[53] argued that dogs were being killed in Berlin in the winter of 1940 not because of scarcity of food but because Germans, as a nation, liked eating dog meat.[54] Similarly Guy Coleridge, the editor of the NAVS magazine *Animals' Defender*, who was shortly to die on active naval service, also explained that the destruction of dogs was for human consumption. However he also thought the carcasses were put to other, unspecified, uses. "It is indeed one of the many foul acts that these foul people have perpetrated."[55] In one of the only accounts to suggest figures shortly after the evacuation of Dunkirk in June 1940, the *Animal Pictorial* declared, "Some three million pet dogs are to be destroyed by order of the government . . . presumably because there is no food for them."[56] Certainly the widespread killing of dogs in Germany in June 1940 was seen to be sufficiently important to be reported in Home Office documents. The explanation emphasized here was that the corpses would provide glycerin and fertilizers.[57] The implication of the report of the German killing is that the corpses of British animals would not be used in this way. This seems true: There had been discussion over whether to use pits to bury dead animals or to burn them rather than any "use value." (There had been no suggestion, for example, that the corpses of animals killed in the massacre in the first week of the war would be "useful" to the war effort. The question had been how to dispose of them quickly.)

ANIMALS WITHIN THE AEGIS OF THE STATE:
DISKS, DEATH, REUNION IN THE TOTALITY OF WAR

Gradually, British state institutions started to acknowledge the positive nature of the interrelationship between animals and humans. Although for
decades Parliament had discussed the treatment of various types of animals
it had not primarily considered how animals played an important part in
the broad affairs of the nation. The war had modified this thinking. The
NARPAC umbrella organization, for the prevention and alleviation of animals' suffering in wartime, was the first body of its kind. While laws protecting animals had, obviously, been passed through state structures, animal
charities that helped both implement and change existing protective legislation were independent of the state itself. State-backed provision for animals had not existed in the 1914–18 war. In many ways the establishment
of NARPAC was a progressive move, almost valuing certain nonhuman
animals as some sort of citizens "for the duration."[58] However, there were
structural problems from the start both with the late set up of NARPAC, as
noted in chapter 3, and with the lack of government finance. The PDSA,
ODFL, and RSPCA had provided some initial funds but the organization
was to be financed primarily through fund-raising: "We need your jumble
more than ever" proclaimed an early NARPAC newsletter. Gramophone records "sound or broken," any kind of rags "particularly woollens," odd
china, "in fact any ware from anywhere" [sic] would be helpful.[59] Some
£25,000 was raised in this way.[60] But the long-standing rivalry between
different animal charities did not disappear within the new organization.
As a subsequent civil service inquiry into the organization's collapse would
note, "anyone who knows anything at all about Charitable Societies knows
that in relation to one another, charitableness is their least conspicuous vir-
tue. The Animal Societies are in competition for public subscriptions . . .
The RSPCA is little concerned with pets: it regards the PDSA and ODFL
as upstarts."[61] Even at NARPAC's inauguration the Home Office had expressed skepticism: "I think it would be unwise to start giving powers over
the public to Inspectors of recognized Animal Welfare Societies," declared
a Home Office official. "Whilst the RSPCA Inspectors would probably be
all right, the Inspectors of the Dumb Friends League have in a short time
acquired an extraordinary reputation for a complete lack of any sort of tact
or discretion."[62] The acrimonious disputes between the veterinary profession and the PDSA over the employment of unqualified staff had not been
forgotten.[63] The later inquiry would also argue, however, that veterinary
surgeons showed themselves "particularly sensitive and reached a degree of

excitement which did not make their case any clearer. They displayed great suspicions of all the societies."[64]

Despite the later disintegration of the organization it was, initially, NARPAC, and in due course, specialist animal charities who did much to monitor and care for domestic animals. Animals were literally signed up to total war. Cats, who had never been recognized by the state as living beings to be taxed or recorded in census form, became numbered and documented alongside dogs, horses, and farm animals.[65] Even though the form of the badges or disks would change and be similar in appearance to those issued by animal charities, the NARPAC scheme was, at least nominally, one run with the approval of the state and was non-profit-making.[66] Animal owners had acted upon the radio appeal by Christopher Stone in the autumn of 1939.

> Now I expect many of you are worried about the terror your animals will experience during an air raid. Of course the noise will be frightening to many animals, and they may dash off, run perhaps for miles and get completely dazed and lost. These possibilities have been provided for. NARPAC though a special department is going to register every animal in the country; even cows and sheep and pigs. Every single one will have a free identification disc with its own number."[67]

A local NARPAC collector—an actor in peacetime—had visited Fryn Tennyson Jesse and her husband Tottie. As Fryn explained to American friends: "It is an association for picking up injured animals after an air-raid and you don't have to pay anything, though as a matter of fact we contributed the large sum of a shilling each for our two cats. They now go about very proudly with large blue and white discs hanging from their collars."[68] Novelist Australian Alice Grant Rosman, a London resident for some three decades, had also registered her own cat, Samuel Penguin.[69] The NARPAC disc, she wrote, "has its use in peace as well, for every wearer has his registered number and can, if found straying, be quickly returned to his rightful family."[70] At first the organization was overwhelmed by the positive response from the public, resulting in a huge backlog of registrations awaiting processing.[71] But by August 1942 three and a half million animals had been registered. Lost animals were identified and returned to their owners. National animal guards established on a voluntary street-by-street and area basis also informed people, who had become separated from their pets, of animals' deaths or helped reunite them.[72] NARPAC reported in June 1942 that 3,000 lost animals were handled each week, of whom the majority

FIGURE 7.2 Child's poster of work undertaken by NARPAC—for a competition? (Ernest Bell Library)

were returned to their owners. It concluded that "although no reliable [national] records are available it is estimated that over the whole country the organisation had handled some 400,000 animals."[73] This was a significant shift in official thinking about the status of companion animals. It is not just that animals become acknowledged as beings important to the nation in war but the state—albeit in a hands-off way—gave official support, though not finance, to such an initiative.

The localized nature of registration meant accounts of which organization actually issued a name tag became blurred and indeed changed over time.[74] Thus Bob the tabby cat, evacuated at one point to Barrow-in-Furness and who had strutted amongst the crockery in the Carnforth station refreshment rooms, returned to London at the end of 1940. Gwladys, his diarist companion, wrote that he was "one of the lucky cats, In spite of upheavals and shortages, he has grown into a fine animal and a joy to behold." She was minded to record that "he is now the proud possessor of an identity card sold to me by Miss Lowenthal, of the Dumb Friends League. He is the 97,354th cat to be so registered through NARPAC."[75] Scamp, the lively office cat living in Notting Hill, had also possessed not one but three such disks, suggesting not only that the cat pulled them off but that his caregiver, Vere Hodgson, was sufficiently minded to ensure replacement: "He loses his disk; we dare not ask for a fourth one." Nevertheless Vere did not give up: "I have bought our cat a puppy collar . . . He is now on file with full description, in case he gets lost."[76] With petrol rationing, more horses had returned to London streets and they too were issued identity discs fixed to their harnesses.[77] Two horses who had improbably "strayed from pasture" in north London were picked up in Horley in Sussex dozens of miles away. They were reunited with their owners thanks to the NARPAC badges they were wearing.[78]

Despite their registration, the status of animals could change very quickly if a whole area had been bombed and people had been relocated speedily. Separated from their human carers animals had a more precarious existence. As the Battersea Dogs and Cats Home had recognized since its founding in 1860, a loved animal companion could quickly become a stray and its status would drastically change.[79] The advice that had been given by animal charities that the safest place for an animal was together with humans would often prove to be true. One lucky dog had a fur coat made for him in case his basket was destroyed in a raid so he wouldn't catch cold. The dog had also got into bed with the family, "so as to be all killed together."[80] In another example, Bill, a large Airedale dog who had been sleeping under his humans' bed, was, like them, affected by a flying bomb that hit their London flat. The people in the family rescued Bill: "The three of us passed out the Airedale, Bill, who was so amenable that he must have been dazed."[81] Less positive are accounts of joint animal-human deaths. Thus in the southeast London suburbs Mr. Dominic, an eighty-year-old Royal Navy

FIGURE 7.3 A hen victim of bombing, Hackney (LHW 18/44, Bishopsgate Institute)

veteran, lived with a little black and brown Pekinese. During the Blitz on 20 September 1940 two heavy bombs fell in the road and both man and dog were found dead, crushed, sitting together in the usual armchair.[82] Similarly in Bexhill a local woman, Mrs. Taylor, was found dead with her also dead spaniel clutched in her arms.[83]

Although animal wardens would look for lost animals and the RSPCA reported rescuing some 256,000 bombed animals,[84] scared cats and dogs who had not been alongside human owners at the time of the falling of a nearby bomb would often have either run to ground or away from the noise in terror. "Hundreds of bombed-out cats slunk through the debris," wrote one antipathetic air raid warden, "hunting the mice & rats, & ransacking the garbage tins. Cats that had been sleek, well-fed pets, grew as thin as their scavenging mangy brothers." In such circumstances charities and individuals did step in. "One little old lady whom I knew, collected sixteen of these 'poor pussies' in her basement flat; she would have collected even more if the 'ground floor' had not protested. The police and the RSPCA did their best, but the animals quickly grew wild and crafty."[85] Animals *were* reunited with their owners even when the people were quickly moved away from bombed-out houses. Exasperated by the cat sitting on top of the rubble of her former house who refused to follow the family, Daisy turned the corner: "and then he came, he came in and he sat straight on that hearth and there he stayed. So the cat came with us."[86] Informal caring for animals in such circumstances, irrespective of "formal" ownership, was often reported: "One old woman, her house in ruins, seized a broom and began to sweep the broken glass from the road. 'Wait a bit, mister, there'll be horses coming along here,' she said to the East London warden waiting to take her to shelter."[87] In a different example, even though there was a time bomb opposite, a woman evacuated from her house insisted on returning daily to feed her cat: "the warden pleaded and argued in vain. She rejected the suggestion that she should take the cat away. She said, 'it wouldn't understand.'"[88]

Nevertheless, despite such institutional and informal measures, the "authorities" were criticized for not making adequate provision for companion animals after raids. Cats wandering through bombed ruins in Southampton, for example, enlisted much sympathy. There were suggestions that the cats needed help; the council should bring round milk, people declared. Then they could also keep the rats down. Cats, like humans, needed sympathy at this difficult time.[89] In Bristol and the southwest, NARPAC had received letters of complaint that people had been evacuated without provision made for the animals. As late as January 1944 people continued to criticize the lack of *government* provision for animals (as opposed to the work of animal charities or vets). Local residents had expressed pity for such abandoned animals, taking them in and looking after them when their owners had been obliged to leave.[90] However, cats who had not been living within homes but working as "warehouse" cats often received short shrift. (These would include the cats who today might be called feral.) Such animals were (wrongly) believed to require little attention. Thus abandoned cats "of the warehouse type . . . require little or no looking after."[91]

ANIMAL INJURY AND DEATH

Wherever they lived inevitably animals—like humans—could be badly injured, traumatized, and killed as a result of bombing. Even though, as Colonel Stordy had predicted, farm animals were not specific targets of bombardment they too would nevertheless be harmed.[92] By July 1941, some 4,500 animal "countryside" casualties had been attended by a network of animal stewards, including veterinary surgeons. Some animals had been blown to pieces, some 15% were treated, and the corpses of 30% were salvaged with the meat made available for human consumption.[93] In rural areas (as well as the cities) local diarists documented the deaths and suffering of animals. Thus in Kent Rodney Foster recorded machine gun fire from a plane near Dymchurch wrecking a farm: Six people suffered from shock and glass injuries—and eleven sheep were killed.[94] And in Wiltshire pacifist Frances Partridge, who seemed inured from much of the war, recording it more as tales on the wireless or stories from friends or—for her—the thankfully temporary sojourn of evacuees,[95] nevertheless noticed that even stray bombs affected animal life: "'Only casualty a skylark' reported one man filling in a bomb crater in a nearby lane." [96]

Badly injured animals were humanely killed, as veterinary surgeons and NARPAC had explained they would be at the start of the war. But others would be "in the world again, some with their old families in new homes, the others with new families in quiet places."[97] As one woman interviewed by Mass Observation explained, her dog was severely hurt in a raid and so "we had to have it put away." The dog was badly missed: "it was a good friend and companion and a good house dog too."[98] In its own publicity the PDSA illustrated its treatment of injured animals with the story of Spot:

> When a flying bomb fell he dug his way out of the debris and then attracted rescuers to the place by barking. They dug for twelve hours to reach Spot's owners, and the dog dug beside them until his paws were raw and bleeding. Unfortunately all efforts were in vain, for the owners were dead when found. Spot was taken to the PDSA Sanatorium for treatment for his paws, an injury to his ear and exhaustion.[99]

Animals, like humans, suffered and remembered the circumstances of bombardment. Thus in one example in Hackney in 1944, a house collapsed "like a pack of cards" on the two men of the household and the dog. Rescuers dug in the rubble to find the two men and when one, Joe, was unearthed, he told them to leave him. "Find the dog and leave me . . . the dog never forgot his rescuer (a brother in law) and followed him everywhere whenever he visited."[100] In another instance a canary who was discovered under the debris was so shocked he had not sung for seven months.[101]

Deaths of various types of animals were recorded both in official records and personal accounts. Thus a chapter of the official history of the Civil Defence is entitled "The Countryman's Blitz," noting, for example, an air raid in Somerset where highly flammable sheep pens caught fire from five incendiary bombs and a sole shepherd ventured into them on six occasions to rescue newly born lambs and their mothers.[102] Less happily, pigeons were often burnt alive as they roosted in the roofs of old buildings: a missing slate would provide an easy entrance for crashing bombs covered with burning metal.[103] Seabirds too suffered a "miserable death" through their feathers being coated with floating oil from sinking ships: "hundreds of tons of oil were released to take new toll of bird life."[104] The rat population had increased and serious concern was expressed by late 1943 about the damage being caused in sewers. A special killing offensive with stale bread spliced with barium carbonate apparently destroyed over a million rats. (Such poison, of course, unless carefully placed could also have killed many other species of animals too.)[105] When the London docks near the Woolwich Arsenal were bombed during the Blitz, both the extensive fires of rum, paint, rubber, and sugar were recorded as well as the hundreds of rats found in the set-alight grain warehouse.[106] The RSPCA routinely reported its local rescue and euthanasia activities as well as the numbers and type of animals killed by bombs or trapped in fires. In a typical report Inspector Miles in Canterbury reported to his RSPCA superiors the death by bombing in the first week of June 1942 of 3 horses, 7 cows, 28 rabbits, 3 pigs, 15 cats, 3 dogs.[107]

Unsurprisingly, personal accounts of animal death often emphasized the relationship between the living human and the dead animal companion and are often commemorative in tone. Diarist Vere Hodgson demonstrated the close relationship that caused, in part, the death of a local man—and his dog. Mr. Bruce, an old actor living in Norland Square in Notting Hill, tried to warn the neighbors about a fire and went upstairs "clutching his dog to alert them." He was 72—and never got there. Overcome by fumes he and the dog were found dead on the landing afterwards. (The neighbors escaped via a balcony.)[108] More emotionally, she recorded Scamp's death. He was the affectionate eight-year-old cat—the cat who had removed his NARPAC disks and complained about his "rations"—who had survived until late in the war. But one morning he was found under the front garden bushes. "His little presence will charm us no more." Seeking to find an explanation for this unexpected death, Hodgson wrote, "The general opinion about our little Scamp is that he was hit by an Army lorry careering along at night and he just lay down in the bushes and died. He had no intention of dying that Friday night. He intended to live on to the piping times of peace, and have a good tuck-in . . . it is lamentable that he should have been an invasion casualty."[109]

More prosaic is an unusual typewritten and archived account by Lilian Margaret Hart, called "Our House Was Bombed," written in February 1941. It described the bombing of her house in Bethnal Green Road in working class East London. Here she had lived with husband George, an ARP warden, and Gyp the dog and Timmy the cat. On the occasion of this particular bombing Lilian was sheltering elsewhere but the animals were still in the house. She was worried about what had happened to both her husband and the animals who had been in the house: "I kept calling and calling for him—Timmy—Timmy—but I couldn't hear a sound. I think he died quick like—didn't know what hit him, I hope. And the dogs too. They found Gyp today, way up on the roof of the vestry—and the black dog was just hanging over a broken rafter there. I hope they died quick, too." After this section of her account she then added, "Then somebody told me George was alright." The next day Lilian had still been looking for Timmy: "I thought there might be, just a chance he was still alive." The account is about her general response to the raids but the deaths of the animals seem to take emotional precedence over the survival of the human.[110]

A PDSA leaflet of 1941 had acknowledged that "many animals are blown to pieces: others so mutilated as to be unrecognizable."[111] However, both companion animal casualties and deaths were less than had been envisaged. Scientists also noted that "many people who had been close to explosions escaped with relatively little injury, and apparently without showing any effects of blasts." Most people who were wounded were in their houses (rather than in some form of shelter).[112] Scientist Julian Huxley reported that far fewer animals were killed through actual bombardment than had been anticipated. The animals' ability to "go to ground" often ensured their survival.[113] Animals would shelter and, as discussed in chapter 6, take humans with them.

ANIMALS AND THEIR TREATMENT
BY LOCAL OFFICIALS

The practice of air raid wardens, demolition workers, and fire fighters towards animals was rather different to that predicted by the Cats Protection League at the start of the war. The League had told supporters, "Wherever you are and whatever happens to you, you will be rescued before long, but rescue parties will not trouble over animals."[114] The organization had based this view on the low status in which cats were held at that time. However, stories of the actual treatment of cats, dogs, and other pets by local officials certainly suggested that their status had changed during the war. NARPAC described its own activities recruiting some 45,000 animal guard volunteers after one radio broadcast and reflecting in late 1943, "There can surely be little doubt that but for the unstinted and unselfish labours of the National Animal Guard the vast bulk of these animals would have to have been recorded as 'missing, believed destroyed.'"[115] The need to reestablish a family unit that embraced animal and human was even acknowledged by the Home Office receiving the report of Sir Robert Gower, the president of the RSPCA, who explained:

> In many districts owners showed great concern for missing pets and on several occasions appeals were made to our van driver to keep a look out for certain favourite cats and on no account to destroy them before the owners could collect them and take them to the new home. In west Kensington, particularly, many such cats were retrieved from ruined buildings and restored safe and sound, to their mistresses.[116]

In an account of her work as an air raid warden, Barbara Nixon often made clear her antipathy toward animals. Yet she vividly recorded many incidents that show her colleagues did not feel the same way. Billy, for example, a tabby cat, had found a refuge during air raids: he always refused to leave the cupboard at the top of the stairs. Usually his human companion stayed with him but on the occasion of a bomb blast, since it was in the morning, she had gone downstairs: "A frail and bedraggled old lady came up and begged us to allow her back into her tottering remains of her house to fetch Billy . . . The house was extremely unsafe, and it was stupid to take unnecessary risks for a cat, but Mackin, the Post Warden, managed to slip past the incident officer unnoticed, and fetched it down."[117] Irrespective of pedigree or species, pets of all types were helped. Thus Bernard Regan, a heavy rescue worker, discovered that the other shift had "brought a parrot in a squashed up cage from Samuda Street [on the Isle of Dogs]. The cage was straightened out and the parrot fed with bacon rind & crusty bread. It was well educated and after preening itself, it gave a most wonderful recital of obscene language."[118]

I noted in the first chapter the off duty firewatcher rescuing a Sealyham puppy from an untimely end but as part of their official duties, firefighters, as well as air raid wardens, would act positively towards displaced animals

and rescue and often temporarily rehome animals. Thus a wire-haired terrier renamed Mick was the only living being to survive a bombing on a
house in Manor Park in East London. He was taken in and made a full-
time member of the local fire station. His character after the rescue was
recorded, particularly his skill in climbing the firefighter's ladder—which
he would perform for fund-raising events. In due course he would find a domestic home with fireman Johnson once he was demobbed and resumed the
role of a "well loved pet."[119] Such rescue activities were not always praised.
Critical of a firefighter who had worked for hours to rescue a puppy, one
journalist defined such activity as "sentimental nonsense." Her remarks
were refuted by the CPL, declaring the value of sentiment against Nazism,
"Better in these times to err on the side of sentimentality than on that of
hardness, for no one can foresee how far the hardening process may take
us."[120] A rabbit from Charlton ended up rehomed with the local warden. On
this occasion the other pet, Gyp, a black and white dog, emerged himself
from the bombed house covered in dust and dirt but it was not until two
or three days later that the pet rabbit was found alive and well under the
rubble, even though his cage had been crushed. The problem was that as the
family had been bombed out there was difficulty taking the rabbit but they
wanted to save the rabbit's life. Ellen Clark has told this story of negotiation
and caution:

> The warden said, "Oh could I have him?" So mum said, "Yes, but don't say any-
> thing to the children. And promise you won't kill him or eat him or anything?"
> The Warden said, "Ooh, no, no, I wouldn't. This is a one off." She didn't tell us
> until a long while after, because she knew that we would want to keep him. So
> the air raid warden had him, and I know he kept him.[121]

It is difficult to unpack what actually *did* happen here. This seems to be a
mother's story specifically constructed for a child about the disappearance
of a family pet. That the child appeared convinced that the air raid warden
would have acted honorably, however, suggests that—irrespective of whatever actually happened to the rabbit—endowing a warden with such benign
characteristics was not improbable. And many accounts exist of similarly
benign behavior.[122] That a couple felt sufficiently confident in the attitude
of those staffing the Poplar warden's post to deposit their dog there with the
request that she be looked after while they went off to a Xmas party says
much about the wardens' reputation with animals. (Unfortunately the ARP
journal does not include the wardens' response.)[123]

However, it was not just a case of animals passively waiting to be rescued
by humans. Incendiaries damaged the stables of the United Dairies, setting

fire to the straw: "One of the horses was busily stamping out the fire with this hooves" before they were led away to safety.[124] And it was Chum, a 12-year-old Airedale companion, who rescued Marjorie French. Her home was demolished and she was trapped in the shelter when she saw the paws of the dog digging furiously to release her, dragging her out to safety by her hair.[125] The RSPCA reported many stories of animals being proactive in rescue. The society's commemorative war book thus recalled a story of a cat who had been rescued from a ruined building returning to direct an inspector to a little wounded dog, both "inseparable pets," or a cat removing her kittens to safety, or animals refusing to leave a human's side. The written narrative was complemented by a visual image of an old man returning to the ruins of his home to find a picture of his dead wife. "His cat, which he had given up for lost, heard his footsteps and appeared from some safe hiding-place, asking to be taken home."[126]

But the rescue of an individual animal did not just affect the particular family where she lived. An example of the ways in which the plight of an individual animal became the focus of *community action* is illustrated by Gwladys Cox's diary entries over a number of days in spring 1944. There had been, she noted, one of the most terrible nights of the war. Her own cat, Bob, had streaked along the passage in sheer terror and she clutched his tail to then hold him and stop him struggling. There were blasts everywhere in the area including huge fires at the local branch of the grocery stores, Cullens. Gwladys "turned faint just now" realizing that the porter would be in the flat above the stores—and Bob's mother would be shut up in the stores below. Some six days later visiting a different branch of the store she inquired, "What had become of Bob's mother?" The grocer explained she had not yet been found but "the demolition men were keeping a look-out for her." A fellow cat lover met on the bus also "promised to keep her eyes open, saying she had already tracked down one bombed out cat." Some fortnight later Gwladys recorded: "Bob's mother is alive! Demolition workers found her, as they dug away debris in the shop and carried her in a sack to the [nearby branch].When I saw her this morning, days without food, she is very thin, but seems none the worse."[127] Gwladys Cox's record of other people's reactions was not simply a noticing of an isolated event. Humans observing the animals around them and rescuing them was more prevalent than has been previously acknowledged. Cox's own empathy is emphasized by the form of writing, rather than because of the rarity of the incident.[128]

Having said that, professional war workers did not always act compassionately towards animals. Jack, a black retriever, was rescued some

FIGURE 7.4 Man and cat reunited after bombing, East London

45 minutes after the rescue squad had given up searching in his bombed home. Fortunately the man of the household was more resolute, finding Jack under the debris. The human family was temporarily living at his office with the dog tied up in the yard: a situation deplored by the man (and no doubt the dog). But he refused to have Jack killed, saying," If the dog is meant to die he would have died under the debris." Instead the Animal Defence Society evacuated him to a home in the country.[129] James Lees-Milne, the wonderful diarist and National Trust employee responsible for saving many stately homes during and after the war, undertook "amateur" firewatching of the Trust's premises. Although pleased to have "something to do" in air raids he was "astonished by the unashamed way in which most of the [firewatchers] admitted that there were not going to take risks in putting out incendiary bombs or rescuing people. I said in surprise, 'But I thought that was what we were here for!'"[130]

Military personnel—British, American, and Canadian—were often fickle in their attentions towards animals they encountered on military bases. They would befriend dogs and cats, leaving them to starve when the camps were abandoned. The Army Council thus instructed units to tell the RSPCA when there was an evacuation so that the charity could "collect and arrange for their disposal."[131] While surveying properties that might be left to the National Trust, James Lees-Milne encountered a distraught housekeeper on the Blickling estate in Norfolk. Not only had the RAF vandalized the house but they had stolen her dog, "the sweetest and cleverest being imaginable, and she loved him more than anyone in the world."[132] This particular problem would increase at the end of the war. Although many animals were rehomed, others were killed. At an American camp in Norfolk, 50 dogs abandoned for months were found wandering albeit in good physical condition. Many had previously strayed from farms, enticed by the food on offer. Some 48 were claimed by their former owners and the remaining two were rehomed. The cats, however, proved less biddable. According to the RSPCA they had become semi-wild and were destroyed "expertly and mercifully."[133]

FRACTIOUS PEOPLE: WHERE ARE THE ANIMALS?

Locally there were fractious disputes about the status of NARPAC since its volunteers did not have the status of those in Civil Defence Services, such as the (also voluntary) Home Guard. The veterinary profession was conscious that, within urban areas, animal charities rather than vets were seen

FIGURE 7.5 Blue Cross rescue of a cat (H98 106/597, State Library, Victoria, Australia)

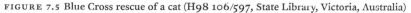

as the leading lights in NARPAC. The records of local NARPAC groups are not widely available but one exception is the correspondence files of the NARPAC Animal Rescue Unit in Wanstead and Woodford on the eastern outskirts of London.[134] The status of individual humans and issues of the division between local authorities dominates the files. Thus the local NARPAC had requested a petrol allowance from the local Civil Defence Department in the event of having to purchase a car for use in emergencies. But the allowance could only be given once the car was purchased and none could be allowed—even to test the car before purchase.[135] The reason given was that the vehicle would not form part of the Civil Defence (General) Services. In similar fashion requests written to receive an allowance of chocolate and biscuits—that the BBC had announced was available to Civil Defence Organisations—were also turned down. More seriously, so was the request for gas protective clothing.[136] Such local bickerings were only one reason for the collapse of the organization.

There was a growing public assumption that NARPAC was only responsible for companion animals. The NVMA was keen to reorient NARPAC to work with "all animals of economic value," that is, primarily animals in rural areas where veterinary surgeons were still of some influence.[137] Thus in rural areas a Technical Branch was established consisting of some eight thousand Parish Animal Stewards, maintaining a network of communication between Veterinary Centres and the farming community in order to give first aid and to "restore [animals] to full productivity" and to "conserve those killed or fatally wounded as a source of food."[138] Nevertheless the scheme in towns as well as the countryside lapsed "into uselessness," according to a Ministry of Agriculture and Fisheries inquiry. For the Ministry the main focus should have been on farm animals not pets.[139] Increasingly individual charities had reasserted their own claims on caring for companion animals. Thus in its printed public letter explaining the reason for its decision to withdraw from NARPAC, the RSPCA stressed not only the financial position it was unwilling to underwrite but its own discrete action for bombed animals: "In one month alone, last year, 10,100 household pets were painlessly destroyed by the Society's officials, and 5,940 were rescued from bombed premises, fed for a time, boarded in the Society's Institutions, or found new homes."[140]

The veterinary profession had had a difficult relationship with some animal charities in the 1930s, particularly the PDSA. The Royal Veterinary College had been highly critical of the PDSA's usage of nonqualified staff to treat animals in its surgeries—and also critical of wealthy potential clients who went to the charity's clinics, rather than employing a veterinary surgeon, to save money.[141] However, the forceful leader of the NVMA, Harry Steele-Bodger, used his presidential address of 1941 to ultimately lay responsibility with the Ministry of Home Security for disowning the urban scheme. Arguing that it would have been possible to form a postwar organization from the nucleus of those involved in NARPAC, the body singled out for criticism was the *state*:

> Born in faith, nurtured with hope, died through charities. This sums up the National ARP Animals' Committee but it is not the whole story. I feel that the villain of the piece is that fairy godmother the Ministry of Home Security which was present at the birth, gave it its blessing, and proceeded to starve it to death.[142]

In the first chapter I referred to the work of Etienne Benson, who has argued that human-authored texts can present insights into animals' experience, and generally I tend to agree with him. Such animal traces are often
hidden away but nevertheless present. But in the relevant National Archives
files and the publications of the veterinary profession there is scant material
to even suggest that NARPAC on a national level was very much concerned
about the animals whom it was intended to support. The experience of injured or stray animals was rarely even mentioned. Instead human organiza-
tional rivalries dominated.

Nevertheless, irrespective of the NARPAC disputes, the existence of an
animal-human relationship was acknowledged, in some way, by the state as
being important for the nation at war. But the tentativeness about interven-
ing too closely into the relationships between existing animal charities—or
funding alternatives—suggested that the wartime experience of some sort
of cooperation would be of the moment rather than a feature of postwar life.
However, that it was considered *at all* demonstrates the impact of animal-
human relationships on the state at this time. Not only had the state changed
its stance but, as we shall see in the next chapter, so had the strength of the
emotional relationship between animals and humans.

CHAPTER EIGHT

Emotion, Utility, Morale on the Home Front: Animal-Human Relationships

Probably dogs do more to uphold morale among their owners than anything else . . . Surely they've earned the privilege of being allowed to live for all their kind?[1]

The previous chapters have shown the ways in which the shared material circumstances of war, including changed diets, enforced common shelter, and physical environments disrupted due to bombardment, affected both animals and humans. Such experiences clearly also disrupt notions of the war as a "People's War." They indicate the central role of animals. In discussing further the different ways in which animals and humans worked, and existed, I now explore the nature of their emotional engagement. The war created emotional responses in animals and humans both discretely *and* in conjunction with each other—and not only in animals narrowly defined as "pets." Certainly the Mass Observation material to which I have referred throughout this book offers a window on the history of emotions that is both transpersonal and trans-species.[2]

EMOTIONAL RECIPROCITY AND BLURRING FORMS OF ANIMAL-HUMAN RELATIONSHIPS

In exploring two examples here of apparently different types of animal-human engagement I want to suggest that they share similar attributes. I have previously looked in chapter 2 at the approach adopted by Colonel Richardson in the First World War training dogs for work in the trenches. For Richardson the key to success was not only the breed of dog but the breed (as it were) of man. Men chosen for this war work had to be fond of dogs, able to relate to them, and, like the dogs, able to be trained into creating an effective working relationship. So effective was his approach that it was also used in the 1939-45 war.[3] As previously noted, dogs were specifically recruited to act as guard dogs on military sites or as mine detectorists.[4] Without compulsion towards human "owners," in March 1942 dogs were "loaned" from families to the military when so requested.[5] Battersea Dogs Home also transferred ownership of stray dogs to the armed forces. These animals who had been kept—and then abandoned—as pets were then in "great demand for accompanying sentries on their night duties."[6] If this had not happened, the Home would have killed them. The RSPCA also proudly reported its own work in sending dogs it had taken in to the army and Ministry of Aircraft Production to guard buildings, patrol, and carry messages.[7] Up to 10,000 dogs were offered for such war work although only 3,500 accepted—many were "gun shy." This was probably unsurprising given their previous role as human companions. The most sought-after breeds were Airedales (the breed trained so enthusiastically in the 1914-18 war by Colonel Richardson), Collies, Lurchers, various cross-breeds—and German Shepherds.[8] Importantly, these were not dogs specifically trained as guard dogs but those who had been part of a family unit. Thus the approach of training based on a positive relationship between human and dog as the "guarantor of successful communication and cooperation"[9] arose not only from Richardson's philosophy but also the background of the *dogs* within a family setting.[10] Rover, a black Labrador retriever, for example, had been useful within his family in different ways, including taking the children to school near Tunbridge Wells. He was volunteered for sniffing out land mines in Belgium and France. Surprisingly, Rover survived this work and was also offered back to the family. This again suggests that the animal-human relationship fostered within the military was complementary to that within the family. War work had not brutalized the dog.[11] But his former family rejected Rover. "He was a very big dog, and in the army he had been well fed. Food was still rationed for us so it was kinder to let him stay in the army," said the daughter of the family, who had been "heartbroken" when he went, remembering this some years later.[12] While both these sentiments may have been her own, the notion of it being "kinder" reads more like the explanations given by a parent to a child. Significantly, in this rejection there is no suggestion that the dog would have become more aggressive because of military practices, it was simply a matter of financial expediency.

This "crossover" between a domestic and a "military" relationship was also evident in the canine-human relationship that operated when humans and animals were "officially" found in bombed buildings after air raids.[13] No animal had been specifically *bred* for seeking out living beings in these

FIGURE 8.1 Memorial to Jet in Calderstones Park, Liverpool

conditions, instead training was the key. Darkie [*sic*], a German Shepherd, was lauded in the press. He had been trained at the Ministry of Aircraft Production at Cheltenham to search for buried people. Other such dogs had been tried out first in Birmingham before being brought to London to assist in locating victims of the flying bombs in the later stages of the war.[14] Jet of Lada, another German Shepherd, had been the companion of breeder Mrs. Badcock Cleaver of Liverpool. He too had been loaned "for the duration" and had then been specifically trained. With Thorn, also a German Shepherd, Jet would be paraded as part of the Civil Defence competitions for his skill in detecting bomb victims.[15] In the course of rescuing two women he had been injured on his right hind hock. Both Thorn and

Jet would be honored with PDSA Dickin medals.[16] Officially, the value of such dogs was "definitely proved as an adjunct to a reconnaissance for live and fatal casualties" since "their positive reactions are reliable."[17] That is, their value was attributed to their abilities to smell rather than to any companionate empathy. In their *official* use, the dogs would have sniffed out humans (or animals) who would not have been personally known. It was not the case that necessarily the excellent ability of a dog (or cat) to smell was not recognized before the war but rather this skill was enhanced—and valued—by the circumstances of war.[18]

More interesting in some ways is the story of Rip. He was a terrier-type dog who had been taken in by Mr. King, an air raid warden of post B132 in Poplar in East London during the Blitz of 1940. As a postwar summary explained, "Homes were found for many [bombed out animals] and a mongrel dog who attached himself to post B132 [Rip] was later awarded the dog's VC for rescue work at incidents."[19] In one account Rip is "found" and "taken in": in another he "attaches himself." This was not a one-sided relationship. The series of photographs of Rip taken by the Ministry of Information and preserved in the local archives shows different aspects of Rip's life. Rip is photographed apparently working alongside the bespectacled Mr. King, burrowing for victims buried after a raid. But he is also shown visiting the street air-raid shelters comforting those sheltering—and being given pats on the head and tidbits for his troubles. Rip is further pictured sitting, watching Mr. King hoeing the tiny allotment adjacent to the warden's post. Thus the dog's role in finding bombed animals and people is only one part of his relationship with Mr. King—as, of course, is the case for Mr. King's relationship with the dog. While he is described as "the first dog on this type of job" he was not unique.[20] The PDSA, describing its own role during the war, also acknowledged animals' proactivity: "These animals frequently ignored their own danger to stand by and help their owners, often they struggled to find and help them in blazing buildings, while they themselves could so easily have escaped to safety alone."[21] Like such dogs—and unlike some of the named dogs who were later rewarded—Rip did *not* require special training. Being a companion of Mr. King seemed to be training enough.[22] I am reminded here of the work of Lynda Birke and Joanna Hockenhull on the nature of animal-human relationships. They have noted that "working together, in the sense of being able to understand at least some of the other species' behavior is part of our dealings with many kinds of nonhuman animals. Both we and they must learn when to approach, when to receive a stroke / lick, or when to keep well away from the potential blow / bite."[23]

FIGURE 8.2 Rip and Mr. King at the warden's allotment, Poplar (courtesy of Tower Hamlets Local History Library and Archives)

Tellingly, they—like Colonel Richardson, in some ways, decades before—focus on a joint animal-human effort rather than simply observing discrete behavior. "To look at human-animal relationships at a micro level, one-to-one, means focusing less on impacts of one on the other and more on how both animals and humans contribute to their engagement, producing something more than the sum of their parts."[24] Certainly, in a variety of ways this behavior was demonstrated and observed during the war.

DIFFERENT NOTIONS OF USEFULNESS

It would, however, be wrong to suggest that there were distinctive and clearly boundaried categories of usefulness in the animal-human relationship. An unusual example is the account of a sparrow, given the name of Clarence, who had been rescued by Clare Kipps, a widow and professional musician who was serving as an air raid warden in London. In July 1940 she had found the sparrow apparently fallen from a nest, less than a day old, and fed him on Bemax, hard-boiled egg yolk, and bread soaked with a drop of halibut-liver oil. Children assisted in the bird's recovery by bringing caterpillars and worms in matchboxes as food. His diet would expand to include Dover sole, Scotch salmon, and roast chicken.[25] The account in the hugely popular book *Sold for a Farthing* was reprinted eleven times in just three years. Prefaced by the zoologist Julian Huxley, the book is "the story—not of a pet, but of an intimate friendship, extending over many years, between a human being and a bird."[26] Clarence was taught various tricks by Clare, such as engaging in a tug of war with a hair pin or running into a small improvised shelter in response to the words "Siren's gone!"[27] But such tricks were not just for Clare's own, domestic, enjoyment. Clarence would accompany Clare in her role of air raid warden to rest centers:

> People who had lost their homes and all their possessions forgot their troubles, at least for the time being, terrified children became merry and carefree, and those who had obstinately refused to allow their gas-masks to be fitted held up their heads at once if promised a game with the sparrow.[28]

The account does not only emphasize the impact of the bird upon humans. It is described as a two-way relationship. The bird is portrayed as also deriving benefits from this relationship: "perhaps no sparrow has ever been privileged to enjoy (or to endure) such exclusive human companionship."[29] Kipps declared that the bird sang "because he knew I loved him."[30] Certainly—if longevity is a sign of contentment—the bird lived for twelve years, seven weeks, and four days and was treated at the end of his life both by a veterinary surgeon with formal medication and by Kipps with sips of champagne.[31] Overall the book describes the "use" of the bird to humans on different levels—both personal joy and as a specific contribution to morale in the aftermath of bombardment. But it also specifically argued (and illustrated) that animals, or at least Clarence, responded to affection.[32]

FIGURE 8.3 Clarence performing a card trick (from Clare Kipps, *Sold for a Farthing*)

The Cats Protection League had also addressed this issue of the nature of "use" in war—to its own supporters—in an article entitled "War Workers," saying that "if the cat were merely a pet, giving no service in return for his keep, the reply to these questions [Is it anti-patriotic to deprive the community of so much foodstuff, for one's own pleasure?] would be— Yes." However, the cat was reinvented as "one of the best food protectors known." The value was embedded in saving "the community" millions of pounds worth of foodstuff annually. Recognizing that cats helped "the community" by killing rats in warehouses was not the same as defending the presence of a pet cat in an individual household, the argument nevertheless developed. The scent of the cat in an individual household was useful in keeping rodents on the move. "They never settle down (and settling down means breeding) in premises continually occupied by a cat. I use the word 'continually' advisedly; the cat that is kept most of the time outside, and sleeps out at night has little chance of leaving permanent traces of his presence in the form of the scent which mice and rats dread." In other words, those who did treat the cat as a pet, through close inclusion inside the home, were also adding to the more conventional definition of utilitarian. The imperative of keeping the cat in at night—which the CPL had consistently promoted since the blackout was introduced—would thus help keep mice away, "even if he does not catch" them. Moreover cats needed to be well fed to be good ratters. "If you neglect to keep up your cat's health and strength you are lowering his value to the community." The article concluded, "To cut down your cat's food because of any difficulty in getting it is almost an unpatriotic thing to do; one can always give up a little of one's ration for the sake of the good work Pussy is doing for his country."[33] The notion of community value was found on other occasions in the writings of the secretary of the Cats Protection League. Again readers were urged not to be perturbed about scares about the possible lack of tinned cat food:

> Things may be a little difficult but please do not take the line of least resistance. Too many cats have been destroyed unnecessarily already. It's so easy to take life but it is equally as easy to exercise common sense and avoid the untimely ending of a life that may be more of an asset than a liability in days to come. Always remember that your cat or kitten has a definite value both to you and to the community.[34]

This expansion of the concept of usefulness was also found in the work of Louise Lind af Hageby of the Animal Defence Society, who sharply contrasted the concept of canine and feline usefulness in Britain and Germany. While Hageby criticized the utilitarianism of the Nazis' approach, she also argued that emotional support was itself utilitarian: "There is no sentimentalism in drawing attention to the sustaining and cheering influence exercised by the family dog or cat."[35] This fudging of notions of use and appeals to a broader notion of national and community interest was not confined to the Cats Protection League nor animal rights campaigners. By spring 1942 the BBC broadcast that "cats [were] doing work of national importance." Frances Partridge heard this on the radio and wrote in her diaries, "And will anyone believe in twenty years' time that the wireless makes [such] pronouncements ?"[36] Her astonishment derived from the BBC giving the cats such status rather than any personal wish to diminish the role of cats per se.

CHANGING FELINE-HUMAN RELATIONSHIPS?

It was not only the BBC that acknowledged the changing status of cats during the war. A pioneering study was conducted in Cardiff towards the end of the war by zoologist Colin Matheson and published in the *Journal of Animal Ecology*. His study was an attempt to estimate the numbers of cats living in Cardiff "in view of the not unimportant role of the domestic cat in urban ecology to-day."[37] This unique research had two distinct starting points. One was the lack of detailed knowledge of the numbers of cats. More significantly, the second was the new recognition of their importance. It also suggested that the study was able to be carried out because of increased human acknowledgment of cats as living within one discrete family. Before the war cats had not been necessarily attached to one family but were overseen by the local community. Thus Christopher Stone in a NARPAC broadcast of 1939 had spoken about: "a cat that drops in to see us several times a week, I don't know whose cat it is, but that doesn't matter particularly."[38]

The Cardiff survey compared ownership of cats in the dock areas of Cardiff "in old property with a racially mixed population" with that of an area with a "rather better type of house." The newer properties were not constrained by council restrictions on the keeping of pets. An assumption was made that better sewers and drains had resulted in less "need for cats as destroyers of rats and mice," although it was accepted that "this is by no means the only factor influencing the keeping of cats, but it is certainly one of them."[39] Thus Matheson calculated that some 74% of households in the dock area kept cats compared to 26% in a municipal housing estate. (No account was taken of dog ownership.) Such cats within homes were estimated to be c. 23,500 with a further c. 6,500 stray or "unwanted" cats. (This begs the question, of course, of the shifting status of strays.)[40] The article concluded that roughly 30,000 cats lived in Cardiff, that is, 13% of the human population.[41] The methodology of the survey may have been questionable: asking schoolteachers to ask pupils to enumerate the numbers of people and cats within their own household. However, the very fact that the survey was undertaken at all suggests some shift in popular consciousness about cats within communities. Something *had* apparently changed in the feline-human relationship. In the same year *Cats and Kittens: The Magazine for Every Cat-Lover* could confidently declare that "Never has the cat been so popular in this country as at the present time." Such popularity was not reducible to a mice catching "use" but to the animals' broader role in helping to provide "relief from the strain of war."[42]

FORMS OF CROSS-SPECIES EMOTIONS IN WAR

In thinking about the varying emotional relationships between animals and humans, an initial observation is the way in which animals were seen to characterize particular emotions. Clearly such characterizations were not about animals per se. Rather these were human projections or representations. However, I am including them here since I think it noteworthy that in a time of war such "crossover" images *are* used. They suggest a reaching out to other species for a sense of language and particular emotions that could not be expressed simply by reference to a separate human condition. For the most part, Lind af Hageby's account of bombed and rescued animals provides a straightforward narrative with material drawn from the press and the experiences of the Animal Defence Society. However, her pamphlet concludes with the story of a canary who, after bombardment, did not sing for some seven months. But the bird had started to sing again and his owner interpreted that as a "prelude to good war news." The Animal Defence Society, she explained, who saw the "righteousness of the cause" for which Britain was fighting, a "cause which is inseparable from justice, freedom, compassion, sympathy, that is life itself are also encouraged by the recovery of that canary."[43] Thus hope has been created in humans not just because of the recovery as such of an injured animal but because of the animal's intrinsic ability to sing.[44] More conventionally some animals were depicted almost as the embodiment of particular human emotions. Thus describing a suburban air raid during the Blitz one child wrote, "This time we somehow sensed it was different. In spite of all the noise, there was a feeling of stillness, and believe it or not, a dog howled. Dad said this was a bad sign."[45] Joan Varley told a similar story about the first night of the Blitz at her home in Streatham, when there was a moment of silence after three bombs fell "and then there was a most unearthly wail, which added greatly to the terror of the moment. It was every dog and cat in the houses howling in terror— but they never did it again in any other bombing."[46] A more positive example might be the language Diana Cooper used to describe the reason she acquired a cow.[47] It was not simply for the milk but because "she represented to me life, riches, sweetness and warmth."[48] In a different vein Vera Brittain had observed St. Paul's Cathedral that had almost miraculously survived the Blitz, and the surrounding pigeons. Rather than the birds "complementing" the Cathedral's status in some sort of pathetic fallacy, she uses them to refashion the Cathedral in the light of the birds' "emotional detachment":

> The usual grey pigeons with green necks and pink feet are walking placidly round the rescued Colossus of St Paul's Cathedral. There is, I believe, no Londoner to-day who could look on the surviving black and grey dome and share the emotional detachment of the pigeons. We stare incredulously at the still barricaded crater where the one-ton time-bomb fell, just missing the structure itself.[49]

FIGURE 8.4 Canaries rescued from a southeast London public house, September 1940 (LHW 18 /30, Bishopsgate Institute)

By way of contrast often understated comments also revealed emotions. The national British characteristic of not saying what one really means or feels or using understatement or euphemism was observable during the war as a way of dealing with extreme emotions. Thus many of the stories I have used here were not written down at the time. It has only been decades later that people have now felt able to speak about their feelings about animals at the time. This is not necessarily because of trauma but rather that people were never asked to acknowledge the role of animals in their wartime lives. In an earlier chapter I discussed Jill Watts' memory of her evacuation to her grandparents' home in Teddington when she was a toddler and enjoying the company of Tinker, a big grey English Sheepdog, and Joey, the canary. But this state of contentment did not continue. As she has only recently written:

And then one day Tinker & Joey just disappeared. There were no fanciful explanations, we were just told to keep quiet in case granddad got cross, so we did, & forgot about it. Some months later, my little brother & I crept into my Granddad's shed, strictly against the rules, and saw Joey's Cage hanging empty amongst my granddad's raffia he tied his plants up with. We didn't ask.[50]

She did remember but did not speak about these events and only wrote about her engagement with these animals for the first time some seventy years later.

Animals became devices for humans not articulating emotions. Thus Gwladys Cox looked out of her window in November 1942, "It is a dark, cold foggy day. I look out on a rather dreary street and watch a neighbour taking the dog out. He walks slowly with bowed head—his only son was killed at the Front last week."[51] Here the man was not speaking; the diarist was not talking to him. But the human isolation was further conveyed by the animal presence. The nonspeaking communication facilitated by animals was again illustrated by a narrative from Nella Last, who described meeting a couple whose soldier son had had his leg shot off and the father said "'t' best horse brekker in't district." Nella confessed to her Mass Observation diary that she could not think of what to say so the three of them sat "and talked of dogs—and their little Yorkshire terrier's balding spot on its head, and told Mrs M of some stuff I'd used: since it was off a market dealer, she seemed to have faith in it. As I got up to go, our eyes met—and then our hands."[52] There was a similar "crossing over" of emotion from grief and sorrow to comfort—without human speech—in another of the diarist's narratives. Here a little spaniel, described as already a pet rather than just a dog, was acquired, it is implied, to comfort a mother in her grief for her dead son. Mrs. Dean, a woman in Barrow-in-Furness, had lost her son at sea. The grieving woman was accompanied by her little spaniel: "a lovely, soft, golden thing with a nose and ears like living velvet. It's a pet already and Mrs Dean said, 'I cannot think of a name for her, can you?' I looked at the sunlight lying on the puppy's back, and thought of the bracken and fern in autumn, and I said, 'What about Fern?'"[53]

I am conscious that such observations tell us more about humans than, of course, animals. I am also very aware that nowadays it has almost become a cliché, at least in Animal Studies circles, to say that animals are useful to think with.[54] The existence of animals, so the argument usually goes, is useful against which to define what it means to be human. And writers did appropriate animals in these ways during the war. Thus, if we return to the letters of Fryn Tennyson Jesse written near the beginning of the war

FIGURE 8.5 A rescued dog and her puppies (H98 106/572, State Library of Victoria, Australia)

to American friends in an attempt to explain the mood in Britain, it first seems that her two cats were incorporated into the narrative to illustrate the household's routines. Perkin and Muff, like her husband Tottie, were all part of the same family unit in extremis. But one letter of March 1940 suggests other, broader, motivations for Tennyson Jesse's writing:

> I watch [our cats] with a sense of relaxation and pleasure because they know nothing about war. I think everybody at a time like this should keep animals, just as royalties and dictators should always keep animals. For animals know nothing of politics, nothing of royalty, nothing of war unless, poor creatures, they also, knowing not why, are wounded and killed.[55]

By situating animals as apart from (human) politics, albeit included in the suffering of war that embraced animal and human alike, Tennyson Jesse suggested that animals conveyed a particular quality needed in warfare: "This quality of something untouched by the social, snobbish and more serious matters that torture us, is what animals give us, and as a contribution to civilisation, believe me it is of inestimable value: it has become our only rest-cure."[56] Although animals are not responsible for the creation of war they were described as embodiments of its antidote, civilization. However, Tennyson Jesse's sentiments remind us how the "absence" of intellect can also promote particular feelings. This is not confined to humans in *contradistinction* to animals. It is a promotion of feeling and emotion that is evident in companion animals *and* their human keepers. For example, near the beginning of the war when animals and humans alike were getting acclimatized to the new sounds of warfare, including air raid sirens, Gwladys Cox wrote about the new routines: turning gas off at the mains, grabbing gas masks, and catching Bob the cat and putting him in his basket.[57] When she writes of Bob, "he must think us mad, such goings-on in the middle of the night," I am not sure we are meant to read this literally.[58] Rather this is a way of showing that prewar routines of the cat as well as those of Gwladys and Ralph were disrupted: Time itself was being almost overturned by warfare.

Relationship implies a reciprocal process. One middle-aged woman explained to Mass Observation interviewers that she had obtained her own small dog after the start of the war, precisely to create domestic companionship for herself: "I've been all alone in the house since my husband went and the children were evacuated—and that dog's been wonderful company."[59] The strength of the cross-species companionship was also evidenced by the account of a middle-aged working class man who confidently attested about his mongrel's behavior: "If I ever go out and leave him, he always sits by my chair never stirs or anything, won't eat or even take a drink not until I come in, then he's as lively as anything . . . they're good companions, better than human beings I think!"[60] Animal-human relationships focused on comfort, support, and companionship were often recounted in the wartime Mass Observation surveys of interviews with individuals with—or without—dogs. One man interviewed by Mass Observation in Euston, having noted that his dog didn't like air raids, explained it thus: "Yes he whines a bit but we all have to put up with something."[61] Here, one imagines, the man is also a being who "whines a bit." Certainly, albeit in an understated way, the strength of the bond is one that is seen to endure despite difficulties. This is emphasized by the use of the conditional mood: "Yes he minds [the raids] a hell of a lot he mopes for days after, he was terrible during last September. I thought *I'd have* to have him destroyed, because you can't find homes for dogs these days"[62] (my emphasis). Another man explained a similar dilemma, "I think *I'd have* a dog put to sleep unless I knew he was going to a very good home where *he'd* be happy"[63] (my emphasis). In such instances the killing of a canine companion has not taken place: Despite the stress of raids this was an unlikely action for the men to have contemplated, as their use of language confirmed.

One young man whose mongrel dog had died some six months previously situated the domestic relationship within the broader context of the mood of the nation. When asked, "How do you feel about people keeping dogs nowadays?" He replied "I take my hat off to 'em." Although he acknowledged that dogs "are unpopular nowadays" and that people had been "downright rude" to him about keeping his dog, the young man expanded:

> It's foolish really. Probably dogs do more to uphold morale among their owners than anything else. And dogs are doing their bit in the war too. Dog messengers at the front always have done a lot of good in wartime. Surely they've earned the privilege of being allowed to live for all their kind—even if it has to include the duchess's spoilt peke feeding on tongue, chicken, cream and orange juice [*sic*].

This account is interesting on different levels. Here "the war" is seen as something happening "somewhere else," the Home Front is not part of the "war." The actions of certain dogs "at the front" are seen to give value to the species as a whole. Dogs have a positive effect on humans ("morale") with whom they live—albeit not generally. The class divisions that still sharply existed during the war are seen, however, not to override a "commonality" of the dog species. When subsequently asked if he thought the government approved of dog-keeping or not, the interviewee retorted: "It certainly does not—but then like all things they haven't given it much thought and won't give it any thought till they've killed every dog in the country and wonder what's gone wrong."[64] Thus the government's perceived stance towards dogs became an exemplum of general incompetence. The dogs may have maintained morale but this was undertaken, he argued, in the face of state neglect of humans and animals alike. In a different example Vere Hodgson described, on the death of Scamp the cat, how he had maintained the humans' morale "so good he was when the bombs were dropping on us" and made them "laugh through many a bad hour."[65] Gwladys Cox, who had written extensively about her joint wartime existence with Bob, her tabby cat, reflected back at the end of the war, "He was our constant companion and consolation in all our war-time trials."[66] Gwladys and Bob were certainly not alone in this experience. As another interviewee explained to Mass Observation in 1941, "Most of the people around still have their dogs. If you treat them well and bring them up properly they appreciate it and they will never leave you."[67] Although dogs, more than cats, are seen to be loyal beings this man made it clear that such behavior needed to be earned by a *human* to create a good relationship for both of them.

SCIENTISTS, HISTORIANS, AND RELATIONSHIPS

Recently cultural historians have started to take an interest in "emotions history," striving, as one recent collection puts it, "to know how history felt to those who lived through it."[68] To date, however, it has largely been left to scientists rather than historians to develop this approach towards animal-human relationships more fully.[69] Recent scientific research, for example, has explored different sources of the creation of oxytocin, the hormone thought to affect bonding within humans. Human-canine interaction by dogs' human-like gazing behavior has brought about social rewarding effects: oxytocin is released in humans and dogs alike. The new research supports the existence of a "self perpetuating oxytocin-mediated positive loop in human-dog relationships that is similar to that of human mother-infant relations." Thus interspecies bonding is deepened.[70] Although this specific research is of the twenty-first century the notion of animals expressing emotions in common with humans is by no means new. Sharing of emotion takes us back to the ideas of Jeremy Bentham over two hundred years ago with his well-known epithet, "The question is not, can they reason? Nor, can they talk? But, can they can suffer?"[71] Here the philosopher was attempting to show the common features that characterized different species, particularly suffering. Instead of promoting the value of speech to separate humans from animals, by emphasizing feeling he promoted a commonality across species. Although Charles Darwin would later famously explore the emotional lives of animals this momentum did not continue.[72] However, in recent years, scientific work by those interested in the emotional lives of nonhuman animals in society has increased. Thus Birke and Hockenhull demonstrate that "coordinating behavior with another entails an emotional component, which both reflects and produces the relationship, and so does interspecies coordination, even if their behavior is not identical."[73] Animals and humans being together share emotional states within particular historical contexts. For example, Sol was valuable to Nella Last in providing both emotional and empathetic support in wartime:

> To me he is more than an animal: he has kindness, understanding and intelligence and not only knows all that is said but often reads my mind to an uncanny degree. He knows when I am sad and dim and lies with his head on my foot, or follows me closely as if to say, "I cannot help you, but please understand I love you and will stand by."

Unlike her human partner who seemed unable to understand his wife, the dog could apparently do this.[74] Instead of dismissing this as simply a product of an imaginative human mind we might consider other possibilities.

As biologist and anthrozoologist John Bradshaw has argued, dogs are very sensitive to "what goes on within relationships — not just those in which they are directly involved, but also those they observe between people."[75] Bradshaw goes further by suggesting "the most basic emotions are so rooted in mammalian physiology and the more primitive parts of the mammalian brain that it is reasonable to assume that they are fundamentally the same whether experienced by a dog or by a human."[76] However, methodologically scientists are not particularly concerned with external cultural contexts and the effect of different historical times. Conventionally, with the scientific emphasis on empiricism, the findings of earlier researchers are ignored unless the same "evidence," certain animal behavior for example, can be personally observed. My argument, however, is that the war itself — and the type of warfare, including rationing of certain foods, changes in accommodation / living arrangements, and aerial bombardment — were contexts that created particular relationships, including the emotional relationships I have been considering here.

FIGURE 8.6 Families including children and a dog at an emergency feeding unit, Chingford January 1945 (LHW 23/6, Bishopsgate Institute)

FIGURE 8.7 Joint canine and human fatigue at Southwark Rest Centre c. 1940 (LHW 19/76, Bishopsgate Institute)

Companion animals and humans were affectionate towards each other. Recently historian Philip Howell has provocatively suggested, in his important book on canine-human relationships in the nineteenth century, that "anthropocentrism being a two-way street . . . we should not simply read such statements as 'really' being about people." It involved both the "animalizing of the human as well as the humanizing of the animals."[77] Similar "blurring" was also occurring within the environment of total war. This was an unprecedented moment of potential stress, fear, and anxiety. It was also a specific time in which otherwise quotidian routines became "more than ordinary" because of the nature of warfare. Thus diarist James Lees-Milne described his own actions in clipping a yew hedge "destroying the silvery spiders' webs as I advance like Atropus with my shears from end to end. I think, 'Who the hell am I, wilfully, mercilessly to wipe out a whole world of insects? I am as bad as Genghis Khan, as bad as Hitler.'"[78] Etienne Benson has argued that historians might need to draw on natural sciences outside the traditional purview of history but that "scientists no more than philosophers can tell them whether it is possible to tell the history of a particular subject."[79] Material conventionally used by historians, such as diaries, may indeed be able to illuminate in different ways the emotional relationship also observed by scientists.

TWO DISTINCTIVE FELINE-HUMAN RELATIONSHIPS

Despite my extensive reading of published and unpublished diaries and memoirs, I have yet to find an account of the last days of a much loved animal companion killed by his keeper to compare with that of Victor Klemperer, a Jewish academic living in Dresden with his non-Jewish wife, Eva, and their cat, Muschel. The cat had provided hope for the humans, "We have so often said to each other: the tom cat's raised tail is our flag, we shall not strike it, we'll keep our heads above water, we'll pull the animal through, and at the victory celebrations Muschel will get a 'schnitzel from Kamm's' (the fanciest butcher here) . . . he was always a comfort and support to Eva."[80] The family—including the cat—faced obvious harassment under the Nazi regime. The daily routines of the cat and humans were inextricably linked in different bonds of emotion to those described above in wartime Britain. The very provision of food for Muschel was a political act that threatened all the family with death. This was never the case in Britain. Fish was, Klemperer wrote in his diaries, exceedingly rare—and completely prohibited for Jews (or their animals). When a kindly Aryan friend sent a fish's head for Muschel it was cooked but the bones were burnt immediately, in case the Gestapo searched the house.[81] On 14 May 1942 the Nazis issued a further decree, this time forbidding Jews either to keep pets or to give them away. This was, Klemperer noted, "the death sentence for Muschel," who had lived with Eva and Victor for some eleven years.[82] Animals had to be given over to the Nazis for collective killing, posing a moral dilemma. "Today, Eva said, 'The little animal plays, is happy and does not know it will die tomorrow'—Is there anyone among us who knows: tomorrow you will die? I constantly have to repeat to myself, muddled feelings about the cat. I feel sorry primo loco for Eva, secondo loco for myself, terto loco for Muschel."[83] The following day as there was news that the "handover" was imminent, Eva, illegally, took the cat to the vet, choosing a time just before the surgery closed.[84] They had postponed the action not wishing to have "the animal, which is healthy and full of life" killed. But recognized that:

> Unless the regime collapsed by the very next morning, we would expose the cat to an even crueller death or put me in even greater danger. (Even having him killed today is a little dangerous for me.) I left the decision to Eva. She took the animal away in the familiar cardboard cat box, she was present when he was put to sleep by an anaesthetic which took effect very rapidly—the animal did not suffer. But she suffers.

Victor too was "haunted by the poor beast."[85] The context, of course, is very, very different to the position in Britain where no human was prevented by the state from keeping an animal companion during the war. Here the extent of Nazi domination into everyday life, including cross-species relationships, created a situation more extreme than any experienced—or discussed in British wartime diaries. However, in a similar way, say, to the accounts of Nella Last or Gwladys Cox, this exemplifies the inextricable links between human and animal forged at a particular moment of war. But Klemperer's account was also about the brutal context for the severing of that relationship.

By way of a very sharp contrast I want to finish this chapter with a story about Nelson, a black cat who enjoyed a very different sort of existence to Muschel. Cats had frequently lived as "warehouse" or "office" cats in government ministries and in Downing Street.[86] But Nelson's status was rather different: He shared a relationship with the Prime Minister, Winston Churchill, at no. 10 Downing Street, the PM's official London residence. His role was useful but not as a mouse catcher. To Nelson, hiding during an air raid under a chest of drawers, the Prime Minister purportedly said, "You should be ashamed of yourself, with a name like yours, skulking . . . while all those brave young men in the RAF are up there fighting gallantly to save their country."[87] Churchill's behavior towards another cat who lived in Chartwell, Churchill's own house in Kent, resembled that of many citizens at that time. Here the ginger cat would eat tidbits of mutton and sit having his eyes cleaned while Churchill composed a speech or complained about the conduct of military affairs in the Middle East. The Prime Minister "expressed his deep regret that cream was not available on account of wartime rationing."[88] While there is no evidence to suggest that Churchill started to form relationships with cats only during the war, it is clear that such feline-human relationships themselves were affected by the very circumstances of war. In a recent radio program exploring the way that state education has generally been neglected as a political priority by successive governments, a particular story of Churchill and Nelson was repeated.[89] Rab Butler, the pioneer of the important 1944 Education Act, came into Churchill's room and, as was often the case, found him in bed. Churchill was smoking a Corona cigar, and there was the black cat curled up on his feet. Churchill started the conversation by claiming, "This cat does more for the war effort than you do!"

One can interpret this story in many ways. The recent program included it as a funny story and to illustrate the lack of importance Churchill gave to education. But it was also about something else, I suspect. Apart from acting as a type of foot warmer, the cat may well have been providing Churchill with the same sort of emotional and moral support that British citizens widely enjoyed. Of course, the cat too was being warmed and enjoying a particular wartime relationship that was also being experienced throughout the land. Even at the highest strata of British society animals were demonstrating the inaccuracies of the excluding term "People's War."

CHAPTER NINE

Conclusion: Change and Continuity. Remembering and Forgetting Animals during the Second World War

There is no evidence in our surviving records of the time of any "massacre" of pets at the start of WW2.[1]

By the end of the war the attitude of dog and cat carers towards their animals had changed in many ways: Often the animal-human relationship became closer than before the war. Knowing this, we can no longer accurately define that time as a "People's War" per se. On the Home Front it was a war experienced and shared by animals and humans alike. "The Animal-Human War" would be a more accurate moniker for the Home Front of 1939–45. The animal massacre had been criticized by those concerned with animal welfare or rights. It was not seen as an inevitable consequence of war. It had been portrayed negatively as "letting war creep into your home."[2] Perhaps what crept out of the total war was a better relationship between humans and companion animals.

But such a summary reads too much like a Whig version of history in which there is almost inexorable progress towards a positive present. It implies that "history" is almost incrementally built up over a long timescale rather than taking place at particular moments. Certainly for the veterinary profession their involvement in the war and NARPAC brought the rewards and recognition for which they had so long campaigned. The Veterinary Surgeons Act of 1948 at last gave only those who were members of the Royal College the right to practice as veterinarians.[3] The veterinary profession started to refocus its attention on the care of domestic animals hitherto neglected as part of the urban rather than rural environment.[4] Those dedicated to the treatment of small animals, such as cats and dogs, established themselves as a distinctive professional group that continues to this day, in the British Small Animal Veterinary Association.[5]

BACK TO NORMAL

But for companion animals there was by no means a steady improvement in their treatment. One recent Mass Observation respondent recalled the arrival of two cats into his home at the end of the war:

> "Tish" and "Tosh" were from the same litter, but were as different as chalk is to cheese. "Tish" was a lean and small-framed tabby while brother "Tosh" was a stunted, rotund khaki-coloured creature whose fur stood up permanently and who was possessed by furious demons.

When the family's trade in horse-shoeing stopped suddenly at the end of the war, the business was disposed of. Only Tish and Tosh remained from that time. There was a wash-house at the end of the main house with a gas stove on which fish roes were boiled:

> I heard that Grandad put plates of food in the upper and lower parts of this stove and shut the cats in before turning on the gas. I was somewhat surprised to hear that no one thought any the worse of Grandad for this. Afterall, working-class folk could never afford to go to the vet. My boyhood was at an end.[6]

The storyteller did as a child express surprise that "no one thought any the worse of Grandad," but it suggests any changes in the war were short-lived. The recent observation of Marc Bekoff is just as relevant for the end of the war—as for the beginning:

> How we treat animals often changes dramatically depending on the context . . . Unfortunately for animals, the relationship with humans has been, and remains, strongly asymmetrical. Human interests almost always trump animal interests.[7]

Animals may have boosted human morale in the war but for many they were now again just disposable things. Pets can function as surrogate humans, where "an animal performs the role of the silent, utterly faithful human companion," but they also exist *concurrently* as a nonhuman animal.[8] The latter "role" was now to the fore. In its own account of its wartime activities published in 1947 the PDSA could still write, "Even today many a cat is destroyed by being tied in a sack with a brick fastened to its neck and thrown into the river."[9] In the same year, the Battersea Dogs Home was continuing to try to persuade owners to take back the increasing number of dogs they were handing in. This was attributable, the annual report suggested, to the rising cost of dog food and more people going out to work feeling unable to leave the dog alone for many hours. Some, large, dogs would survive since there was now a demand for watchdogs, owing to an increase in postwar burglaries. Such an outcome was unlikely for dogs older than 5 or 6 years. If the staff's persuasive powers could not work then the dogs would be destroyed.[10] Over 15,000 "stray" dogs and 560 cats were killed. (I use "stray" since this included animals who were deliberately abandoned and dumped far from home.[11]) In its first postwar report the local Windsor, Hillingdon, and Uxbridge branch of the RSPCA reported the problem of performing

FIGURE 9.1 Animals in War memorial, Park Lane, London, c. 2010

cats and dogs and a menagerie at the Slough August bank holiday carnival. The branch would try to persuade the Provost of Eton College not to allow such an "attraction" on its land in future.[12]

I said at the start of the book that as a nation the story of the massacre does not fit with the tales we like to tell ourselves about ourselves. Nor does the animal human relationship of 1939-45 fit with the idea of a "People's War": "These stories we tell ourselves about our lives are not necessarily those lives as they are lived, but these stories become our experience of those lives."[13] In a culture obsessed with heritage, historical "anniversaries," and nostalgia for the "good old days," the general role of animals as part of our history is mostly evident through the *absence* of public commemoration.

AMNESIA IN MEMORY AND MEMORIALS

An exception is the Animals in War memorial in London, unveiled in 2004 to both acclaim and controversy. After many years of campaigning, novelist Jilly Cooper together with most animal welfare groups in Britain had managed to raise the £1.4 million necessary and had commissioned an imposing sculpture by David Backhouse. They secured a site, albeit not their first choice, alongside (but not in) Hyde Park in a traffic island on busy Park Lane.[14] At first glance the Animals in War memorial seems impressive: a memorial privileging animals' role in war rather than seeing them just as a human adjunct. The absence of human figures is striking.[15] But it is more complicated than this. The very images, including elephants, camels, donkeys, horses, and dogs[16] sculpted in white Portland stone, and two bronze donkeys carrying heavy loads, suggest animals' role in warfare is placed in a much earlier era—bees and rats on twenty-first century battle and minefields are absent, as are the animals whose bodies are employed for experiments in the military establishment at Porton Down.[17] But humans are far from absent in the Park Lane memorial. On the right-hand side there are the words "They had no choice." This implies that animals have and had no agency, no ability to think or to choose how to relate to the wars of which they were an integral part. This suggests too that humans did have agency, a claim that is by no means always the case in war.[18] But the memorial is not commemorating all animals who have died in warfare, say, German dogs in the trenches of France in 1914-18, Finnish horses in the Winter War of 1939-40, or Japanese animals killed in Tokyo Zoo in 1943.[19] The statement makes it clear that these were animals who served and died in their millions for the British and Allied cause, playing "a vital role in every region of the world in the cause of human freedom."[20] On the one hand animals are depicted as having neither choice nor agency but on the other they are seen as simultaneously apparently choosing to give their lives for a particular nation and its causes, resulting not in their own "freedom" but that of humans. The explicit role of *people* in creating the conditions for such death is barely acknowledged. There is no reference to animals' role in the Second World War in general nor to their particular deaths at the hands of the "Allies" in September 1939. Similarly although in the National Memorial Arboretum there is a memorial to animals of the Second World War, this is dedicated only to those animals (such as Jet of Lada) working "officially" in Civil Defence.[21] In the PDSA cemetery where the corpses of thousands of pet animals were buried in the autumn of 1939, there are memorials to animals of the Second World War but these are gravestones of individual animal "heroes" who typically worked with civil defense. There is no similar recognition for those thousands of animals who died not as "heroes" within a self-congratulatory framework of a "good" war but as victims of human action and humans' refusal to acknowledge responsibilities for all beings in the household.

Most humans alive in Britain today were born after the war. The adults who would have taken the decision at the time to kill—or keep within the bounds of the family—pet animals are now few in number. Many of those who have passed on to me stories of that time (or who have been recorded by others) recalled their wartime childhood. Asta, the dog who had written to the child of the family, was introduced in the first chapter. As an adult obviously Jean Brant realized that Asta had not written her letters, but as a child she had thought he was still alive. When they were children, some of the harshness of wartime life was hidden from them, including the killing of pets. As previously noted, the cat and dog massacre was never hidden from the population at large. Indeed it was the subject of national press coverage. However, children were often protected from such distressing accounts and thus may not have remembered some 70 years later what *did* happen to family pets. It is thus no wonder that tales of "being kind" have been transmitted: These are the stories we tell children—they are not necessarily the stories we should tell ourselves as adults.

It is, of course, difficult for those of us who have not had to suffer the fear and actuality of total war to imagine what we would do with the animals who live with us in such circumstances. But we have had more recent experiences, albeit vicarious ones for those of us living in Britain, of what happens to the human-animal relationship in extremis. The state-enforced human abandonment of animal companions at gunpoint in the Katrina hurricane and floods resulted in massive animal death—and human trauma. As Sarah Lowe has noted, "[Animal] guardians who are not monetarily privileged or who are otherwise socially marginalised, may be those most at risk of prolonged and intense grief following companion animal loss."[22] In an excellent account that privileges the plight of animals in the aftermath of the Christchurch earthquakes in New Zealand of 2010, Annie Potts and Donelle Gadenne can nevertheless assert the "trivialisation of animals affected by disasters."[23] That the position of companion animals in Afghanistan and other zones of British war activity is being recognized in the press and through animal charities such as Nowzad is laudable.[24] But, as Nowzad honestly notes, many of the dogs and cats it is now seeking to re-home either in Afghanistan or Britain were those taken in and then abandoned by troops or contractors—even though the charity is able to organize repatriation if they are approached.[25] I refer to these present examples of animals in war and disaster to reinforce the idea that history is not about the past. Rather, it is about bringing the past into the present, and creating the sort of histories we consider that we need for the present.[26] The role of animals in supporting humans through the Second World War and the regret felt by many who had killed them unnecessarily might be relevant when thinking today about animals in war—and our responsibilities towards them.

People's attitudes towards animals were—and are—not fixed but changed and developed through the war in response to animals' own behavior. Diarist Nella Last, whom I frequently mentioned in previous chapters for the close relationship she enjoyed with her dog Sol and cat Mr. Murphy, had been one of the many who at the end of August 1939 had contemplated killing her companions: "Wonder if I should give my faithful old dog, and my funny comedian cat 'the gift of sleep.'"[27] But unlike others who considered this course of action she chose to keep—and love—her animals, who seemed to reciprocate.

Although as a historian and researcher I have looked at wartime materials garnered over many years, my initial fascination was with the September massacre. It took me a while to think through that such a decision to kill would *not* have been taken by most humans who lived with animals in 1939. Thus I returned to Peter Townsend's *The Family Life of Old People: An Inquiry in East London*, a key sociological text alongside the better known and similarly romanticized publication from the Institute of Community Studies, *Family and Kinship in East London*. At first I was perturbed by the many accounts of older people's daily interactions with companion animals, such

as, "had another sit down talking to Mr Bird (budgie)" or "12.30 had my dinner, bacon and potatoes, fed the dog."[28] Needless to say, although Townsend
acknowledged the existence of relationships, albeit in tactless wording, "Attachment to flowers and pets is almost universal . . . Well over half the old
people interviewed had a pet, most of these a cage-bird," he chose not to
analyze these relationships within his framework of family life.[29] At the
time I made the (wrong and hasty) assumption that these elderly people
had previously killed their pets and that those discussed in such affectionate terms were mere expendable "replacements." My thinking has changed
over the years it has taken me to write this book. While realizing that the
lifespan of pets would mean that many of those companions alive in the
1950s would have been born after the war, I suspect that many were and
had been living in the same households. For many people, I remind myself and reiterate, there was never any question about destroying their own
companion animals. They were not facing edicts that instructed them to
kill animals or face severe personal consequences—the predicament faced
by Victor Klemperer and his cat, Muschel, discussed in chapter 8. Despite
personal difficulties they valued animals and their part in their own family.

THE RETURN TO NORMALITY

Ironically, through diaries, official records, and particular memories, the
war has provided researchers with glimpses into the lives and experiences
of companion animals that otherwise are not necessarily available in "ordinary" times. It is the wide range of material that can make the 1939–45
war a moment during which traces of animal experience might be glimpsed
more easily than the years immediately afterwards or before. And such materials do include the memories of individuals transmitting family stories
across the generations into a present and enabling them to be transformed
into broader histories of the nation at war. As my endnotes show I have
many people to thank for materials for this book, including very helpful individuals at animal charities such as Cats Protection and the RSPCA. They
have shown themselves keen to acknowledge the past role of animals in
Britain's cultural life. I am not sure it has always been like this. Some time
ago when I first started the research for this book I wrote to the then archivist of the RSPCA seeking to read the council minutes during the war. The
reply was not as helpful as I had hoped:

> There is no evidence in our surviving records of the time of any "massacre" of
> pets at the start of WW2. Unfortunately, our minutes are closed to external re-

searchers for 100 years, due to issues of confidentiality, so you will be unable to verify that personally but I can assure you that we have researched this matter a number of times and have found nothing to support the anecdotal reports we have heard over the years.[30]

There was nothing either, I was told, in the published annual reports. I had been rather surprised by this assertion, given that the RSPCA's published account of its own role during the war that I had already read in the British Library stated unequivocally that "four hundred thousand cats and dogs, chiefly cats, were painlessly destroyed in Greater London during the first four days of war."[31] Undeterred I asked to visit to see what was not there and although this was agreed, on *that* occasion I did not receive a warm reception.

But over time I have come to look at the archivist's defensive statement in a more nuanced light. The RSPCA is the only animal welfare charity to have powers invested in law to prosecute people for cruelty to animals.[32] A reading of the annual reports did indeed confirm that there was an increase in killings but, as I noted in the first chapter, it was certainly not the case that no unnecessary killings of animals had taken place before the events of September 1939. It was not just the RSPCA but all animal welfare charities that killed animals. They killed them in the war. They killed them before the war. They killed them after the war. And many continue to kill them now. This is what humans in "animal-loving Britain" want them to do. The reasons for this may vary, including giving animals relief from painful illness; private landlords forbidding animals in rented accommodation; and unwillingness to take responsibility for an animal throughout her life. It was not the mass killing of pet animals that took place during that first week of September 1939 that was an aberration—but what developed in the remainder of the war.

The physical conditions of total war—restricted food, enforced sheltering from bombs, potential and actual homelessness—and its mental / emotional states, including anxiety, stress, and trauma, were characteristic of a particular type of warfare. In that moment there started to grow cross-species relationships that benefitted both humans—*and* animals. These were exceptional times. Rather than choosing to forget the varying treatment humans meted out to animals in the war, we might chose to remember those times in different ways and to create new histories of the animal-human war as a reminder of the past and as a possible guide to future living.

Acknowledgments

I have many people and institutions to thank for their assistance in various ways while researching for this book. Many archivists went out of their way to give advice and to suggest materials. I am most grateful for being allowed access to the following archives. In some cases this was not a formal archive but just a cupboard with a minute book or magazines but these materials were all nevertheless of great value: Battersea Dogs and Cats Home, BBC archives, Bishopsgate Institute, Blue Cross, British Library at Colindale and Euston, Camden Local Studies Centre and Archives, Cats Protection, Dogs Trust, Hastings House, Hastings Local Studies Library, Havering Archives, Hillingdon RSPCA, Imperial War Museum, London Metropolitan Archives, Mass Observation, Onekind, RSPCA, Royal Veterinary College, The National Archives, Tower Hamlets Archives. Particularly thanks are due to Stefan Dickers, the library and archives manager at the Bishopsgate Institute; David Allen, Head of Education at the RSPCA; John Edmundson of the Ernest Bell Library; and the very helpful staff in the Rare Books Room of the British Library, who help ameliorate the dire experience of entering the noisy internet cafe at Euston Road.

Apart from using formal archives I was assisted by many individuals who agreed to be interviewed, contacted me via my website, passed on family stories, or agreed to raise my queries with older family members. This has been incredibly helpful and provided insights not necessarily contained in conventional written materials: Sylvia Berliner, the late Dr. Mary Brancker, Clare Brant, Jean Brant, Gwen Brown, Julia Courtney, Maureen Hirsch, David Johnson, Ken Jones, Brenda Kirsch, Caroline Morrell, Jon Newman,

Elizabeth Paul, Jean Paul, Paul Plumley, Anne Reese, Adrienne Roche, Alison Skipper, Chris Sladen, Peter Townsend, Jill Watts.

I also wish to thank all the individuals who forwarded me information, looked up queries, and suggested things to read. Others shared their knowledge, passed on books, were willing to discuss ideas, and helped with queries. Thanks in particular to Maggie Andrews, Ben Annis, Jim Aulich, Paula Bartley, Malachy Billingsley, Lynda Birke, Veryan Boorman, Joanna Bornat, John Edmundson, Brian Edwards, Nadine Finch, Jonathan Fishburn, Andrew Flack, Paul Foley, Andrew Gardiner, Jenny Green, Andrew Gritt, Felicity Harvest, James Hinton, Christian Høgsbjerg, Laurie Holden, Val Horsfield, Angela V. John, Dave Juson, Marilyn Kinnon, Robert Kirk, Paul Knight, Robert Lentell, Alison Macnair, Anne Marshall, Roger McCarthy, Jennifer McDonell, Steve Mills, Lucy Noakes, Neil Pemberton, Anthony Podberseck, Wendy Robertson, Mieke Roscher, Richard Ryder, Dorothy Sheridan, Jan-Erik Steinkruger, Emma Tait, Helen Tiffin, Abigail Woods.

Many of the ideas contained in these pages were previously presented at a range of conferences, seminars, and media events resulting in feedback and input from many people. This included feedback from appearances on *The One Show* (BBC1) and *Saturday Live* (Radio 4) and radio in Australia and New Zealand. Other feedback resulted from public lectures at the Animal Worlds series at the Humanities in Public Centre, Manchester Metropolitan University; Birkbeck College, University of London; London Metropolitan Archives; Massey University, New Zealand; University of Greenwich; Vero series at Mansfield College, University of Oxford. Academic events included "Britain as a Nation of Animal Lovers? Representing Animals" conference at the University of Rennes; lecture and seminar at the Centre for Animal Studies at the University of Kassel; "Cosmopolitan Animals" conference, University of Kent; International Veterinary History Conference at Imperial College, London; ISAZ conference at the University of Cambridge; "Memories of War: New Narratives and Untold Stories" conference at the University of Greenwich; Minding Animals international conference at University of Newcastle, Australia; Centre for Animal Welfare, Department of Veterinary Science, the University of Cambridge; "The Second World War, Popular Culture and Cultural Memory" conference at the University of Brighton; "Women on the Home Front" conference of the Women's History Network at the National Memorial Arboretum. I would also like to thank the anonymous reviewers of the book proposal and manuscript for their helpful comments and also all the helpful staff at the University of Chicago Press.

Last, but by no means least, I want to thank most warmly those friends and colleagues who read drafts (often more than one version), engaged in endless accounts of various animals (and approaches to history) discussed during a number of meals, drinks, and conversations over a period of years. In their critical comments (both positive and negative) they helped keep me on track: Keren Abse, Russell Burrows, Philip Howell, Ken Jones, Brenda Kirsch, Di Parkin, Farhana Sheikh, Kim Stallwood, Jo Stanley.

Needless to say neither these readers nor any other person who has made comments, suggested material, or offered advice is responsible for the contents of this book. That is my responsibility alone. If I have inadvertently overlooked an individual's suggestion or input this is not intentional but a product of the length of time it has taken for this book to see the light of day. Those who in some ways have made me think most carefully about this topic are Sidney Trist, Tommy Atkins, and Albert Chevalier, to whom this book is dedicated.

Notes

CHAPTER ONE

1. Harrisson, *Living through the Blitz*, 51.

2. Eley, "Finding the People's War," 818.

3. Gray and Bell, *History on Television*, 102–23.

4. Given that W. C. Sellar and R. J. Yeatman published *1066 and All That* in 1930 they did not refer to the Second World War. See Fielding, "The Good War 1939–1945."

5. Eley, "Finding the People's War," 818.

6. Gray and Bell, *History on Television*, 123.

7. M. Smith, *Britain and 1940*, 7.

8. Overy, *The Bombing War*, 73–93.

9. Addison, "National Identity and the Battle of Britain," 236.

10. Field, "Nights Underground in Darkest London: The Blitz 1940–1941," 27. See too A. H. Bell, *London Was Ours*, 12.

11. Finney, " Remembering the Road to World War Two," 217; S. O. Rose, *Which People's War?*

12. Nesbo, "Guardian Book Club."

13. This is not to say that fascists did not operate in Britain during the war but rather that this is known and widely written about. It was also known at the time and many were interned.

14. Kean, *Animal Rights*.

15. A. Calder, *The People's War*, 34.

16. Turner, *The Phoney War on the Home Front*, 113–15.

17. *The Oxford English Dictionary*, 2nd ed., vol. 7, prepared by J. A. Simpson and E. S. C. Weiner (Oxford: Clarendon Press, 1989), 315.

18. I realize that humans are also animals but for sake of clarity I will use the term animal. I will on occasion use the term pet (as well as companion animal) although I accept that this can be seen to be demeaning. It was, however, a term often used during the war.

19. N. Rose, *Governing the Soul*, 24.

20. Anon., *A Woman in Berlin*, 54.

21. Shirer, *Berlin Diary*, entry for 19 April 1940, 319.

22. When the Germans entered Paris on 14 June 1940 they found large parts of it deserted. Instead of the usual cacophony of car horns, all that could be heard was the lowing of a herd of cattle, abandoned in the city center by refugees passing through from the countryside further north. J. Jackson, *The Fall of France*, 174–82. Thanks to Steve Mills for this reference.

23. The huge popularity of the National Memorial Arboretum is but one sign of this; the majority of its memorials commemorate the Second World War. Gough, "'Garden of Gratitude': The National Memorial Arboretum and Strategic Remembering."

24. Howell, "The Dog Fancy at War," 564.

25. MacNeice, *Autumn Journal*, stanza 7, 113. Thanks to Ken Jones for this reference.

26. MacNeice, *The Strings Are False*, 209.

27. Burt, "The Illumination of the Animal Kingdom," 203–4. See also Cronin, "'Can't You Talk?'"

28. Photocopy of letter dated 21 September 1940 to Miss Beryl Myatt, Imperial War Museum archives, 05/56/1.

29. Account of Jean Brant told to Clare Brant and emailed to author. My thanks to both Jean and Clare Brant.

30. Shirer, *Berlin Dairy*, 183 and 202.

31. Henderson, *Hippy in Memoriam*, 7 and image in *Daily Mirror*, 8 September 1939, 1.

32. A. Calder, *The People's War*, 34. His statement about dachshunds being stoned in the street has recently been debunked. See Howell, "The Dog Fancy at War," and Alison Skipper, "The Dog as National Symbol in World War One: 'All-British Bulldogs' and 'German Sausages on Legs'" (unpublished paper given at 41st Congress of the World Association for the History of Veterinary Medicine, Imperial College, London, 12 September 2014).

33. Henderson, *Hippy in Memoriam*, 46–48.

34. Peter Neville, "Sir Nevile Meyrick Henderson (1882–1942)," Oxford Dictionary of National Biography website, http://www.oxforddnb.com/view/article/33814?docPos=1 . Henderson finished writing the manuscript in July 1942 and died a few months later, with the book published posthumously in March 1943. Henderson, *Hippy in Memoriam*, 48.

35. *Daily Mirror,* 8 September 1939, 3.

36. "By the dog that Ribbentrop deserted!" *Daily Mirror,* 7 September 1939, 10.

37. *Daily Mirror,* 8 September 1939, 1.

38. Turner, *The Phoney War on the Home Front*, 114.

39. Kathie Jennie, "The Power of the Visual in Animal Liberation," *Philosophy and Policy Journal* 2, no. 4 (2005): 1-2, as quoted in Baker, *Artist / Animal*, 145.

40. See the church's image of Faith in Kean, *Animal Rights*, 194.

41. See, for example, letter from Robert Gower to Herbert Morrison 14 March 1944 in Ho 186/1417, The National Archives.

42. Kean, *Animal Rights*,194.

43. See for example Rainer Pöppinghege, *Tiere im Krieg* (Paderborn: Schöningh, 2009); Gervase Phillips, "Writing Horses into American Civil War History," *War in History* 20, no. 2 (2013): 160–81 and "'Who Shall Say That the Days of Cavalry Are Over?' The Revival of the Mounted Arm in Europe, 1853–1914," *War in History* 18, no. 1 (2011): 5–32; John Singleton, "Britain's Military Use of Horses 1914–1918," *Past and Present* 139, no. 1 (1993): 178–203.

44. F. M. L. Thompson, *Victorian England*, 3.

45. McShane and Tarr, "The Horse in the Nineteenth-Century American City," 227; McShane and Tarr, *The Horse in the City*. They have been recently criticized by Sandra Swart for defining a horse as a living machine rather than as an animal possessing agency (Swart, *Riding High*, 200).

46. E. P. Thompson, *The Making of the English Working-Class*, 12.

47. Charles Phineas [pseud.], "Household Pets and Urban Alienation," *Journal of Social History* 7, no. 3 (1974): 339 as quoted in Fudge, "A Left-Handed Blow," 4.

48. Certainly the diaries of Queen Victoria recently published online indicate the huge attention given to companion animals, such as Islay, about whom Victoria wrote regularly and sketched. http://www.queenvictoriasjournals.org/quick/executeSearch.do;jsessionid=A01A83F76B2 8839EDE8CEC5162AE08BC.

49. Hodder-Williams, *Where's Master?*, 53.

50. See Gordon, *Noble Hounds and Dear Companions*; MacDonogh, *Reigning Cats and Dogs*; and Hall, *These Were Our Dogs*.

51. Burt, "Invisible Histories," 159.

52. Burt, "Review of Cary Wolfe, *Zoontologies* and *Animal Rites*," 168.

53. Fudge, "A Left-Handed Blow," 9; Kete, *The Beast in the Boudoir.*

54. Wolfe, *What Is Posthumanism?*, 123-24. For further discussion see Kean, "Challenges for Historians."

55. See, for example, Steedman, *Dust*, 81.

56. Kean, "The Smooth Cool Men of Science"; Mayer, "Representing the Experimental Animal"; Li, "Mobilizing Christianity in the Anti-vivisection Movement in Victorian Britain"; Guerrini, *Experimenting with Humans and Animals*; Rothfels, *Savages and Beasts*; Litten, "Starving the Elephants."

57. Tansey, "Protection against Dog Distemper and Dogs Protection Bills."

58. British Union for the Abolition of Vivisection (BUAV), "The National Health Service Act and Vivisection."

59. Brantz, *Beastly Natures*, 5.

60. "To admit that other animals have no sense of history is a quite different thing from claiming that animals cannot be held within the embrace of history." Smail, *On Deep History and the Brain*, 69.

61. See for example Rosenzweig and Thelen, *The Presence of the Past*; Ashton and Kean, *Public History and Heritage*; Kean and Martin, *The Public History Reader.*

62. The argument goes along the lines of how can women as a group, or a category, be apparently treated in a collective, undifferentiated way. (Rowbotham was not writing about "all" women but looking at radical and socialist change in political movements.)

63. Animal agency will be discussed particularly in chapters 5 onwards.

64. Benson, "Animal Writes," 5.

65. Anon., *Front Line*, 30.

66. NARPAC, *Wartime Aids for All Animal Owners* in HO/ 144/ 21418. There were also other aims particularly focused on "farm" animals. See chapter 7.

67. Lewey, *Cockney Campaign*, 93. See chapter 7 for images of rescued animals.

68. Vale, *Bethnal Green's Ordeal*, 5. The parliamentary constituencies have changed in recent years within a newly defined borough of Tower Hamlets. In essence, during the war Stepney and Poplar were near the docks and Bethnal Green was nearer Hackney.

69. Edward Heslop Smith, "For Members of the Wardens' Services Only," *Poplar Civil Defence Wardens' Organisation Bulletin*, no. 67. Victory issue typescript , June 1945, 10, Tower Hamlets Archive.

70. See, for example, Smith, *Poplar Civil Defence*,10; Demarne, *The London Blitz*, 65; Lewey, *Cockney Campaign*, 92.

71. *Hornsey Journal, Finsbury Park & Muswell Hill Standard*, 21 July 1944, 2.Thanks to Joanna Bornat for this cutting.

72. See material about Jumbo in Cab /50/7. There had been a cat employed in the Home Office since the nineteenth century albeit not receiving a food allowance until 1929 (HO 223/43, National Archives).

73. See Kean, "The Home Front as a 'Moment' for Animals (and Humans)."

74. Millgate, *Mr. Brown's War*, 3.

75. Cox, diary entry, 11 March 1942.

76. Cox, diary entry, 2 October 1940.

77. Benjamin, "Theses on the Philosophy of History," 247-49.

78. Tennyson Jesse and Harwood, *London Front*, letter 4 October 1939, 67.

79. Tennyson Jesse and Harwood, *London Front*, letter 16 October 1939, 106.

80. Tennyson Jesse and Harwood, *London Front*, 203.

81. Irene Fern Smith, diary entry, 2 February 1941, in Bishopsgate Institute.

82. Photocopy of letter dated 21 September 1940 to Miss Beryl Myatt, Imperial War Museum archives, 05/56/1.

83. For discussion of the responses to the sinking of the Arrandora Star, see Wendy Ugolini, *Experiencing War as the "Enemy Other": Italian Scottish Experience in World War II* (Manchester: Manchester University Press, 2011).

84. Perry, *Boy in the Blitz*, entry for 9 July 1940, 13.

85. Broad and Fleming, *Nella Last's War*. This aspect was not included in the BBC Film adapted by Victoria Wood, *Housewife 49* (2006), nor on the BBC website that included extracts from the diaries. http://www.bbc.co.uk/history/british/britain_wwtwo/nella_last_01.shtml. Accessed 1 May 2016.

86. Mass Observation Archive. Original Mass Observation Project. http://www.massobs.org.uk/original_massobservation_project.htm . Accessed 1 September 2013.

87. Mrs. Jean Brant, email to author from Clare Brant.

88. "Blitz Kitty by Brazen 67." Story of John Healey Article ID A4660481 in http://www.bbc.co.uk/history/ww2peopleswar/ .

89. B1654 Male widower 78 Rugeley Staffs, Animals and Humans Summer Directive 2009, Mass Observation. Similar types of naming were not uncommon. Thus three Birmingham-based kittens were named: "Stalin—because he is always before schedule—climbing etc. Roosevelt—because he feels he is important. Winston—because he never minds being mentioned last." Hodgson, *Few Eggs and No Oranges*, 3 April 1945,574.

90. A883, Married man born in 1935 in Eastbourne, Animals and Humans Summer Directive 2009, Mass Observation.

91. Anthony Giddens, *Modernity and Self Identity*, 77, in Kean, "Continuity and Change: The Identity of the Political Reader."

92. S. Williams, *Climbing the Bookshelves*, 5.

93. S. Williams, *Climbing the Bookshelves*, 65.

94. Overy, *The Bombing War*,128.

95. Mackay, *Half the Battle*,18.

96. King and Andrews, "Second World War Rationing," 185–86. See also Kirkham, "Beauty and Duty."

97. Fielding, "The Good War: 1939–1945," 37-38. The George Cross, created as a way of commemorating the service of civilians, would be awarded most frequently to firefighters and rescue workers, often posthumously. Sokoloff, "The Home Front in the Second World War and Local History," 27.

98. Sir Harold Scott, *Scotland Yard* (Harmondsworth: Penguin, 1957), 68, as quoted in Thomas, *An Underworld at War*, 16.

99. Overy, *The Bombing War*, 194.

100. Harrisson, *Living through the Blitz*. He tells the story of the dog who had to be walked directly the alert sounded or the cat who remained placid during raids but hysterical when hearing the voice of a radio broadcaster giving vigorous physical training instructions over the airwaves (p. 51).

101. Harrisson, *Living through the Blitz*, 51.

CHAPTER TWO

1. Croxton-Smith, *Tailwaggers*, 57.

2. Ritvo, *The Animal Estate*, 23.

3. Kete, "Introduction," *A Cultural History of Animals in the Age of Empire*, 3.

4. *Times*, 29 April 1918, 11. *Hansard*, 14 December 1916, vol. 88, cc831-8.

5. *Hansard*, 29 November 1916, vol. 88, cc344-5.

6. See Pemberton and Warboys, *Mad Dogs and Englishmen*.

7. *Times*, 6 December 1916. The use of dogs in rural areas had also included those working as hounds since fox hunting had not been suspended "for the duration" in order to maintain morale.

8. Gardner, *Cavies or Guinea Pigs*, 21.

9. Hunt, for example, discusses both food shortages but also domestic food riots in response. "A Heroine at Home."

10. NCDL, *Annual Report*, 1916, 15.

11. "Dogs and Dog Owners," *Times*, 29 April 1918, 11.

12. F. W. Norris, *Times*, 3 May 1918, 9.

13. *Times*, 28 April 1917, 8.

14. *Hansard*, 14 May 1918, col. 199, as quoted in Howell, "The Dog Fancy at War," 557.

15. Howell, "The Dog Fancy," 564.

16. *Times*, 18 August 1915, 7.

17. James Buckland, Letter to *Times*, 27 March 1916, 9.

18. Richard Pearce, Letter to *Times*, 27 March 1916, 9.

19. Richard Pearce, Letter, 9.

20. Robert Wallace, *Times*,1 April 1916,8. This letter suggestion was not as fanciful as it might appear. As records in the National Archives show, cats had been employed by the Home Office to catch mice and rats since the 1800s—although it was not until 1929 that Emily, the cat then in post, received a food allowance. (HO 223 /43). Later cats were named, including Peter 1949-64 and Jumbo working for the War Cabinet. They were also employed in the Post Office, National Gallery and British Museum (and in the latter until well into the 1990s in the basement housing books until the transfer to Euston Road). Similarly Mike, who for some twenty years from 1908 had stalked pigeons at the British Museum for a reward of a slice of beef or mutton and milk was recognized as providing a useful role. Mike's food was paid for (six old pence weekly) by Sir Wallis Budge, the keeper of Egyptian Antiquities. Joseph, *Cats Company*, 66 -71.

21. *Times*, 15 December 1916, 5.

22. This was also the case for Kennel Club shows that continued during the war. Crufts also continued in some form between 1914-17. See Howell, "The Dog Fancy at War."

23. "Pet Dogs," *Times*, 2 December 1916.

24. Ethel Bilbrough, diary entry for April 1917 in Blue Cross Archives.

25. Fudge, *Pets*, 107. See Kean, *Animal Rights*, 46-47, 77, 97 for a range of examples of animals kept as companions.

26. How people view their space has been seen to embody their very world: "our house is our corner of the world . . . it is our first universe, a real cosmos in every sense of the world." Bachelard, *The Poetics of Space*, 4, 17.

27. *Times*, 9 December 1939, 9.

28. Clabby, *A History of the Royal Army Veterinary Corps*, 33.

29. The figures are less in overall terms than the 2005 *national* estimates by veterinary scientists of over 10.3 million owned cats and 10.5 million owned dogs (J. K. Murray et al., "Number and Ownership Profiles of Cats and Dogs in the UK," 163) or the Pet Food Manufacturers' Association (PFMA) 2015 estimate of 12 million households (46%) caring for some 58.4 million animals, including fish, birds, hamsters, horses, rats, and snakes and nearly 16 million each of cats and dogs. They nevertheless give some indication of the durability of the companion animal-human relationship during the twentieth century. Pet Population 2015-PFMA http://www.pfma.org.uk/ pet-population-2015 . Accessed 28 November 2015. Tellingly the figures are lower than 10 years previously.

30. Bradshaw, *In Defence of Dogs*. He suggests domestication could have taken place at some time between 100,000 and 15,000 years ago, 31-32.

31. A work of 1907, suggesting that particular types of kennel should be provided, confirmed that dogs were generally kept outside: "Dogs of the ordinary breeds are perhaps best housed at night in a kennel out-of-doors, but this abode should be roomy, perfectly dry, and free from damp,

and placed out of the way of hot sun in the summer and cold winds in the winter." Finn, *Pets and How to Keep Them*, 20.

32. E. Bell, "British War Dogs," 25-26. Thanks to John Edmundson for sharing this cutting.

33. R. G. W. Kirk, "In Dogs We Trust?," 8.

34. Croxton-Smith, *Tail Waggers*, 30. Popular dog author Edward C. Ash was also highly critical of the chaining of dogs, arguing that it led to shorter life expectancy. Instead a kennel was to be placed the nearer the house the better, close to the back door "but just far enough away to prevent kind hearted errand boys from feeding and fondling the puppy." Ash, *Puppies*, 46-47.

35. As an elderly respondent to the 2009 Mass Observation directive on Animal Human relationships stated, "Of course in my childhood days the dogs stayed outside in kennels." H260 woman married 79, Brentwood. This sentiment was echoed by another memory of a respondent's grandfather who never allowed the pet dog inside the house. R470 male 75, Basildon in Animals and Humans, Mass Observation.

36. Croxton-Smith, *Tail Waggers*, 30.

37. Croxton-Smith, *Tail Waggers*, 57.

38. NCDL, *Dog Welfare*,10. The RSPCA advocated a running chain to enable dogs to exercise outside, albeit confined and constrained. RSPCA "Chained Dogs. The Value of the Running Chain." Postcard, RSPCA, c. 1930s. Thanks to John Edmundson for a copy of this image.

39. The Tail-Waggers Club, *The Tail-Waggers Club*.

40. Caged birds were usually kept inside-but could be moved outside on warm days. Mice, however, were kept in small cages inside with an "appallingly cramped play wheel." As one animal lover has recently recalled, her parents sold off the mice litters to the pet shop but the mice also ate their offspring: "Even today, when I am agitated or distressed I have nightmares about baby mice in piles, each with its head chewed off. Guilt haunts these memories. But neither I nor my parents, knew better." N1592 77 Woman in Animals and Humans, Mass Observation.

41. Cocker spaniels, for example, were bred to be larger than 25 lb in weight in the early twentieth century—and the red or golden color was specifically developed in the aftermath of the Great War. Croxton-Smith, *British Dogs*, 26.

42. Galsworthy, *The Dear Dogs*, 40.

43. Croxton-Smith, *British Dogs*, 40.

44. Allan and Allan, *The Essential German Shepherd Dog*, 24.

45. Howell, "The Dog Fancy at War," 549.

46. Very large dogs, such as the St. Bernard, became a favorite of feminists such as socialist campaigner Annie Besant; Louise Lind af Hageby, founder of the Animals Defence and Anti-Vivisection Society; and Charlotte Despard, president of the Women's Freedom League. No longer simply a *symbol* of Christian charity (the dogs were originally kept by the monks of Mt. Saint Bernard to rescue travelers stuck in the snow), they became popular as women's pets. Despite their large size they became popular in cities, no longer acting simply as "working" dogs. Frederick Whymper, "Great Pets," *Animals Guardian* 2, no. 1 (October 1891): 3-5; Hageby, *On Immortality*,13; NCDL, *Annual Report* (London: National Canine Defence League, 1910), 20; Ash, *Dogs*, vol. 2, 604. Dogs bred for particular "working" functions included terriers, such as Dandie Dinmot bred for "sport" on land and water. They had been kept as pets by the royal household of Victoria and Albert. Ash, *Puppies*,128-29; Kean, "The Moment of Greyfriars Bobby."

47. Richardson, *Forty Years with Dogs*, 203. In an early manual for cat breeders most of the text is devoted to a variety of Persian cats. Of Siamese the author remarks, "though favoured by many exhibitors, [the Siamese] is practically unknown to the general public. People who do not attend any cat shows are never likely to see a good Siamese sitting on a window-sill, or washing its face on the area steps." Mrs. L. Williams, *Sidney Appleton's Handbooks for Animal Owners*, 185.

48. Si-unsurprisingly a Siamese cat "White and fawn and black with blue eyes and a kink in his tail—a true Siamese"—who lived in Charmouth (in Dorset) in the 1920s was "a great darling" to his human companions. His diarist fan made no mention of the distinctive voice of this breed but his characteristics were perceived, positively, to be those of a dog: "Sometimes he looks more

like a pug than a cat. I am very fond of Siamese. They have a lot of the dog about them and get very attached to persons and will follow people about." Gerald Gray Fitzmaurice, diary entry 27 June 1927, Bishopsgate Institute.

49. Joseph, *Charles*, 9. James Mason, the film actor, described meeting his future wife at a party in 1935 and talking about Gemma, her cat: " I said quite truthfully that I had seen and admired Siamese cats at a distance but had never actually met one." Mason, *The Cats in Our Lives*, 21.

50. Joseph, *Charles*, 18–19.

51. Joseph, *Charles*, 10.

52. Bob Martin, *Bob Martin on Dogs*, 4.

53. PDSA "Annual Reminders" *Annual Report*, 1946, 20.

54. NCDL, *Dog Welfare: A Helpful Book on Dog Ailments* (London: NCDL, nd [1920s]), 32.

55. Queen Victoria had given her patronage to Spratt's dog biscuits that had been used alike in the royal kennels and the Battersea Dogs Home. Beetroot was an added key ingredient to appeal to dogs' sweet tooth and to encourage them to eat vegetables. Kean, *Animal Rights*, 80–84.

56. See, for example, *Queen Victoria's Journals* for Tuesday, 24 September 1839. http://www .queenvictoriasjournals.org/search/displayItem.do?ItemNumber=2&FormatType=fulltextimgsrc &QueryType=articles&ResultsID=2924936319074&filterSequence=0&PageNumber=5&ItemID =qvj02587&volumeType=ESHER. Islay was frequently present when the Prime Minister, Lord Melbourne, visited. There are many references to the dog and other companion animals in her journals.

57. "Blitz Kitty by Brazen 67." Story of John Healey Article ID A4660481 in http://www.bbc .co.uk/history/ww2peopleswar/.

58. Recently cat owners have been advised to provide "a nutritionally balanced diet" containing certain "proteins, vitamins and fatty acids." That is, a cat's need for a balanced diet reflects, at least in its categorization of different food sources, the same discourse used for humans. Oddly, this phrase was included in the DEFRA, *Consultation Code of Practice for the Welfare of Cats*, November 2008, but omitted in the final document, which simply called for a balanced diet. DEFRA, *Code of Practice*, 2009.

59. A menu of breakfast of porridge of oats and minced meat or gravy and vegetable and meat from the kitchen stockpot and a supper of fish and brown bread was recommended. To this were added liver and lights, of which cats were apparently very fond, and, from an early age, vegetables. Croxton-Smith et al., *Animals Home Doctor*, 196.

60. Croxton-Smith et al., *Animals Home Doctor*, 198.

61. L1696, Male 92 in Animals and Humans Directive, Mass Observation.

62. Jones, "A Short History of British Small Animal Practice," 115.

63. Hobday, *Fifty Years a Veterinary Surgeon*, 53–56, 91–92.

64. Lane, *All About Dogs*, 394.

65. P2034 man 82 in Animals and Humans Directive, Mass Observation.

66. Cousens, *Dogs and Their Management*, 101–21. The vaccine had allegedly been discovered through experiments on dogs at the government laboratories in Mill Hill. This discovery was a reason given for the lack of success of legislative attempts to ban experiments in dogs in the 1920s.

67. Galsworthy, *The Dear Dogs*, 26.

68. Croxton-Smith et al., *Animals Home Doctor*, 192.

69. Sherley, *Sherley's Dog Book*, 17–18.

70. Anon., "The Veterinary Profession and Poor People's Clinics," *Veterinary Record* 6 (1926): 530–31. The speaker is Captain R. Cornish-Bowden, MRCVS, as quoted in Gardiner, "The 'Dangerous' Women of Animal Welfare," 7.

71. Gardiner, "The 'Dangerous' Women of Animal Welfare"; and Kean, "Vets and Pets."

72. B1654 in Animals and Humans, Mass Observation.

73. W. H. Kirk, *Index of Diagnosis*, 2–4. Animal charities such as the RPSCA, ODFL, and PDSA also provided treatment for companion animals.

74. W. H. Kirk, *Index of Diagnosis*, 2, 71, 402.

75. Mrs. L. Williams, *Sidney Appleton's Handbooks for Animal Owners*, 67-68.Thanks to Veryan Boorman for sending me a copy of this book.

76. W. H. Kirk, *Index of Diagnosis*, 2.

77. The lack of human knowledge about feline enteritis also led to assumptions that cats had been poisoned: "It is not uncommon for neighbours or servants to be suspected of furtive and malicious poisoning when in reality, they are innocent." Illustrating that knowledge of feline illnesses was not widespread, this also shows that poisoning a cat was a way of taking revenge on a human, perhaps suggesting an affectionate relationship was being destroyed. W. H. Kirk, *Index of Diagnosis*, 354. (Red squill was commonly used as a poison for rats; in small quantities it was not poisonous to cats and dogs, W. H. Kirk, *Index of Diagnosis*, 361).

78. There were, inevitably, exceptions, thus Tigger, a moggie living in Dartmoor, was the recipient of medical expertise even though his human companion, Beatrice Chase, thought it unlikely a vet "would condescend to attend poor ordinary little cats"–especially since the nearest was some ten miles away. The vet came, however, and came back regularly even though Tigger was a moggie and not a "valuable" cat. But as the vet replied, "There's values, and values, madam!" Beatrice Chase, "The Dartmoor Vet," *Animal Lovers' Annual*, no. 1 (Autumn 1933), printed in aid of the RVC Camden Town Rebuilding and Endowment Fund, 19-25.

79. See chapter 7 for the dispute between the veterinary profession and the PDSA.

80. RSPCA Poplar Free Animals' Clinic, *Annual Report*, 1937, 3.

81. RSPCA Poplar Free Animals' Clinic, *Annual Report*, 1937, 2.

82. Croxton-Smith et al., *Animals Home Doctor*, 198.

83. Pegasus, *Horse Talks*, 25, 30.

84. Holman, Diaries, 2 December 1942, Camden Archives.

85. Pegasus, *Horse Talks*, 57; Dashper, "Tools of the Trade or Part of the Family?,"356. Recently Katherine Dashper has juxtaposed the classical riding and training traditions stressing harmony and cooperation between horse and rider with the contemporary requirements of competitive equestrian sport. These ideals, she concludes, are still placed within a context of equine "submission and a hierarchical relationship, which the human 'partner' ultimately dominates." Also see recent developments in "natural horsemanship," such as Parelli, being promoted by Mark Rashid in Colorado. Thanks to Laurie Holden for this information.

86. The homing orientation was important in various ways. Thus Welsh terrier Lerry was able to lead the way home for his human companion Molly, disoriented in a new rural environment: "One day I lost my directions among the many paths; so I sat down, and Lerry flung himself panting beside me. After a rest I said firmly, 'Home Lerry!' Immediately he started off, and I meekly followed. How charming, I felt, to be able to lose my way, and to have a dog who could find it!" Hughes, *A London Family between the Wars*, 10.

87. The Tail-Waggers Club, *A Dog Owner's Guide*.

88. In today's culture when less agency is desired and dogs have less opportunity to behave autonomously and roam on their own, nevertheless their methods of defecation are not controlled. Instead a responsible human is supposed to collect warm feces to be disposed of, often in specially designated bins.

89. See Kean, "The Moment of Greyfriars Bobby," and Kean, "An Exploration of the Sculptures of Greyfriars Bobby."

90. There had been several different human responses to this aspect of dogs' behavior. One was increased theft. As the 1844 *Parliamentary Select Committee on Dog Stealing* had explained, dogs were usually stolen for two reasons. Particular breeds were taken abroad where "fancy" breeds would fetch high prices or individual dogs were effectively held to ransom since they were highly valued as pets by their owners. Reporting to the committee, the London commissioner of the metropolitan police noted that sheep and horses were not enticed away like dogs since "you do not find them straying about as dogs do" (statement of Richard Mayne, commissioner of Metropolitan Police to *Parliamentary Select Committee on Dog Stealing*, p. 3/301, as discussed in Kean, "The Moment of Greyfriars Bobby"). As comical as this might sound, it also reinforces the idea

that dogs were so enamored of a specific human's company that they intentionally returned after a peregrination of many miles.

91. For nineteenth-century changes and particularly the impact of rabies scares, see Howell, *At Home and Astray*.

92. Mrs. L. Williams, *Sidney Appleton's Handbooks for Animal Owners*, 197.

93. W. H. Kirk, *The Diseases of the Cat*, 284. Even when the 1919 Act was repealed by the Protection of Animals (Amendment) Act in 1954, male cats were still exempted. The requirement to apply anesthetics for the castration of male cats under six months was not finally enforced under law until 1964 in the Protection of Animals (Anaesthetic) Act 1964. My thanks to Nadine Finch for this information.

94. W. H. Kirk, *The Diseases of the Cat*, 284–89, 348–52.

95. "We have never taken to the idea of spaying females. . . . We cannot speak of spayed cats with the authority of those who have lived with them. But we have met them in other people's houses many a time and have always come away with the impression that such cats are somewhat vacant, much more so that [*sic*] the average neutered tom . . . It is a difficult operation, too difficult perhaps for many practising vets." Mason, *The Cats in Our Lives*, 45. Charles, a Siamese cat, was the first of many cats who had lived with Michael Joseph to be castrated. On recovery from a serious bout of gastroenteritis the vet advised this procedure fearing he might otherwise pick up some infection from other cats. Joseph, *Charles*, 33.

96. Cornish, *Animals of To-day*, 33.

97. Anon., "They Our Friends We Their Guardians," *Animals Pictorial* 1, no. 6 (November 1938): 18–19.

98. This tradition had been established in the nineteenth century when cats were abandoned from middle-class homes in London Squares when houses were shut during the summer months for "the season," or as the RSPCA named it in the late nineteenth century, "the cat starvation season." An integral part of the critical narrative is that cats are no longer solitary but gathered in groups. The RSPCA secretary recalled, for example, seeing a gathering of 22 cats with "cries for help." Some were also simply shut up in the houses to suffering a lingering death of starvation: those in streets were liable to be chased, drowned, or given to vivisectors. RSPCA, "The Cat Starvation Season," *Animal World* 9, no. 108 (September 1878): 132–33.

99. Alger and Alger, *Cat Culture*. Pet manuals did not suggest putting cats on leads to take for walks, indicating that this "independence" was seen as an *integral* part of the feline make-up (hence the human wariness of cats in groups). There was greater freedom of movement and ability to exhibit agency for those not confined in a cattery for pedigree cats compared to dogs, who were bound by collars and leads or a chain. Restraint was required only if a cat was a spectacle outside the home as in a cat show. But she was not expected to be–and was not—a companion of the human in thoroughfares outside the house.

100. The incident described in this earlier twentieth-century purple prose was not restricted to that time: "'When the purchase arrives it is already in the grip of disease, a wretched-looking little object, only half the size it ought to be, dirty, with a staring coat and eyes half full of matter. It has been sent in a crazy box, gaping with cracks, and what little life it had in it when it started is soon snuffed out by the bad cold it has caught on the journey." Mrs. L. Williams, *Sidney Appleton's Handbooks for Animal Owners*, 190. Such inauspicious beginnings no doubt influenced future behavior. Mimi, for instance, a dachshund pup, had "arrived trembling in a crate from Harrogate. She was our pet for many years, but was never a cuddly little dog." N 1592 female 77 Animals and Humans, Mass Observation. (Today, in similar vein, animals can be bought and sold on eBay— legally—despite campaigns against this: http://www.change.org/petitions/ebay-classifieds-stop -selling-live-animals.)

101. R1418 Derby male 87 Animals and Humans Directive, Mass Observation.

102. W1893 man b. 1924 Animals and Humans, Mass Observation.

103. Author's interview with Dr. Mary Brancker.

104. B1654 Male widower Rugeley in Animals and Humans, Mass Observation.

105. R1418 male 87 Animals and Humans, Mass Observation.

106. Ken Jones, correspondence with author.

107. Croxton-Smith, *Tailwaggers*, 56.

108. Kinney and Honeycutt, *How to Raise a Dog in the City and in the Suburbs*,142. (Although some references are American the book was published in Britain.)

109. Cousens, *Dogs and Their Management*, xi–xii.

110. Cousens, *Dogs and Their Management*, 172.

111. Cousens, *Dogs and Their Management*, 174. John Bradshaw some 80 years later takes this further with his idea of dogs experiencing "fifteen kinds of love" in *In Defence of Dogs*, 223.

112. Cousens, *Dogs and Their Management*, 178.

113. This approach, suggesting that it is indeed possible for humans to understand dogs, is very different to the more famous approach of philosopher Thomas Nagel. He argued that it was impossible for humans to imagine what it was like to be an animal, specifically, a bat. As he put it, "there is no reason to suppose that it is subjectively like anything we can experience or imagine" and that even if we could, we could not know "what it is like for a bat to be a bat." Choosing a bat, rather than a companion animal, was deliberate: Although many people like bats and try to save their environment they are unlikely to share their homes or leisure time with such animals. Unsurprisingly, his position has been challenged. Animal advocate Kim Stallwood has recently explored the animal-human relationship and what he calls altruistic love or "the magical connection." He describes, for example, his relationship with a Chihuahua-type dog, Honey, a "feisty spirit": "I imagined that if Honey were a human being she'd be living on her own, getting by on gin and cigarettes, and making sure she knew everyone's business in the neighbourhood." As he explores, his connection with Honey enabled him to "imagine what it could be like to be them" and also understanding their wants such as treats, going for walks, or running on the beach. Less extravagantly radical theologian Andrew Linzey has also challenged Nagel, saying that we do not need to know precisely how a bat thinks, or feels, or "mentally encounters the world" to "know basic things about how it can be harmed." Like Linzey, Stallwood has emphasized the importance of lack of harm: "When she lay against my chest, I hoped that each beat of my heart reassured her that no harm would ever visit her again." Whether he is successful in his imagining is not the main point, rather that he hopes his benign practice is beneficial to the animal. That is, humans can at least engage with an animal and her environment without causing harm. Linzey has argued that humans can know things about a bat's consciousness and concludes, "We can know these things at least as reasonably as we know them in the case of most humans." Linzey intimates that understanding *human* experience is impossible. But nevertheless this is a task that routinely historians undertake in relation to human history. Nagel, "What Is It like to Be a Bat?"; Stallwood, *Growl*, 146–47; Linzey, *Why Animal Suffering Matters*, 50.

114. Just "being" is not enough to be chosen for a "forever home." The timid cat who shivers in terror near the back of the cage in the animal sanctuary is unlikely to be picked by humans who are looking for emotional reciprocity in an animal. And the black moggie who apparently doesn't show up well in "selfies" has a bleak future. According to the RSPCA 70% of the 1,000 abandoned cats in its care are black. They are less popular as their features do not show up in photos. "Hundreds of black cats are being abandoned by their owners because they don't look good in selfies," *Daily Mail*, 29 July 2014. http://www.dailymail.co.uk/news/article-2709721/Hundreds-black-cats-abandoned-owners-don-t-look-good-SELFIES.html

115. See for example Light, *Mrs. Woolf and the Servants*.

116. Croxton-Smith et al., *Animals Home Doctor*, 198.

117. B1654 widower 78 Rugeley Staffs, Animals and Humans, Mass Observation.

118. B1654 widower 78 Rugeley Staffs, Animals and Humans, Mass Observation.

119. Pierce, *Memories of the Civilian War*, 73.

120. K310 F married 80 Burgess Hill retired part-time shoe shop assistant in Animals and Humans, Mass Observation.

121. In 2009 DEFRA issued Codes of Practice for the Welfare not only of cats but dogs and horses, encouraging carers to observe and interpret animals' behavior.

122. Similarly the "office cat" was given a particular diet to positively encourage the catching of mice as a food supplement. The cat "must be given a penny worth of cats' meat every day" and clean water and, if desired, poor quality milk (Croxton-Smith et al., *Animals Home Doctor*, 198.) These suggestions contradict an earlier manual that argued that it was an "old idea" to underfeed a cat to make it a good mouser: "as a matter of fact, a well-fed cat will hunt more, because she does it for the pure love of sport, whereas a hungry one is satisfied when she has caught enough mice to satisfy her internal cravings" (Finn, *Pets and How to Keep Them*, 5).

123. Mrs. L. Williams, *Sidney Appleton's Handbooks for Animal Owners*, 201.

124. Mrs. L. Williams, *Sidney Appleton's Handbooks for Animal Owners*, 202.

125. As a work of 1898 described it, "It has been observed of the whole race . . . that though they will often obey the order 'Come,' they absolutely refuse to entertain the command 'Go'; and as most useful service involves this as an initial idea, the animal which refuses obedience is practically useless except as a volunteer." Cornish, *Animals of To-day*, 38.

126. AGM of Windsor, Eton and Staines RSPCA, *Minute Book*, 7 April 1937. However, unsurprisingly attitudes and treatment were contradictory. While the publication of a weekly encyclopedia devoted to the treatment of pets indicated a proactive stance to animal welfare, as did the establishment of the Tail-Waggers committed to philanthropic work for dogs, cats were still routinely ejected from homes or killed, with their bodies being dumped in disused burial grounds. Robinson, "Cats Must Be Taxed"; Robinson, "Cats and Legislation."

127. RSPCA, *Annual Report*, 1938, 239. Indeed the work of the respectable organization at the heart of the British establishment was so well known that it could be the butt of satire. Novelist Winifred Holtby wrote:

> The RSPCA has been at it again. I do not wonder at the extensive membership of that organization . . . If the meetings of housing associations, societies for penal reform or the League of Nations Union could stir one-tenth of the feeling that regularly manifests itself at any function concerning the welfare of the dear animals, we could revolutionize society within a year.

Emily Pinto Leite, an anti-vivisection activist, was caricatured attending the meeting despite her ill health: "'Yes,' cried Mrs Pinto-Leite, passionately. 'I know that some of you would like to see me dead: but I am going to live—live—live—to fight for suffering animals.'" As Holtby wryly commented, "I call that drama." But the RPSCA was also being challenged as insufficiently proactive against all animal cruelty. At the same meeting Holtby had satirized, an anti-vivisectionist colleague of Mrs. Pinto-Leite was ejected from the meeting having tried to question the inclusion of Sir William Gentle, a proprietor of the Belle Vue Circus in Manchester, on the RSPCA council. (Emily Pinto-Leite was the sister of Norah Dacre Fox, the fascist and activist in LPAVS. See McPherson and McPherson, *Mosley's Old Suffragette*, 114, 124; Winifred Holtby, "Let's Abolish the Dear Animals!" *Time and Tide*, 30 January 1932, 118; "RSPCA Meeting Disturbance," *Times*, 17 July 1931, 11; "RSPCA Meeting Disturbance," *Times*, 20 July 1931, 9.)

128. There were 400,000 members by January 1931. The organization did fund-raising for the Royal Veterinary College in Camden and Guide Dogs for the Blind. The Tail-Waggers Club, *On to the Million*.

129. Cats Protection League, "Is Apology Necessary?," *Cats' Mews-Sheet*, no 1 (January 1931): 1–2.

130. Cats Protection League, "The Tailwavers Second Anniversary," *Cat*, July 1942, 88.

131. *Hansard*, 3 October 1939, 2116.

132. Comben, *Dogs, Cats and People*, 136–37.

133. Tansey, "Protection against Dog Distemper and Dogs Protection Bills," 20. It was again defeated in 1933, partly on the grounds that apparently an improved distemper vaccine had been found through vivisection (p. 23).

134. Hobday, *Fifty Years a Veterinary Surgeon*, 177; Turner, *All Heaven in a Rage*, 262. Various animals were exempted from the 1933 Act to Provide for the Humane and Scientific Slaughter of Animals, namely pigs, boars, hogs, and sows killed in a knacker's yard or slaughterhouse where there was no supply of electricity or when the Jewish or "Mohammedan" method of killing was used. Burt, "Conflicts around Slaughter in Modernity,"132–33.

135. Little was actually achieved by the Performing Animals (Regulation) Act of 1925. Turner, *All Heaven in a Rage*, 274; Wilson, "Racial Prejudice and the Performing Animals Controversy in Early Twentieth-Century Britain,"149–65.

136. The assumption was that vast numbers of people would be without shelter and sanitation. An air raid precautions committee had been appointed in 1924. In 1937 the Committee of Imperial Defence had forecast 1.8 million human casualties in the first two months, of which one-third would die. Mackay, *Half the Battle*, 18, 20, 21, 31.

137. Aside from the cost involved, the state had been generally reluctant to intervene in matters to do with "pets." Martin's Act, the internationally pioneering legislation of 1822, was around "farm" animals and those in public places; legislation to cover domestic animals only came later and was strengthened particularly by the Protection of Animals 1911 Act. See Kean, *Animal Rights*, 31–35, 144.

138. Letter from C. R. D. Pulling, New Scotland Yard, 24 March 1939, in HO/144/21418.

139. Letter from C. R. D. Pulling, New Scotland Yard, 24 March 1939, in HO/144/21418.

140. The Cats Protection League was founded in 1928. Cats Protection League, "Is Apology Necessary?," 2.

141. This concern about status was reflected in the ongoing disputes with the PDSA. See Gardiner, "The 'Dangerous' Women of Animal Welfare."

142. There were stories of cats and dogs having been eaten. Montague, *Let the Good Work Go On*, 88–90.

143. The NVMA was formed in 1919. The Royal Veterinary College was the professional body regulating the profession. Thus both bodies could be seen to speak in different ways for the profession. W.R.Woolridge, "The Veterinary Profession and Air Raid Precautions for Animals," *Veterinary Record* 27 (April 1940): 315–24.

144. Editorial, "ARPs for Animals," *Veterinary Record*, 24 June 1939, 789.

145. It was not until January 1938 that the Home Office convened an official grouping, with nominees invited by the Home Secretary from the Minister of Agriculture, RAVC, RCVS, NVMA, and officials responsible for Air Raid Precautions. In February 1939 there were discussions between the ARP department of the Home Office and the veterinary profession about the production of a booklet of advice to owners of animals and the establishment of an ARP (animals service), but little public activity took place. "National Emergency Committee Report," *Veterinary Record*, 29 April 1939, 557.

146. "ARPs for Animals," *Veterinary Record*, 24 June 1939, 789. Although it was thought unlikely that animals would be prime targets of enemy attacks, nevertheless animals would be caught by gas raids and incendiary bombs. Editorial, "Animals and ARPs," *Veterinary Record*, 19 August 1939, 1011; Clabby, *A History of the Royal Army Veterinary Corps*, 32; NARPAC, *Wartime Aids for All Animal Owners*, 21–23.

147. "Air Raid Precautions for Horses in Towns," *Veterinary Record*, 6 May 1939, 598.

148. It was estimated that drivers /owners of some 18,000 horses attended the conference. *Veterinary Record*, 6 May 1939, 598.

149. Editorial," The Present Prospects of the Commercial Horse," *Veterinary Record*, 28 October 1939, 1285–88.

150. RSPCA, *Animals and Air Raids*, 13–15.

151. The *Veterinary Record* attributed the delay to a scarcity of "animal-minded persons" in urban local authorities, since although this would be a national body it would be organized by people on the ground in different localities. Editorial, "ARPs for Animals," *Veterinary Record*, 24 June 1939, 790.

By June 1939 veterinary surgeons were still very concerned that the public "still remains largely oblivious to the need for ARP measure for animals." Editorial, "ARPs for Animals," *Veterinary Record*, 24 June 1939, 789-90.

152. Report of enquiry into the affairs of NARPAC. MAF 52/18 National Archives 1.

153. Letters from PDSA in HO 186/1417; C. R. D. Pulling, 24 March 1939, HO 144/1418; Pulling to Col. Vince, 14 April 1939, HO 186/1417 National Archives.

154. "Animal Welfare Societies and the NVMA," *Veterinary Record*, 18 March 1939, 366.

155. "NVMA and NARPAC," *Veterinary Record*, 7 October 1939, 1234. See also Jones and Boulton, "Robert Stordy 1873-1943," 394-407.

156. "NVMA and NARPAC," *Veterinary Record*, 7 October 1939, 1234.

157. "ARPs for Animals," *Veterinary Record*, 24 June 1939, 789.

158. Mr. Franklin, File Note memorandum 9 January 1941 in MAF 52/118. For discussion of the black market generally, see Thomas, *An Underworld at War.*

159. Radford, *Animal Welfare Law in Britain*, 124.

160. Woolridge, "The Veterinary Profession," 316.

161. Woolridge, "The Veterinary Profession," 316. There was a later change of direction in NARPAC with animal clinics being supplemented by surgeries and mobile units. This arrangement included up to 1,500 veterinary surgeons working to county veterinary officers. Vets were paid for attending animals-3 shillings, 6 pence for first aid for animals injured as a result of hostile enemy action or otherwise, 2 shillings, 6 pence for destroying if gravely injured, and 10 shillings, 6 pence for giving a lecture on elementary first aid ("National ARP for Animals Service; Reorganisation in Urban Areas," *Veterinary Record*, 9 August 1941, 466). This tardiness and lack of Home Office action would later be seen as reasons for the collapse in due course of NARPAC. Steele-Bodger, "Presidential Address NVMA," *Veterinary Record*, 11 October 1941, 589.

162. Pets were not discussed in general public information leaflets of July and August 1939, in which advice was given about gas masks, blackouts, evacuation of children, and not panic-buying foodstuff. Public Information Leaflet 1, *Some Things You Should Know If War Should Come*, July 1939; Public Information Leaflet 3, *Evacuation: Why and How?* July 1939 .

163. NARPAC, *Wartime Aids for All Animal Owners*, 1.

164. NARPAC, *Wartime Aids for All Animal Owners*, 5.

165. "ARP for Animals: London Arrangements," *Veterinary Record*, 26 August 1939, 107.

166. "The Unwarranted Destruction of Small Animals," *Veterinary Record*, 16 September 1939, 1154.

CHAPTER THREE

1. Script of Christopher Stone radio broadcast ,19 November 1939, "Animals: Protection and Treatment," HO 186/1417, the National Archives.

2. Glover, "Notes on the Psychological Effects of War Conditions on the Civilian Population," 142.

3. Thomson, *Psychological Subjects*, 225.

4. N. Rose, *Governing the Soul*, 15.

5. Spillane, "A Survey of the Literature of Neuroses in War," 3.

6. Titmuss, *Problems of Social Policy*, 345.

7. Bion, "The War of Nerves," 183, 190-95. In the months before the war passivity was seen negatively; a sense of helplessness was expressed by half of their interviewees. Madge and Harrisson, *Britain by Mass Observation*, 48-50.

8. Bion, "The War of Nerves," 190.

9. *Daily Telegraph*, 4 September 1939, 9.

10. J. F. C. Fuller, *The Reformation of War*, 1923, 150, as quoted in Quester, "The Psychological Effects of Bombing on Civilian Populations," 203.

11. *Daily Mirror,* 8 September 1939, 1.

12. Kirby and Moss, *Animals Were There,* 18–19; Clabby, *A History of the Royal Army Veterinary Corps,* 41.

13. The figure of 750,000 was given by Sir Robert Gower, president of the RSPCA. "RSPCA Annual General Meeting," *Veterinary Record,* 22 June 1940, 475.

14. *Times,* 7 September 1939, 3. The *Veterinary Record* had estimated that in London the number of "small animals alone is stupendous." See British Veterinary Association, "ARPs for Animals," *Veterinary Record,* 24 June 1939,789.

15. Gilbert gives 60,595 as the total number of "civilian deaths by bombing." Gilbert, *Second World War,* 746.This figure is corroborated by Overy, *Bombing War,* 194.

16. Gilbert, *Second World War,* 17.

17. It is difficult to calculate the routine figure for pet slaughter since not all charities provided them. Suffice it to say that killing of companion animals was a routine practice. During 1937 the RSPCA killed 61,179 cats and dogs at its headquarters and 43,505 at its branch clinics, some 104,684 in total. Police in London took stray dogs (and cats) to the Battersea Dogs Home (and its branch in Bow). If they were not retrieved after a few days they would be killed. In 1937, some 3,125 dogs and 2,034 cats were brought in by their owners for killing at Battersea and 435 dogs and 229 cats in Bow. In the same year 11,166 stray dogs and 881 stray cats were killed at Battersea and 6,222 stray dogs and 103 stray cats at Bow. To this total overall figure of 116,499 (Battersea and RSPCA combined) of animals killed by their owners need to be added the strays, who were often animals dumped by owners, of 18,371. However, there is no specific way of telling why the animals were killed, so the figures will include elderly or very sick animals. In addition the NCDL, ODFL, Mayhew Home, PDSA, and the Wood Green animal Shelter provided facilities for killing pets at cheap rates. Battersea Dogs Home, *77th Annual Report, 1937; 78th Annual Report, 1938; 79th Annual Report, 1939;* RSPCA, *114th Annual Report, 1937; 115th Annual Report, 1938.*

18. NCDL, "September Holocaust," *Dogs' Bulletin* 114 (December 1939): 2 . The same term was used in Ziegler, *London at War,* 74; A. Calder, *The People's War,* 34; Cox, diary entry, 15 September 1939. See chapter 1, note 17.

19. *Times,* 7 September 1939, 3.

20. The RSPCA had been asked to keep its surgeries open twenty-four hours by the police in order to kill the numbers of animals brought in by owners. See *Animal World* (October 1939): 185. The RSPCA had many London clinics, including those in Camberwell, Willesden, Eltham, Fulham, Islington, North Kensington, Poplar, Kilburn, and Southwark. See RSPCA, *115th Annual Report, 1938,* 127–28.

21. RSPCA, "Emergency Arrangements. To be adopted at outbreak of war." Undated archive file, 1F/85/6. I am grateful to the RSPCA for permission to quote this archival material.

22. RSPCA, *Animal World* (October 1939): 185.

23. As a result dogs were then electrocuted. See NCDL, "September Holocaust," 2.

24. PDSA, *Annual Report,* 4.

25. Kirby and Moss, *Animals Were There,* 18–19.

26. PDSA, *Annual Report,* 4.

27. BUAV, "Appeal from Wood Green Shelter," *Abolitionist* (November 1939):12.

28. BUAV, "Appeal from Wood Green Shelter," *Abolitionist* (November 1939): 12.

29. The Home worked with the police in receiving stray animals. Animals were killed (or offered to other humans) after they had been in the home unclaimed for some days. Howell has recently argued that the Home was a bargain for the state in regulating stray animals at no cost. Howell, "At Home and Astray," 87ff.

30. Battersea Dogs Home,*79th Annual Report,* 1939, 24.

31. Forty tons of lime, additional labor, and transport were needed to carry out this task. See PDSA, *Annual Report,* 4.This is now the site of the Ilford PDSA animal cemetery. In 2006 Heritage Lottery Funding of £50,000 was obtained to restore memorials in the cemetery to individual

animals, mainly dogs. However, although the animal welfare charity highlights the restored individual memorials in its exhibition at the cemetery and gives short summaries of the animals'
achievements, it fails to even mention that in the same site are buried thousands of animal corpses
deposited there in September 1939. As it recorded in its *Annual Report* of 1945, as other animal
societies and veterinary surgeons were:

> "unable to cope with the burial of these poor Animals [*sic*] [the PDSA offered] the use of a
> meadow in the grounds of our sanatorium. Then, our real difficulties began, for, as far as
> can be estimated, we buried half a million Animals [*sic*]." PDSA, *Annual Report*, 1945,4–5.

32. Script of Christopher Stone radio broadcast, 19 November 1939, "Animals: Protection and
Treatment," HO 186/1417.

33. *Times*, 16 November 1939, 6.

34. Douglas, *The Chronicles of Ferne*, 19.

35. Douglas, *The Chronicles of Ferne*, 19.

36. Hewison, *Under Siege*, 10.

37. Letter, 5 September 1939, Tennyson Jesse, *London Front*, 18.

38. Beatrice Webb wrote on 5 October 1939: "Everyone . . . seems utterly bewildered and
downcast . . . There is no war enthusiasm—at best a dull acquiescence." Webb, *The Diaries of
Beatrice Webb*, 572.

39. Entry for Sunday, 3 September 1939, Woolf, *The Diary of Virginia Woolf*, Vol. 5, 233–34.

40. Nicolson diary, 24 September 1939, 32.

41. Entry for 24 September 1939, Nicolson, *Diaries and Letters 1930 –1939*, 32.

42. Harrisson, *Living through the Blitz*, 51.

43. Langdon-Davies, *Air Raid*,109, 113. See too Haldane, *ARP*, who essentially argued that
the government should take air raid precautions such as the building of shelters and evacuation
programs seriously: "People will only remain calm under such a trial if sure they are dying for
something worthwhile," 64.

44. W. Schmideberg, "The Treatment of Panic," 167–68.

45. Madge and Harrisson, *Britain by Mass Observation*, 49–50.

46. A. Calder, *The People's War*, 22.

47. Glover, "Notes on the Psychological Effects of War Conditions on the Civilian Population," 133.

48. Glover, "Notes on the Psychological Effects of War Conditions on the Civilian Population," 133.

49. N. Rose, *Governing the Soul*, 24.

50. Burney, "War on Fear," 50.

51. Padley and Cole, *Evacuation Survey*, 4; Stonebridge, "Anxiety at a Time of Crisis."

52. Padley and Cole, *Evacuation Survey*, 4. (The authors describe less blind panic in September
1939 than in September 1938.) See too Titmuss, *Problems of Social Policy*, 31; Glover, "Notes on the
Psychological Effects of War Conditions on the Civilian Population," 142; Trotter, "Panic and Its
Consequences," 191.

53. Lloyd-Jones, *The Animals Came in One by One*, 54. The NCDL also facilitated the evacuation
of dogs through advertising offers of accommodation. *Annual Report* 1939, 11.

54. Trotter, "Panic and Its Consequences," 191.

55. Charles Madge and Tom Harrisson, *Britain by Mass Observation*, as quoted in Hennessy,
Never Again, 6.

56. MacNeice, *The Strings Are False*, 174.

57. Mrs. I. Byers, "Me and Mine," typed memories, written in 1986, Imperial War Museum
88/10/1, 6.

58. RSPCA, *115th Annual Report*,1938, 235.

59. NCDL, *Dogs Bulletin*, no. 109, December 1938, 6.

60. Battersea Dogs Home, *78th Annual Report*, 1938, 22.

61. ODFL, *18th Annual Report*, 1938, 9.

62. ODFL, *18th Annual Report*, 1938, 9.

63. See Best, *Churchill: A Study in Greatness*, 151–57.

64. Steward, "A. R. P. or E. D. (Emergency Decisions)," *Cat*, October 1938, 75–76.

65. Cousens, *Dogs and Their Management*, 142.

66. Cousens, *Dogs and Their Management*, 142–43.

67. Interview with Dr. Mary Brancker, October 2008. According to Brancker it was only in the 1930s that barbiturates were introduced for humane killing. "They came in first of all in capsule form and you could make a solution in water. But you couldn't do it in London water because they wouldn't dissolve." The animal would then be injected.

68. All quotes taken from "Humane Killing of Pets: Animal Lovers Discuss Rival Merits of Poison, Gas, Gun, and Electricity," *Manchester Guardian*, 15 June 1933, unpaginated cutting in SSPVS archive now called Onekind.

69. Battersea Dogs Home, *74th Annual Report*, 1934, 25.

70. Battersea Dogs Home, *74th Annual Report*, 1934, 25.

71. NVMA, *Report of the Special Committee*, 5.

72. NVMA, *Report of the Special Committee*, 56.

73. NVMA, *Report of the Special Committee*, 56.

74. NVMA, *Report of the Special Committee*, 54–56.

75. In 1937, for example, the RSPCA killed 288,519 animals *nationally*. The reasons for the killing are not included in the annual reports so these figures would include elderly and sick animals as well as those who were unwanted (RSPCA, *114th Annual Report*, 1937, 255). In the same year the Battersea Dogs Home destroyed at its Battersea premises 14,291 dogs and 2,915 cats. These figures included strays brought in by the police as well as animals brought in by their owners (Battersea Dogs Home, *77th Annual Report*, 1937, 22).

76. "He is very appealing and has a remarkable digestion. I am very proud of this. He has never been sick, although almost daily he finds in the garden bones that no eye can have seen these twenty years and has eaten several rugs and a number of chairs and stools." Letter from Eileen Blair to Norah Myles, New Year's Day 1938, from Orwell, *George Orwell: A Life in Letters*, 94–99. My grateful thanks to Brian Edwards for this reference.

77. Orwell, *Facing Unpleasant Facts 1937–1939*, Appendix 4, 451.

78. Orwell, "The English People," 4.

79. Transcript of BBC radio broadcast "The World Goes By," 27 March 1940, BBC sound archives, Caversham, Reading.

80. Douglas, *The Chronicles of Ferne*, 17, and ODFL, *Annual Report*, 1938, 9.

81. Douglas, *The Chronicles of Ferne*, 17. I am aware that the current Ferne sanctuary that continues the work of Nina and the ADAVS is based in Somerset. The first such named sanctuary was, however, near Salisbury.

82. This was captured by Humphrey Jennings during his filming of *The First Days 1939* (K. Jackson, *Humphrey Jennings*, 220–22). One sees a London cat staring up at a barrage balloon and images of animals being safely evacuated—and the killing of thousands of others noted. The film *The First Days 1939* was made in collaboration with Harry Watt and Pat Jackson (K. Jackson, *Humphrey Jennings*, 220–23). It can be seen on YouTube.

83. CPL, "Lulu," *Cat*, January 1941, 39.

84. CPL, "Lulu," *Cat*, January 1941, 39.

85. CPL, "Lulu Concluded," *Cat*, March 1941, 63–64.

86. CPL, "Lulu Concluded," 64.

87. CPL, "Lulu Concluded," 64.

88. Jon Newman, email to author 21 January 2009. I am very grateful for this account.

89. C. Smith, *The Blue Cross at War*, 44.

90. C. Smith, *The Blue Cross at War*, 44.

91. It suggests not just that emotions shape history but that emotions themselves have a history, as Matt and Stearns have argued. *Doing Emotions History*, 2. See also Reddy, *The Navigation of Feeling*.

92. Penny Green, comment on author's website, 1 September 2012. http://hildakean.com/?p=863

93. Paul Plumley, comment on author's website, 3 September 2012. http://hildakean.com/?p=1323

94. Sewell, *Outsider*, 25.

95. Cox, diary entry, 15 September 1939.

96. Gwen Brown, written interview by daughter Alison Skipper, 24 September 2014, in response to my questions. I am extremely grateful to both of them for this interview.

97. F40E Euston, 11-14 July 1941, Pilot survey, Dogs, TC 79 1/B, Mass Observation.

98. Minutes of the Bristol Zoo General Committee Meeting, 20 September 1939, 271. My thanks to Andy Flack for these minutes.

99. Letter from RSPCA inspector to Snelling, 28 June 1940, HO 186/1419, the National Archives.

100. Kean, *Animal Rights*, 39-42.

101. *News Chronicle*, 4 September 1939, 3.

102. *Times*, 14 October 1939, 4.

103. "Animals and ARPs," *Veterinary Record*, 19 August 1939, 1011.

104. "Zoos," *Veterinary Record*, 16 September 1939, 1156-57.

105. *Times*, 14 October 1939, 4.

106. *Times*, 14 October 1939, 4.

107. *Times*, 16 September 1939, 5; *News Chronicle*, 4 September 1939, 3; "Zoos," *Veterinary Record*, 16 September 1939, 1156-57.

108. *Times*, 9 December 1939, 9; Cox, diary entry 9 December 1939. 1/- means one shilling.

109. H260 woman aged 79 in Animals and Humans Directive, Mass Observation.

110. Turner, *The Phoney War on the Home Front*, 118.

111. Enabling legislation was first enacted in October 1939. Sheial, "Wartime Rodent-Control in England and Wales," 56-57.

112. *Scottish Daily Express*, 4 July 1940, as quoted in Raymond Challinor, "Class War in the Blitz," *Workers' Liberty*, no. 18, February 1995, http://marxists.catbull.com/history/etol/writers/challinor/1995/02/class-war-blitz.html. Thanks to Christian Høgsbjerg for this reference.

113. Turner, *The Phoney War on the Home Front*, 118.

114. Front, later Griggs, diary entry for 29 December 1939, IWM 02/27/1.

115. Front, diary entry for 28 March 1940.

116. Animal Studies Group, *Killing Animals*, 4.

117. Animal Studies Group, *Killing Animals*, 198.

118. Kean, "Human and Animal Space in Historic 'Pet' Cemeteries," 21-42.

119. To date the cat and dog massacre has never been commemorated or represented within the public landscape. See conclusion.

120. See for example Lind af Hageby, *Bombed Animals*, 19: "Of the massacre—the word is appropriate—of dogs and cats on the days preceding the outbreak of war and immediately after it is difficult to give accurate figures."

121. http://news.bbc.co.uk/1/hi/world/asia-pacific/64344.stm site visited 20 June 2014.

122. Galvayne, *War Horses Present and Future*, 53-56; Bell and Baillie Weaver, *Horses in Warfare*, 4-6; Kean, "Animals and War Memorials," 244-47; Swart, "Horses in the South African War."

123. Death was frequently due to glanders, epizootic lymphangitis, and mange. Clabby, *A History of the Royal Army Veterinary Corps*, 13-14.

124. Clabby, *A History of the Royal Army Veterinary Corps*, 13.

125. It is ironic that the memorial has recently been severely attacked by the Economic Freedom Fighters as an imperialist memorial since the memorial was critical of the "imperialist" treatment of animals. Kean, "Animals and War Memorials," 246–47.

126. Jacobs, "The Great Bophuthatswana Donkey Massacre," 485–506.

127. Jacobs, "The Great Bophuthatswana Donkey Massacre," 487.

128. Jacobs, "The Great Bophuthatswana Donkey Massacre," 505. See also Jacobs' account of the erection of memorials to donkeys by white people while ignoring the plight of black humans, p. 506.

129. The account is based on the quasi-fictional narrative of Nicolas Contat written some twenty years after the event. Darnton, "The Workers' Revolt," 78.

130. Darnton, "The Workers Revolt," 77.

131. Darnton, "The Workers Revolt," 100.

132. http://asbarez.com/81613/cannes-film-festival-winner-barking-dog-to-screen-in-yerevan/ site visited 20 April 2014; http://divergences.be/spip.php?article2340&lang=fr site visited 20 April 2014.

133. In this respect it is also different to the horrific killing of animals, especially elephants, in Ueno Zoo in Tokyo, Japan, when the elephants refused to eat poisoned food and were slowly starved to death while simultaneously the slaughter was being glorified by a state ceremony in the zoo. See Litten, "Starving the Elephants"; and I. J. Miller, *The Nature of the Beasts*.

134. NARPAC, *Wartime Aids for All Animal Owners*, 1939, 5.

CHAPTER FOUR

1. M. W., "Cats at Home," *Cat*, September 1939, 67.

2. H. Smith, *A Horseman through Six Reigns*, 169–72.

3. *Times*, 8 December 1939, 5.

4. H. Smith, *A Horseman through Six Reigns*, 175.

5. A. Calder, *The People's War*, 63.

6. Ziegler, *London at War*, 68.

7. Nicolson, *Diaries and Letters*, 1 September 1939, 411.

8. Robertson, *I Saw England*, 118.

9. Robertson, *I Saw England*, 118.

10. Cockett, *Love and War in London*, 21. (This was a diary written for Mass Observation.)

11. CPL, "One Year," *Cat*, September 1940, 140–41.

12. Steward, "The Secretary's Comments," *Cat*, August 1940, 131.

13. Steward, "Wartime Problems," *Cat*, July 1940, 117–19.

14. This was later in the war. By being outside Nigger had avoided a bomb that killed people locally in November 1943 but "ordinary" events resulted in his demise. Correspondence with author from David Johnson, March 2009. A. Calder noted a 100% increase of human deaths through road accidents. *The People's War*, 63.

15. M. W., "Cats at Home," *Cat*, September 1939, 67.

16. Bradshaw explains that cats can see in the "near-dark" but in full daylight they see less well than humans. *Cat Sense*, 110.

17. M. W., "Black-out," *Cat*, October 1939, 3–4.

18. NCDL, *The "Safety-First" Code for Dog Owners*, unnumbered, 1.

19. Martin, *How to Care for Your Dog and Cat in Wartime*, 8.

20. NCDL Card 1, June 1940, from Charles R. Johns, secretary NCDL in Wanstead and Woodford Borough Council Civil Defence Dept 90/30/1 and 90/167: 94 ARP for Animals 1 / 4.

21. FitzGibbon, *With Love*, 159.

22. Advertisement in the *Times* as reproduced in Greene, *Ways of Escape*, 102.

23. Tennyson Jesse, letter of 12 June 1940, *London Front*, 426.

24. Thomas, *An Underworld at War*, 276. See Thomas for discussion of prewar practices of dog doping and race fiddling, 281.

25. Titmuss, *Problems of Social Policy*, 97. See also MacNicol, "The Evacuation of School-children."

26. Titmuss, *Problems of Social Policy*, 103.

27. The LCC reported that parents of 83% of schoolchildren wanted them evacuated (p. 34) but only half this figure went and many were brought back quickly. The government thought the figure "unexpectedly low." Titmuss, *Problems of Social Policy*, 103.

28. Woolf, *The Diary of Virginia Woolf*, Vol. 5, 234.

29. *Daily Mirror*, 4 September 1939, 6.

30. *Daily Express*, 2 September 1939, 16.

31. Photograph of Frederick Croly in Balshaw and Lundin, *Memories of War*, 23.

32. Isaacs, *The Cambridge Evacuation Survey*, 9.

33. Isaacs, *The Cambridge Evacuation Survey*, 9.

34. Isaacs, *The Cambridge Evacuation Survey*, 68–70.

35. Isaacs, *The Cambridge Evacuation Survey*, 72.

36. Griffin, *Lost Identity*, 22.

37. Isaacs, *The Cambridge Evacuation Survey*, 189.

38. Isaacs, *The Cambridge Evacuation Survey*, 71.

39. Burlingham and Freud, *Young Children in War-Time*, 1942.

40. N. Rose, *Governing the Soul*, 159.

41. Burlingham and Freud, *Young Children in War-Time*, 27 ff.

42. Burlingham and Freud, *Young Children in War-Time*, 64.

43. Sylvia Berliner, interviewed by her niece Brenda Kirsch. I am very grateful to both of them for answering my questions.

44. I am grateful to Maggie Andrews for this Midlands story.

45. Minutes, Hillingdon RSPCA, 17 October 1939.

46. Goodall, *Voices from the Home Front*,185. This evacuation actually occurred later during the Blitz but the example is still relevant.

47. Advertisement in *Tail-Wagger* 12, no. 10 (October 1940): 237; Minutes, NARPAC F & GP committee, 7 November 1940, Ho 186/1418.

48. PDSA statement 12 May 1939 in HO 186 /1417; Pulling, New Scotland Yard to Vince Home Office 14 April 1939 in HO 186/1417.

49. CPL, "Wartime Problems (2)," *Cat*, 1940, 127.

50. Lind af Hageby, *Bombed Animals*, 26.

51. *Times*, 30 October 1939, 9.

52. *Tail-Wagger* (July 1941): 166.

53. Account from Chris Sladen describing his mother-in-law in email to author May 2008.

54. Lloyd-Jones, *The Animals Came in One by One*, 75.

55. Examples of two contrasting approaches might be Mary Davis, *Comrade or Brother? A History of the British Labour Movement* (London: Pluto Press, 1993), in which a paragraph on women and ethnic minorities was routinely added at the end of a chapter, and Joan Scott, *Gender and the Politics of History* (New York: Columbia University Press, 1989), challenging and gendering the seminal work of E. P.Thompson.

56. Robertson, *I Saw England*,172.

57. Brantz, *Beastly Natures*, 3.

58. Donaldson and Kymlicka, *Zoopolis*, 65. Criticizing other scholars for failing to give due status to animals as agents, Jason Hribal analyzes the absence of treatment of animals as "active, as laborers, prisoners, or resistors" (Hribal, "Animals, Agency and Class,"102-3.) In more nuanced fashion in her exploration of horses, humans, and history in South Africa, Sandra Swart has

argued that the fact that instruments of control such as whips or reins were needed by humans indicates horses' own resistance. While attempting to blur the distinctions between horses and humans she nevertheless notes that humans are not able to see like a horse. However, Swart has argued that "many [people] have tried to think like a horse," since this "was essential in the process of domesticating and training them." Swart, *Riding High*, 202, 217. See also Dashper, "The Elusiveness of 'Feel' in the Horse-Human Relationship."

59. F. W. Norris, Letter, *Times*, 3 May 1918.

60. "The Animal Welfare Societies in War-Time," *Animal Pictorial* 3, no. 2 (March 1940): 103.

61. Lind af Hageby, *Bombed Animals*, 19.

62. Cox, diary entry,15 September 1939.

63. Tennyson Jesse, *London Front*, letter 4 October 1939, 67.

64. The cost was 10/6d each [52½ new pence]. Cox, diary entry, 8 December 1939.

65. W. Shipley MRCVS of Yarmouth in *Eastern Daily Press*, quoted in *Animal Defender and Zoophilist* 59, no. 6 (October 1939): 50.

66. ARP Department Circular no. 267/1939, "Animals in War Time," Ministry of Home Security, 7 October 1939, to all local authorities and chief constables. In Ho 144/21418, National Archives.

67. Report of Stordy dated 11 September 1939 HO NARPAC 186 / 1418, National Archives. As noted in chapter 3, the figure of 750,000 was also given at the time.

68. Ziegler, *London at War*, 74.

69. Foster, *The Real Dad's Army*, entry for 12 November 1939, 10.

70. The first bombs on the mainland fell in Canterbury 9 May 1940 and the first bombs on London 18 June 1940. The Blitz started 7 September 1940 with bombing on 56 nights out of 57. Stansky, *First Day of the Blitz*, 21, 28.

71. Lukacs, *Five Days in London, May 1940*, 130; A. Calder, *The Myth of the Blitz*, 90–101.

72. Lukacs, *Five Days in London, May 1940*, 196.

73. Michael Foot, Frank Owen, and Peter Howard, who called themselves "Cato," created this image in their hugely popular book, *Guilty Men*. See A. Calder, *The Myth of the Blitz*, 90–101.

74. Partridge, *A Pacifist's War*, entry for 17 December 1942, 152. (This was the first occasion she had seen her brother-in-law since Dunkirk.)

75. RSPCA *117th Annual Report*, 1940, 10. It praised its own inspectors serving in the Dunkirk army who "'did useful work in shooting animals which were hopelessly injured by bombing or shelling." RSPCA *117th Annual Report*, 3. This seems to have been a spontaneous act by inspectors who happened to be serving in the army rather than an organized response. When approached by the Calais Ligue de Protection des Animaux in February 1940 to give assistance with stray dogs, the RSPCA decided it could take no action but suggested the Royal Army Veterinary Corps might be able to assist. RSPCA Emergency War (Executive) Committee, 13 February 1940. My thanks to the RSPCA for allowing me to cite this.

76. Levine, *Forgotten Voices of Dunkirk*, 43–45.

77. Levine, *Forgotten Voices of Dunkirk*, 101.

78. See, for example, Fudge, *Pets*.

79. Private Frank Curry in Levine, *Forgotten Voices of Dunkirk*, 134.

80. Ordinary Seamen Stanley Allen in Levine, *Forgotten Voices of Dunkirk* 240.

81. Story of Norman Battersby told to Alan Battersby, 20 January 2004, Article ID: A2217566 http://www.bbc.co.uk/history/ww2peopleswar/

82. Able Seaman Ian Nethercott in Levine, *Forgotten Voices of Dunkirk*, 213.

83. Foster, *The Real Dad's Army*, diary entries for Friday 31 May and Saturday 1 June 1940, 31.

84. Bell, *London Was Ours*, 4.

CHAPTER FIVE

1. Hodgson, *Few Eggs and No Oranges*, 8 February 1942, 259.

2. A. Calder, *The People's War*, 71-72.

3. *Hansard*, House of Commons Debates, 28 February 1940, vol. 357 c2064.

4. Minute 94 by B. C. Burt 29 July 1942 in MAF 84/61, National Archives.

5. Dogs in Wartime, 1/C Mass Observation.

6. Brands as listed by the CPL included packet foods such as Livabrex, Spratts cat food, and Spillers cat food and Red Heart, Jiffy, Stamina, and Kit-e-Kat tinned food. CPL, "For Your Information," *Cat*, November 1939, unnumbered back page. See also RSPCA, *Feeding Dogs and Cats in Wartime*, nd [1942?] RSPCA archive 1F/108/56.While emphasizing that as a charity the RPSCA could not recommend any particular brand, it nevertheless noted the existence of Red Heart, Kit-e-Kat, Ken-L-Ration, and Chappie.

7. RSPCA, *Feeding Dogs and Cats in Wartime*, nd [1942?] RSPCA archive 1F/108/56. I am grateful to the RSPCA for permission to quote from this leaflet.

8. RSPCA, *Animals and Air Raids*, 5.

9. NARPAC, *Wartime Aids for All Animal Owners*, 14.

10. *Cat*, November 1939, 17. It was also suggested in *Cat*, January 1940, 40. Other suggestions to keep a cat healthy included cocksfoot or cat condition powders, beef or mutton boiled or raw, and cooked unsalted fish. Liver should be provided once a week if there was no grass. Town cats apparently liked rabbits.

11. RSPCA, *Animals and Air Raids*, 5.

12. *Breadless Diet for Dogs*, NCDL leaflet no. 492, nd [1942] in MAF 84/61, National Archives.

13. Report of questions to dealers in Walham Green etc. 30 July 1941, Dogs in Wartime, Mass Observation.

14. Hodgson, *Few Eggs and No Oranges*, 18 March 1941, 143.

15. NCDL typed leaflet of suppliers of cat and dog food March 1940 in Dogs in Wartime 79/1/A, Mass Observation.

16. FitzGibbon, *With Love*, 32.

17. FitzGibbon, *With Love*,139, 159.

18. Hodgson, *Few Eggs and No Oranges*, 8 March 1941, 136.

19. Hodgson, *Few Eggs and No Oranges*, 20 May 1941, 176.

20. Hodgson, *Few Eggs and No Oranges*, 1 September 1944, 526.

21. Hodgson, *Few Eggs and No Oranges*, 2 July 1941, 190.

22. Written account from Chris Sladen to author 2008.

23. Cox, diary entry, 22 January 1942.

24. Cox, diary entry, 2 February 1942.

25. Cox, diary entries for 22 January 1942, 2 February 1942, 24 December 1942, 20 February 1943.

26. Landen 13 January 1941 Miss M. Landen Transcription of Margaret's diary. 03/42/1, Imperial War Museum.

27. Landen entry for 9 May 1941.

28. Alan Windsor entry on Evelyn Dunbar, http://www.oxforddnb.com/view/article/63781

29. "Although fresh fish was in short supply, being perishable it was never rationed. Fish queues were therefore always long and even air raids could not disperse them. Dunbar's canvas size emphasizes the length of the queue (a cat has joined in, rather hopefully)." Roger Tolson, "Art and Daily Life in World War Two." http://www.bbc.co.uk/history/trail/wars_conflict/art/art _daily_life_gal_01.shtml archived page visited 16 Feb 2015; http://www.iwm.org.uk/collections/item/object/8171 16 February 2015.

30. Hodgson, *Few Eggs and No Oranges*, 8 February 1942, 259.

31. Lloyd-Jones, *The Animals Came in One by One*, 80.

32. Minute 94 by B. C. Burt 29 July 1942 in MAF 84/61, National Archives.

33. FitzGibbon, *With Love*, 139, 159.

34. Cox, diary entry, 20 February 1943.

35. Cox, diary entry, 27 November 1941.

36. Animal products were rationed (vegetables were not) so vegetarians were urged to offer their meat rations to those feeding cats. *Cat,* January 1940, 40.

37. Landen, diary entries for 6 March and 2 April 1941.

38. Ellen Clark in Age Exchange Reminiscence, *Londoners Remember Living through the Blitz*, 37.

39. Broad and Fleming, *Nella Last's War*, 2 January 1943.

40. *Nella Last's War*, 10 November 1943, 216; 2 January 1943, 227-28.

41. Cox, diary entry, 22 December 1941.

42. Pam Ashford, 19 September 1940, in Garfield, *We Are at War*, 369. It should be noted that even small amounts of "human" chocolate are extremely unsafe for dogs, causing vomiting and possibly muscle tremors, seizures, or a heart attack.

43. "Blitz Kitty by Brazen 67." Story of John Healey Article ID A4660481 in http://www.bbc .co.uk/history/ww2peopleswar/

44. CPL, advertisement, *Cat,* November 1939, 25.

45. Partridge, *A Pacifist's Diary*, 7 April 1942, 130.

46. Holman, diaries, 30 September 1940, 3 October 1940, 4 October 1940, 12 October 1940. He routinely described his daily diet (and often its cost) as well as his daily rides.

47. Cox, diary entry, 24 November 1941.

48. Hodgson, *Few Eggs and No Oranges*, 28 November 1941, 230.

49. BUAV, *Abolitionist* (July-August 1942): 43.

50. *Hansard*, House of Commons Debates 6 February 1941 vol. 368 cc1108-10W Question from Colonel Carver to Major Lloyd George, Parliamentary Secretary to the Board of Trade.

51. *Hansard*, House of Commons Debates 11 November 1941 vol. 374 c2088W Mr. Rostron Duckworth to Mr. Hutton Minister of Agriculture. See too Hodgson, *Few Eggs and No Oranges*, 7 October 1942, 321.

52. Holman, diaries, 12 August 1942.

53. Holman, diaries, 15 January 1942, 4 March 1942.

54. Holman, diaries, 30 April 1944, 26 June 1944.

55. Holman, diaries, 24 August 1945, 21 August 1945. I realize the war had ended but rationing and restraints were still in place.

56. *Hansard*, House of Commons Debates. HC Deb 28 February 1940 vol. 357 c2064 .

57. Maggie Joy Blunt in Garfield, *We Are at War*, diary for 25 August 1940, 345. (Pseudonym of Jean Lucey Pratt.)

58. Of the 280,000 tons c. 170,000 tons were carbohydrates and the remainder proteins. Minute 94 by B. C. Burt 29 July 1942 in MAF 84/61, National Archives.

59. G. D. Lundis to Sir Bryce Burt 2 February 1942 MAF 84/61.

60. G. D. Lundis to Sir Bryce Burt 2 February 1942 MAF 84/61.

61. 20 February 1942 Burt to Minister Sir John Bodinnar. MAF 84/61, National Archives.

62. 4 August 1942 Minister's secretary Mr. Broadley response to Burt's proposals. Feeding stuff, MAF 84 /61.

63. Feeding stuff note, 71, 10 July 1942 MAF 84 /61, National Archives.

64. Pratt, *A Notable Woman*, entry for 12 August 1941, 245.

65. Roodhouse, *Black Market Britain*, xi.

66. In New Zealand there was meat rationing for humans and no provision for domestic animals. The Christchurch SPCA distributed horse and goat meat for pets. A petition and a deputation to the Minister of Supply followed. As a result meat companies were asked to deliver meat for animals to butchers' shops. Swarbrick, *Creature Comforts*, 228.

67. Harcourt-Brown and Chitty, *BSAVA Manual of Psittacine Birds*, 130, 140.

68. http://www.pdsa.org.uk/pet-health-advice/budgerigars/diet visited 18 March 2015.

69. Finn, *The Budgerigar*, 3.

70. "Budgerigars by the Million: The Twentieth Century Pet," *Times*, 9 December 1939, 9.

71. Finn, *The Budgerigar*, 4 and 15. Grit and cuttlefish were also emphasized, 14.

72. Melville in Finn, *Budgerigar*, 30.

73. HC Deb 10 April 1941 vol. 370 cc1712-3W. George Mathers questioned the amount of 600 tons annually needed for feeding but Major Lloyd George said, "Before the war over 9,000 tons of canary seed, nearly 9,000 tons of millet and 5,000 tons of dari were imported each year, and I regret that in view of the shipping situation the decision cannot be reconsidered."

74. HC Deb 30 April 1941 vol. 371 cc534-6. Comments by Mr. Mathers MP for Linlithgow. George Mathers, a Labour MP, was a supporter of the BUAV and president of the National Temperance Federation. (Fox hunting was banned from March 1943 in the interests of food production, thereby overcoming the arguments that fox hunting was necessary for efficient farming. Tichelar, "Putting Animals into Politics," 222.)

75. RSPCA, *Feeding of Canaries, Budgerigars and Parrots*, RSPCA, nd [1941?] RSPCA Archive 1F/108/57. My grateful thanks to the RSPCA for allowing me to quote from this.

76. RSPCA, *Weed Seeds for Birds*, RSPCA leaflet no. 329, nd. RSPCA Archive 1F/108/58. My grateful thanks to the RSPCA for allowing me to quote this.

77. Ian Coleman letter to author, 29 September 2014.

78. Email to her brother Tim from Joy, 18 April 2012. Thanks to Maggie Andrews for forwarding this with permission.

79. Harcourt-Brown and Chitty, *BSAVA Manual of Psittacine Birds*, 136, 137.

80. "Budgerigars by the Million: The Twentieth Century Pet," *Times*, 9 December 1939, 9.

81. Les Martin helped his father during the war. Tom Meltzer, "The Battle of the Budgies," *Guardian G2*, 20 October 2010. Viewed online 2 December 2015 http://www.theguardian.com/lifeandstyle/2010/oct/20/budgies-battle-of-the-breeders

82. Letter of Jerry Park, *Guardian*, 22 October 2010. Viewed online 2 December 2015 http://www.theguardian.com/theguardian/2010/oct/22/budgerigars-rspb-rolling-stones-cobbles

83. Orwell, "The English People," 4.

84. See, for example, Irene Fern Smith, Diary, 19 April 1941, Bishopsgate Institute.

85. Cooper, *Autobiography*, 566-67.

86. Partridge, *Pacifist's Diary*, entry for 16 March 1941, 84.

87. Broad and Fleming, *Nella Last's War*, 10 March 1943, 235.

88. Scott, *Your Obedient Servant*, 8.

89. Ellen Clark in Age Exchange Reminiscence, *Londoners Remember Living through the Blitz*, 37.

90. RSPCA, *Feeding Animals in Wartime: "Waste" and Common Sense*, 1940, RSPCA Archive 1F/108/55 . My grateful thanks to the RSPCA for allowing me to quote from this.

91. Hodgson, *Few Eggs and No Oranges*, 25 July 1941, 194.

92. Cutting from *Bristol Evening Post*, 20 January 1943. Thanks to Paul Foley for passing me this extract that bizarrely found its way into a General Certificate of Secondary Education examination paper in recent years.

93. Thomas, *An Underworld at War*, 35. This suggests, at least to me, that this was probably an easier prosecution rather than one based on health regulations.

94. Brander, *Eve Balfour*, 135.

95. "Birds in Wartime," *Animal World* (November 1939), cutting in Dogs in Wartime, Mass Observation.

96. Dobson, *The War Effort of the Birds*. Not everyone was convinced. Organic farming pioneer Eve Balfour, for example, reported that not only had pigeons destroyed her young cabbages but that, "they are far worse all over the country than they have ever been before [since] they come from Norway." Brander, *Eve Balfour*,135.

97. Garfield, *A Notable Woman*, entry for 10 January 1942, 258.

98. Lind af Hageby, *Bombed Animals*, 15.

99. Report of Inspector Miles forwarded by Sir Robert Gower, chair of the RSPCA, to Ellen Wilkinson MP on 19 June 1942 HO 186 /1417, National Archives.

CHAPTER SIX

1. Male Euston 45 D, Dogs in Wartime, TC1/B, Mass Observation.

2. For an image of a family sheltering with the family cat under a table see Woon, *Hell Came to London*, 52.

3. There is much literature on this topic. In essence people themselves in inner London took over tube stations because of the lack of appropriate shelters built by the authorities. There was much hostility towards the provision for shelter available to those in expensive hotels, including demonstrations against this. See Kirkham, "Beauty and Duty"; Ziegler, *London at War*, 116–18, 135–37.

4. Age Exchange Reminiscence Group, *Londoners Remember Living through the Blitz*, Account of Ellen Clark, 42–44; *Hansard*, House of Commons Debates 19 September 1940, vol. 365 cc179–81 179; O'Brien, *Civil Defence*, 517, claimed that by mid-October closets had been installed in almost all of London's public shelters but emptying them was a problem since the facilities of nearby buildings were used for this purpose. There was no concerted attempt at that time to provide washing facilities.

5. NCDL report 41 in Dogs in Wartime, Mass Observation.

6. NAVS, editorial, *Animals' Defender* (October 1940): 45.

7. RSPCA, Emergency War (Executive) Committee, Minutes 13 August 1940; cutting from *Animal World* 35, no. 11 New Series (November 1940): 90–91, in Cuttings and Leaflets in Wartime Work of the RSPCA. My grateful thanks to the RSPCA for allowing me to quote this.

8. NCDL, *Dogs' Bulletin* no. 114 (December 1939): 4.

9. NCDL poster and covering card from Charles R. Johns, the secretary, dated 1 June 1940 in Wanstead and Woodford Borough Council Civil Defence Department 90/30/1 and 90/167:94 ARP for Animals 1/ 4, Redbridge archives.

10. *Mainly about Animals* 1, no. 10 (October 1940): 230.

11. Local minutes 17 October 1939 Windsor, Uxbridge and Hillingdon RSPCA.

12. RSPCA, Emergency War (Executive) Committee CM/80, minutes of 14 November 1939. My grateful thanks to the RSPCA for allowing me to quote this.

13. Holman, diary entry Monday 30 September 1940. Also 8 September 40. Despite heavy bombardment on the previous night with 400 human deaths, 300 injured, and 3 big fires Holman still went riding but "went into [the] Life Guards anticipating the all clear."

14. Nixon, *Raiders Overhead*, 37–38.

15. Woman F 35 D Euston, Dogs in Wartime 1/B 11–14 July 1941, Mass Observation.

16. Lewey, *Cockney Campaign*, 26.

17. Eleanor Hardingham appeared at Westminster Magistrates Court 14 December 1940. Thomas, *An Underworld at War*, 72.

18. NAVS, *Animals' Defender* (October 1940): 45.

19. Rip ARP dog and Post B 132 Southill Street Poplar, MOI photos 1–19, in Tower Hamlets Archive. See chapter 8, p. 144, for an image of the dog.

20. Newman and York, *What to Do When the Air Raid Siren Sounds*. Thanks to Jon Newman for drawing my attention to this and then providing me with an extract from his work.

21. Hodgson, *Few Eggs and No Oranges*, diary entry 1 January 1942, 248.

22. Eileen Potter, Mass Observation diary for 25 June 1940 as published in Garfield, *We Are at War*, 282.

23. Those unable to afford such animal shelters devised their own alternatives: "A wet towel handy, and hoped for the best" was how one middle class woman described her strategy for her small terrier. F 50 B Hammersmith Dogs in Wartime 1/B Mass Observation. Another alternative was a wooden box covered with wire netting and glossy paint to counteract gas absorption to be covered with a flannel soaked in bicarbonate of soda in water. NCDL leaflet Air Raid Precautions for Dogs and Cats, nd [March 1940] MO TC79/1/A, Mass Observation.

24. Letter from Boulton and Paul 6 Sept 1939 to Thompson room 412 of ARP Home Dept in NARPAC HO 186 /1418.

25. Advertisement for the Frank-Heaton Protective Enclosure against gas, splinters, and blast for small animals in Dogs in Wartime 1939–42 file in TC 79 /1/A, Mass Observation.

26. NCDL leaflet Air Raid Precautions for Dogs and Cats, nd [March 1940] in TC79/1/A, Mass Observation.

27. Unnamed child in Westall, *Children of the Blitz*, 112–13.

28. Stansky, *First Day of the Blitz*, 61.

29. Bradshaw, *In Defence of Dogs*, 230.

30. Fudge, "What Was It Like To Be A Cow?," 4. She is discussing the argument of Alan Mikhail that self-reflexive intentionality generally is not a prerequisite to historical agency.

31. Brenda Watkinson, Article IDA2879526, contributed 30 July 2004. http://www.bbc.co .uk/history/ww2peopleswar/

32. Croucher, in Hostettler, *The Island at War*, 31.

33. Written account from Anne Reese, Swansea, to author 2009.

34. Broad and Fleming, *Nella Last's War*, entry 5 May 1941, 135.

35. Male Euston 45 D, Dogs in Wartime, TC1/B, Mass Observation.

36. Natural caves were used elsewhere for similar purposes, for example in Hastings, now packaged as the Smugglers' Caves.

37. Ellen Clark in Age Exchange Reminiscence Group, *Londoners Remember Living through the Blitz*, 42–44.

38. Wilbert, "What Is Doing the Killing?," 35; Steve Hinchliffe et al., "Urban Wild Things," 643. This argument is developed in Kean, "Traces."

39. Fudge, *Pets*, 20.

40. Taylor, *Humans, Animals, and Society*, 18.

41. Holman, diary, Thursday 19 September 1940.

42. Holman, diary, Friday 18 October 1940.

43. Letter to Partridge, *A Pacifist's War*, recorded in entry for 15 September 1940, 60.

44. Stansky, *First Day of the Blitz*, 46.

45. Hodgson, *Few Eggs and No Oranges*, entry for 9 March 1941, 137. There was no Anderson shelter in the garden and no record of the residents above the offices, or the office workers themselves, going to a communal shelter outside the building. The Greater World Association Trust was founded in 1934 as a Christian Spiritualist organization undertaking welfare work. Hodgson, xxi–xxii.

46. Cooper, *Autobiography*, 552.

47. W 1893 b 1924 from Wirral, Animals and Humans directive. Mass Observation.

48. I am very grateful to Peter Townsend for permitting me to include this story, originally written in an email May 2010 to Adrienne Roche, who kindly brought this to my attention.

49. F30 B Mill Hill 23 July 1941 1D, Dogs in Wartime, Mass Observation.

50. Eileen Blair to Norah Myles, New Year's Day 1938 from The Stores, Wallington, Herts in Orwell, *George Orwell: A Life in Letters*, 94–99. My grateful thanks to Brian Edwards for this reference—and related research help on Orwell.

51. War-time diary, Orwell, *The Complete Works of George Orwell*, vol. 12, 262–63, 17 September 1940. Marx was looked after by Marjorie and Humphrey Dakin (Orwell's sister and brother-in-law) while the Blairs were in Morocco. Dakin maintained that Marx was later given away "to

complete strangers," who had the dog killed, although the Dakins would have liked to keep him permanently. This account is not corroborated. See 232n1.

52. Pierce, *Memories of the Civilian War*, 22-23.

53. Some dog questions,1D, 23 July 1941 Dogs in Wartime, Mass Observation.

54. "Animals' Reactions to War," *Times*, 7 September 1940, 9. Although anonymous, the author is likely to be Julian Huxley, director of the London Zoo.

55. "Animals and Air Raids," *Times*, 14 October 1940, 5.

56. RSPCA, *Animals and Air Raids*, 3-4; CPL, *Cat*, September 1940, 138-39; NCDL, Air Raid Precautions, Dogs in Wartime 79/1/a, Mass Observation. See also Kean, "Nervous Dogs Need Admin, Son."

57. Martin, *How to Care for Your Dog and Cat in Wartime*, foreword, 2.

58. M40C 15 Neasden Js 27 /8/1941 1E, Dogs in Wartime, Mass Observation.

59. Schmideberg, "Some Observations on Individual Reactions to Air Raids," 151.

60. RSPCA, *Animals and Air Raids*, 4.

61. Steward, "War Time Problems (3)," *Cat*, September 1940, 137-38. A veterinary surgeon has advised me that aspirin *might* act in these ways but that it is extremely difficult to ascertain the correct dosage, hence the advice nowadays not to give human medicines to animals.

62. Broad and Fleming, *Nella Last's War*, entry for 15 April 1941, 119.

63. Cox, diary entry, 26 September 1940. This does mean sleep literally: not a euphemism for death.

64. Advertisement in *Tail Wagger* (October 1940): 233. See discussion around Nazis and dogs in chapter 7.

65. A vitamin B tonic, Metatone, was also given to cats. Gwladys Cox gave Metatone to Bobby as he was out of condition. The vet attributed this to insufficient meat in his diet. Diary entry 2 September 1944.

66. Age Exchange, *Londoners Remember Living through the Blitz*,17-18.

67. Babs Downes in Age Exchange, *Londoners Remember Living through the Blitz*, 40.

68. Cattermore, "Cats in the Blitz," *Mainly about Animals* (May 1944): 26.

69. It included the destruction of the Swan Hotel and 16 human deaths. Its absence is marked today by a memorial park in the High Street of the Old Town. http://victoriaseymour.com/ww2/. Accessed 5 February 2015.

70. Handwritten and anonymous account of raid on Sunday 23 May 1943 in Cuttings on Second World War file (no number), Hastings local studies library.

71. Folkes, *Dogs, Goats, Bulbs and Bombs*, introduction, 17.

72. Folkes, *Dogs, Goats, Bulbs and Bombs*, entry for Friday 26 February 1943, 166.

73. Folkes, *Dogs, Goats, Bulbs and Bombs*, entry for 15 May 1942, 137.

74. Miss Cox 06/26/1 Imperial War Museum. This is an account of her childhood. Her mother ran a sick bay for evacuated children in Speldhurst.

CHAPTER SEVEN

1. Note of Minister (HIF) 4 August 1942 in MAF/61, National Archives.

2. As George Beardmore, employed to track down rate payers for Wembley council, observed: "At one house I found the back door open, walked inside, and a Marie-Celeste situation presented itself: breakfast things unwashed, a half-smoked cigarettes dipped in tea to put it out, fruit going mouldy in a bowl." Beardmore, *Civilians at War*, 45. The ODFL reported cats being left shut up in houses and being "almost starving before they were rescued." "Cats Left in Empty Houses," *Times*, 25 October 1939, 2.

3. Cox, diary entry, 21 October 1940. It is difficult for me (and I am sure others) to disassociate this image from the iconic film *Brief Encounter*, which was shot on location in this station.

4. Joan Herring in Age Exchange Reminiscence, *Londoners Remember Living through the Blitz*, 24–26.

5. Cox, diary entry, 19 November 1939.

6. http://www.winstonchurchill.org/resources/speeches/1940-the-finest-hour/we-shall-fight -on-the-beaches site visited 7 April 2015.

7. At that time Harold Nicolson, then working in the Ministry of Information, alerted his wife Vita Sackville-West to be prepared to evacuate their Kent home at Sissinghurst and to fill the Buick with petrol, take food for 24 hours, and pack "your jewels and my diaries." Four days later he wrote that the government might decide to evacuate Kent and Sussex and there was need to get tablets from medical friends to end things quickly. Letters from Harold Nicolson to Vita Sackille-West for 22 May and 26 May 1940 in Nicolson, *Diaries and Letters 1939–1945*, 84 and 86.

8. Thus Field Marshal Lord Alan Brooke noted on 13 September 1940, "Everything looks like an invasion starting tomorrow from the Thames to Plymouth." Some three weeks later his diary stated: "Still no invasion! I am beginning to think that the Germans may after all not attempt it. And yet! I have the horrid thought that he [Hitler] may still bring off some surprise on us." Entry for 3 October 1940. Alanbrooke, *War Diaries*, 107, 112–13.

9. Addison and Crang, *Listening to Britain*, 11 September 1940, 410.

10. Hylton, *Kent and Sussex 1940*, 139.

11. Burton, *Bexhill in World War Two*, 5.

12. Hylton, *Kent and Sussex 1940*, 39, 109, 132.

13. From typed memoir of Betty Morrell. Many thanks to Caroline Morrell for this.

14. Correspondence from Caroline Morrell.

15. Thornton, *Hastings: A Living History*, 55. He is describing events on 10–13 September 1940. In Eastbourne the RPSCA, including local hero "Teddie" Winn, responsible for rescuing many a dog in peacetime at Beachy Head, has been remembered for feeding and caring for pets abandoned in their homes when families were obliged to temporarily move due to an unexploded bomb. Thus Smut, a black cat, was popped into a sack—on hand for such an emergency—and safely evacuated. As the daughter of the family recalled, "Poor Smut was the only pet evacuated with his family, only to be put to sleep the next day! 'Not fair to him – it may happen again' said my mother." Letter from Jean E. Paul to author summer 2012 (via email and daughter Liz Paul). More positively Ted-die Winn is recorded visiting in hospital the owner of a wrecked Eastbourne house to cheer her up with news of her dog's safety. Humphrey, *Eastbourne at War*, 38–39.

16. Appendix E to letter to the principal officers at Cambridge and Tunbridge Wells, from D. J. Lidbury, Ministry of Home Security, 20 June 1940, in Correspondence regarding evacuation HO 186 /1419, National Archives.

17. Minutes of Emergency meeting of committee 23 August 1939 HO 186 -1418; NARPAC de-clared in their 1939 pamphlet on wartime treatment of animals, "a good many people have the idea that if air raids come, official steps will be taken to send all animals out of the danger area, This Is quite untrue." NARPAC, *Wartime Aids for All Animal Owners*, 5.

18. Correspondence 3 July 1940 to Snelling from Storey. HO 186 /1419, National Archives.

19. Internal memorandum to Mr. Barrow 1 August 1940. HO 186 /1419, National Archives.

20. At the time such large dogs were not permitted in carriages but had to travel in the separate guard's van. Letter from RSPCA 27 June 1940 to Snelling Ministry of Home Security, HO 186 /1419, National Archives.

21. 4 July 1940 letter from Stordy to Sir William Wood, vice principal of London Midland and Scottish Railway Co., subsequently copied to Barrow of ARP department on 30 July 1940, HO 186/1419, National Archives.

22. Porter, *Hastings in Peace and War*, 64.

23. File note from Snelling, 23 November 1941, HO 186 /1419, National Archives.

24. Snelling to Sir Gordon Johnson, 12 October 1942 HO 186 /1419, National Archives.

25. File note from Snelling of meeting with A. W. Moss of RSPCA, 22 November 1941; Note

from Snelling to Sir Gordon Johnson, 12 October 1942, Correspondence regarding evacuation, HO 186 /1419, National Archives.

26. M40C 15 Neasden 27 August 1941, Dogs in Wartime TC 79/1E, Mass Observation.

27. M20 C Hendon 27 August 1941, Dogs in Wartime TC 79/1E, Mass Observation.

28. M60 C 14, JS 27 August 1941 Neasden 1E, Dogs in Wartime TC 79/1E, Mass Observation.

29. Typed analysis sheet 1D Dogs in Wartime (1941), Mass Observation.

30. B. C. Burt to the Minister St. John Bodinnar 20 February 1942 and B. C. Burt to Mr. Lundie 9 May 1942 in MAF 84/61 Feeding stuff for dogs. This was a similar argument to that considered in the 1914–1918 war. See chapter 2.

31. Minute 94 by B. C. Burt 29 July 1942 in MAF 84 /61, National Archives.

32. Mr. Broadley response to Burt's proposals 4 August 1942 in MAF 84 /61, National Archives.

33. Mr. Broadley response to Burt's proposals 4 August 1942 in MAF 84 /61; Note of Minister (HIF) same day, National Archives.

34. As emphasized in the BBC broadcast of Christopher Stone HO 186 /1417, National Archives.

35. Howell, *At Home and Astray*, 1.

36. Germans—as opposed to just Nazis—were depicted as having an almost inbred brutality towards animals. A radio program "Animals in Wartime," broadcast at the end of August 1940, is a case in point. The writer and presenter was Cicely Hamilton, a well-known feminist and former suffragette. The talk noted that as a consequence of the previous war Peacock butterflies were comparatively rare in Germany. Hamilton also recalled meeting a kitten in a Viennese soup kitchen in the aftermath of the 1914–18 war who turned out to be a cat stunted to kitten size through lack of nourishment; "that soup-kitchen dwarf was the only cat I set eyes on during my stay in Austria . . . cats were equally scarce in the Rhineland." Turning her attention to the current war she continued, "From what we hear of the food supply of Europe, it is more than likely that the domestic cat—and the domestic dog—will again be rare in parts of the [German occupied] Continent." Due to the Allies' naval blockades there was a shortage in linen, wool, and flax: substitutes were made from stinging nettle fiber—the favorite nourishment of the Peacock's caterpillar, then a commercial product. Transcript of broadcast "Animals in Wartime" by Cicely Hamilton 20 August 1940, BBC Archives.

37. See chapter 1, pages 7–9.

38. A correspondent to the *Times*, 29 August 1939.

39. Another suggested that the dogs with German associations were Alsatians, Boxers, and Rottweilers. Letters 4 September 1939, *Times*.

40. These included Zerline, Boy, Berghina, and Waldman VI, a favorite brought over from Baden in April 1872. Gordon, *Noble Hounds and Dear Companions*, 17, 19, 105.

41. Vivian, "The Dachshund," *Animal Pictorial* (May 1940): 203.

42. Carl Olsson, "How Germany Conscripts Her Dog Population," *Animals and Zoo* (May 1940). My thanks to Mieke Roscher for forwarding me a copy of this cutting.

43. "Our Dog," Story of Sue Hill and mother A5952567, http://www.bbc.co.uk/history/ww2peopleswar/

44. Carl Olsson, "How Germany Conscripts Her Dog Population," *Animals and Zoo* (May 1940).

45. See chapter 5.

46. Bowker, "When the War Is Over," *Animals Defender* (March 1940): 89.

47. Transcript of oral account: Memories of the Jersey Animal Shelter during the Occupation, p. 4, Jersey Archive Ref L/D/25/A/2. My grateful thanks to Malachy Billingsley for these materials.

48. Joseph, *Cat's Company*, 81.

49. Shaffer and Barrows, *The Guernsey Literary and Potato Peel Pie Society*, 57. (See also p. 128 story of smashing a cat's head against the wall then chopping his head off and skinning and boiling him in a billy can.) I am well aware that this is fiction but the book is based on letters and oral testimony. Thanks to Wendy Robertson for drawing my attention to this lovely book.

50. Transcript of oral account: Memories of the Jersey Animal Shelter during the Occupation, p. 4, Jersey Archive Ref L/D/25/A/2. "There was also a lot of meetings about people only keeping one dog—the idea being to conserve food—there were a lot of meetings about this but no animals were put to sleep as a result of this."

51. Animal Studies scholars, such as Mieke Roscher, working in Germany are starting to research the treatment of domestic animals in war. Until very recently it was impossible to access relevant records, including those of animal charities.

52. See for example, Garfield, *Notable Woman*, 206. Entry for 14 June 1940.

53. See for example James, "A Visit to the Leipzig Veterinary College and Public Abattoir," *Veterinary Journal*, May 1939, 174–77.

54. Editorial, "Animals in Germany," *Veterinary Record*, 23 November 1940, 826. It reported that in 1912 Germans had consumed 10 tons of dog meat. (Based on an unspecified article in the *Times*.)

55. Coleridge, "Dog Murder in Germany," *Animals' Defender* 60, no. 3 (July 1940): 19.

56. "Dogs of War," *Animal Pictorial* 3, no. 5 (June/July 1940): 266–71.

57. This was discussed in the context of potentially compulsory evacuation from the south coast of England in the event of invasion. Letter to Mr. Snelling from A. Johnston of the Home Office, 24 June 1940, HO 186/1419, National Archives.

Even today it is common in Germany for the corpses of companion animals to be recycled as combustible, meal, etc., rather than to be buried by their owners. Thanks to Jan-Erik Steinkruger for this information. He is currently researching on animal commemoration in contemporary Germany.

58. See Donaldson and Kymlicka, *Zoopolis*, for discussion of extending a form of citizenship to certain animals.

59. The treasury had made only an initial grant of £1,000 and a further grant of £1,500 for equipment (2 April 1941 *Hansard*; NARPAC, *Now for Animals' ARP* 1, no. 1; December 1939–January 1940, Mass Observation.) The RSPCA gave £500 in cash together with £3,500 worth in humane killers and ammunition while the PDSA and ODFL together gave £6,000 in cash and £1,500 in goods (MAF inquiry, 4, National Archives). Although signed up to NARPAC as early as 30 August 1939 the RSPCA wrote to the War Office seeking to be recognized as the *only* society empowered to raise funds for animals working with the armed forces. This was agreed and the RSCPA then donated £20,000 from funds remaining for such purposes from the 1914–18 war. (Minutes of RSPCA Council, 20 September 1939, RSPCA Archives, CM/46.) By way of contrast only equipment to the value of £775 had been offered to NARPAC. (Minutes of Emergency War [Executive] Committee, 25 January 1940, RSPCA Archives, CM/80.) My grateful thanks to the RPSCA for permission to quote from these unpublished records.

60. Out of this there was expenditure on producing animal registration discs, although the MAF alleged that £22,000 had been spent on actually raising the money. MAF 52/118. There were flag days too, by animal charities. For example on 19 August 1944 the RSPCA raised £65 in Folkestone alone. Scott, *The Real Dad's Army*, 19 August 1944, 296.

61. Report of inquiry into the affairs of NARPAC. MAF 52/118, 2, 7, National Archives. The observation regarding the RSCPA and pets was accurate in terms of their minuted discussion. Dogs are barely mentioned—and cats not at all—in their wartime minutes.

62. Letter to Ross from Home Office 19 September 1939 in HO 144/21418, National Archives.

63. In January 1939 a subcommittee of the RCVS council together with the NVMA had been authorized to enter into negotiations with PDSA representatives. With Mrs. Dickin in the chair there was preliminary agreement with the PDSA that all vets in the vicinity of a PDSA dispensary would be invited to act as a veterinary surgeon; that PDSA would pay a uniform fee for services in permanent hospitals and for inpatients; PDSA would employ a vet at a salary (*Veterinary Record*, 13 January 1939, 101). W. Hamilton Kirk remained concerned that unqualified people were charging fees and making a living from this at the PDSA (*Veterinary Record*, 18 March 1939, 368–69) but

suggested a year-long trial that would benefit animals and the public would approve (*Veterinary Record*, 15 April 1939, 482-83). In the months before the war the College and NVMA were still discussing a scheme to protect their status (and level of animal treatment) and refrained "from committing themselves too deeply" to ongoing collaboration (Editorial, "The NVMA and the PDSA of the Poor," *Veterinary Record*, 15 April 1939, 482-83).

As an editorial in the *Veterinary Record*, 27 April 1940, 326, said, "Some have thought it unfortunate that the profession should become so closely linked with the animal welfare societies." One reason for this was "the erroneous impression grew in the minds of some that the Committee was essentially concerned with the protection of the dog and cat population."

64. Report on inquiry MAF 52/118, 7, National Archives.

65. Nowadays in Britain companion animals have been routinely microchipped to aid reunion if lost, but such schemes fall under the aegis of private profit-making businesses, not the state. However, from April 2016 all dogs are legally obliged to be microchipped at the owners' expense (more to aid prosecution than to facilitate recovery of lost dogs.)

66. Registration had not brought in the anticipated funds. The PDSA and ODFL helped get a bank overdraft offering themselves as guarantors. The inquiry described Mr. Bridges Webb of PDSA as a most able man, "I think there is no doubt that he has foreseen most things," concluding that affairs of NARPAC were really in his hands "and he is in a position to force matters for them and almost to dictate terms, e.g. he was been active with the Registration scheme; he was asked to register the badges; whether with the authority of NARPAC or not the badge is hardly distinguishable from the Blue Cross; it is registered in his name . . . He is accused by the veterinary profession of having so worked the scheme that it shows no profit or loss, hoping thus to induce NARPAC to surrender it to him, when he will exploit it thoroughly." MAF 52/118, 6, National Archives.

67. Suggested script, 10 October 1939, NARPAC, HO 186/1417, National Archives.

68. Tennyson Jesse, *London Front*, letter 5 March 1940, 259-60.

69. Rosman, *Nine Lives*, 11.

70. Rosman, *Nine Lives*, 153.

71. It required 30 staff working in shifts to get the information up to date. Staff were employed up to midnight and at weekends dealing with pet owners' inquiries (NARPAC registration branch. Mr. Colthurst's report 14 May 1940: HO 186-1418, National Archives). A letter to NARPAC from the RPSCA Acting Chief Secretary S. G. Pelhill of 13 May 1941 both suggests that the problem was ongoing and implies that animal owners were paying for disks that did not materialize. Minutes of Emergency War (Executive) Committee May 1941, RSPCA Archives CM/76.

72. NARPAC, "National ARP for Animals Service: Reorganisation in Urban Areas," *Veterinary Record*, 9 August 1941, 466.

73. NVMA, "A.R.P. for Animals: N.A.R.P.A.C. Services in Action: A Review," *Veterinary Record*, 20 June 1942, 252. The MAF inquiry would later argue that what was really needed was kennels and detention posts for strays and for animals left by temporarily evacuated people—and a means of disposal of carcasses (Report of the enquiry, 5).

74. Different examples of various tags that change form and name over time can be regularly found on e-Bay, for example, often in multiples. Inter alia this surely suggests that the concern over lack of distribution of disks was accurate.

75. Cox, diary entry, 30 December 1940.

76. Hodgson, *Few Eggs and No Oranges*, Friday 2 May 1941, 166.

77. Rosman, *Nine Lives*, 167.

78. NARPAC registration branch. Mr. Colthurst's report 14 May 1940: HO 186 -1418, National Archives.

79. Kean, *Animal Rights*, 88.

80. Pamela Ashford, diary entry for 26 October 1940, in Garfield, *We Are at War*, 406.

81. Account of Mr. Jory, a journalist in Goodall, *Voices from the Home Front*, 290.

82. David Johnson, letter to author, 13 March 2009.

83. This happened on 12 November 1940. Burton, *Bexhill in World War Two*, 53.

84. Kirby and Moss, *Animals Were There*, 139.

85. Nixon, *Raiders Overhead*. She is referring to October–November 1940, 37.

86. Daisy Woodard in Hostettler, *The Island at War*, 33.

87. Rosman, *Nine Lives*,161.

88. R. Calder, *Carry on London*, 95.

89. Harrisson, *Living through the Blitz*, 161.

90. Snelling to Philipson M I division HO 10 December 1943 and 5 January 1944, HO 186 /1419, National Archives.

91. Copy of Letter from Herbert Morrison to Lt. Cdr. A. L. Tufnell MP 19 November 1942 in HO 186/1419, National Archives. This quote is in the context of potential forced evacuation of people but the point is valid regarding varying treatment of different types of cats.

92. He had shown how stables, byres, and other farm buildings could be protected from the effects of blast and splinters by the erection of an "improvised wall or revetment with iron sides on timber posts filled with sand, earth, chalk, clinker etc." Stordy, "Air Raid Protective Devices," *Veterinary Record*, 26 August 1939, 1059–60.

93. "National ARP for Animals Committee: An Informative Bulletin," *Veterinary Record*, 5 July 1941, 388–90.

94. Scott, *The Real Dad's Army*, 10 July 1944, 288. In Lydd, also in Kent, Home Guard member Frank Paine and George Coleman led horses to safety when the cowsheds in which the horses were sheltering were blasted by incendiary bombs. For this act of bravery they received a RSPCA certificate. Scott, *The Real Dad's Army*, 6 December 1941, 143.

95. Partridge, *A Pacifist's War*, 13 September 1940, 59–60.

96. Partridge, *A Pacifist's War*, 5 November 1940, 66. Nevertheless the total nature of the war meant that Frances's domestic pigeons were obliged to be "executed" for fear of being appropriated to facilitate invasion. The pet birds were killed and eaten "but one snow-white managed to escape and now wheels about against the green landscape. We feel we can hardly bear to condemn it to death also." Partridge, *A Pacifist's War*, 7 June 7 1941, 95. In a different example on the coast Colonel, a horse employed by the Bexhill Corporation, became the first casualty in the town in July 1940. Although he was hit in the ear by shrapnel, he was working again the following day. Burton, *Bexhill in World War Two*, 49.

97. Rosman, *Nine Lives*,126–27. This was not always the case, of course. Rosman tells a story of a terrified tabby cat sojourning in an animal post. As one neighbor noted, "It was sitting on [her owner's] knee when they saw her last . . . but it must have jumped in time." The previous day the now dead woman of whom they spoken had given a donation to the animal post and entreated: "If anything should happen to me, don't let my poor cat be left, will you?" The tabby cat was duly killed, as requested. Rosman, *Nine Lives*, 206.

98. She was sure, she said, she would get another dog after the war. Willesden F 35c JS 24/7/ 41 in Dogs in Wartime 1/D, Mass Observation. A somewhat humorous picture article in *Picture Post* attempted to reassure people that their animals would be looked after. In a staged enactment, a very large Dalmatian cross is seen lying in a road: "Perhaps it's been hit by shrapnel. Perhaps it's been knocked out by blast. Perhaps it's been run over. Perhaps it's just having a rest." Pictures follow of the dog on a stretcher and being treated at a veterinary hospital: "Might as well be in Harley Street!" "Animals A.R.P.," *Picture Post*, 7 December 1940, 22–23. Many thanks to John Edmundson for a copy of this.

99. PDSA, *Christmas Appeal Leaflet*, 1944. Thanks to Jonathan Fishburn for a copy of this. Such attention to animals was not without its critics. In his customary hostile vein George Orwell wrote scathingly of NARPAC providing "miniature stretchers for cats." Orwell, *The English People*, 4. Tennyson Jesse posed more sympathetically the ethical question of whether an animal ambulance should stop if it found wounded humans on the pavement or carry on with its legitimate business. *London Front*, 260.

100. "Bombed Out," mother's story contributed anonymously. A4626092,30 July 2005. http://www.bbc.co.uk/history/ww2peopleswar/

101. Lind af Hageby, *Bombed Animals*, 38.

102. Anon., *Front Line*, 128.

103. Lind af Hageby, *Bombed Animals*, 11.

104. "Animal Welfare in War-Time," *Animal Pictorial* 3, no. 3 (April 1940): 166–67 and 183.

105. Ziegler, *London at War*, 245.Thus the RSPCA Council agreed to advise local authorities when poisoning rats to "advertise the fact in order that owners of domestic animals may take special care to prevent their animals from picking up the poison." Minutes of RSPCA Council Meeting 25 May 1944. My grateful thanks to the RPSCA for allowing me to quote this.

106. Fitzgibbon, *The Blitz*, 63, describing 7 September 1940.

107. Report of Inspector Miles forwarded by Sir Robert Gower, chair of the RSPCA, to Ellen Wilkinson MP on 19 June 1942 HO 186 /1417, National Archives. There is some similar material in the National Archives and also in NARPAC reports. However, unfortunately, no such details now exist in the RSPCA archive.

108. Hodgson, *Few Eggs and No Oranges*, 11 February 1943, 361.

109. Hodgson, *Few Eggs and No Oranges*, 29 May 1944, 477; 11 June 1944, 480.

110. Lilian Margaret Hart, "Our House Was Bombed," unpublished typewritten account, Tower Hamlets Archive, February 1941.

111. PDSA, "A Typical Rescue Case: Only One out of Many Thousands," nd [1941 /2]. Thanks to Jonathan Fishburn for a copy of this.

112. Zuckerman, *From Apes to Warlords*, 133–38.No scientific study of air raids commenced until about a year after the start of the war (p. 138).

113. "War-Time Reactions of Cats," *Cat*, May 1941, 88–89.

114. *Cat*, November 1939, 16.

115. Letter from E. Bridges Webb, "controller" of NARPAC to Snelling at Ministry of Home Security 10 November 1943 HO 186 /1417, National Archives.

116. Letter from Robert Gower to Herbert Morrison 14 March 1944 regarding the work of the RSPCA in London HO 186/1417, National Archives.

117. Nixon, *Raiders Overhead*, 118.

118. Bernard Regan in Hostettler, *The Island at War*, 52–55.

119. Demarne, *The London Blitz*, 66.

120. CPL, "Notes of the Month," *Cat*, January 1941.

121. Ellen Clark in Age Exchange Reminiscence, *Londoners Remember Living through the Blitz*, 42–44.

122. In Gravesend two men and a woman returned to feed animals who had temporarily been left behind in a speedy evacuation from the area due to delayed action bombs. For this action they received a RSPCA silver medal. *Animals' Defender* 61, no. 3 (July 1941): 85. By January 1941 already twenty RSPCA inspectors had been awarded gallantry medals for "rescuing creatures of one species or another." *Animals' Defender* 60, no. 9 (January 1941): 61.

123. Warden's Post, *Journal for ARP and All Civil Defence Services, District C Poplar* 1, no. 1 (February 1940): 3.

124. Hodgson, *Few Eggs and No Oranges*, Sunday 27 February 1944, 455.

125. *Daily Mail*, 30 December 1940, as quoted in Lind af Hageby, *Bombed Animals*, 3.

126. Kirby and Moss, *Animals Were There*, 41 and picture opposite 63.

127. Cox, diary entry, 19 February, 25 February, 1 March, 3 March 1944. Such animal rescues even merited inclusion in quasi-official accounts. Commenting on the work of local animal wardens, Frank Lewey, the mayor of Stepney, suggested, " It needs as much—perhaps more—pluck to wander among blazing and tottering ruins, looking for a maddened dog or trying to pick up a crazed cat, as to go to try to help sensible humans." Lewey, *Cockney Campaign*, 93. See also Demarne, *The London Blitz*, 65.

128. This is also reflected in the rather sentimental and patronizing account of novelist Alice Grant Rosman, for example: "There must have been some people no doubt who, in their own tragic extremity, forgot their stricken animals, but generally even the most humble showed the greatest devotion to them and did not rest until they were in safe hands. 'My house was bombed, miss, and my two cats are in there.' 'You mean you've lost everything.' 'Oh yes, but it's not that. It's my poor cats. Would the lady get them out? They won't let me by, you see, the wardens won't.'" Rosman, *Nine Lives*, 165–66.

129. Lind af Hageby, *Bombed Animals*, 1941, 5.

130. Lees-Milne, *Prophesying Peace*, entry for 23 February 1944, 22. Thanks to Anne Marshall for introducing me to the writing of this wonderful diarist.

131. RSPCA, *118th Annual Report*, 1941, 13–14.

132. Lees-Milne, *Ancestral Voices*, 1942–43, entry for 30 October 1943, 116. He distracted the housekeeper by getting her to speak about her favorite subject, Blenheim. "She told me how Gladys Duchess of Marlborough would have her spaniels in the stateroom in order to annoy the duke who was inconceivably fussy. He would spend hours examining the curtains looking for stains made by the dogs, and was very disappointed if he failed to find any." (Lees-Milne does add that he believed none of the stories of Bleinheim to be true!)

133. RSPCA, *122th Annual Report*, 1945, 147.

134. They read to me much like source material for the comedy series *Dad's Army*.

135. Letter from Hon Sec Winifred Byles, Wanstead and Woodford NARPAC (volunteer) Animal Rescue Unit, to Captain Barge of Civil Defence department, 25 August 1942.Wanstead and Woodford Borough Council Civil Defence department 90/167:90 ARP for Animals 1 /4 Correspondence from 1942.

136. Letter from Mrs. Byles 2 December 1941 to Wanstead Civil Defence and reply 17 December from Controller RHSF/DE; in Wanstead and Woodford Civil Defence Department 90/30/5 and 90/167: 96 ARP for Animals 1 / 4; Letter from H E Bywater to ARP Officer, Wanstead and Woodford BC, Wanstead and Woodford Borough Council Civil Defence Dept 90/30/1 and 90/167: 94 ARP for Animals 1 / 4.

137. There were tensions here too between veterinary surgeons and the National Farmers' Union. Because of the time elapsing between attendance at an incident, voluntary parish animal stewards were recruited to help farmers, rather than the vets taking a key role. "Air Raid Precaution for Animals," *Veterinary Record*, 27 April 1940, 325–26.

138. File Note memorandum, 9 January 1941 MAF 52 /18. There were mobile veterinary sections equipped to render first aid, decontaminate gas casualties, or humanely destroy animals fatally injured. "National ARP for Animals Committee: An Informative Bulletin," *Veterinary Record*, 5 July 1941, 388–89.

139. MAF 52/118, National Archives.

140. One Hundred & Twenty-Second Letter to Branch & Auxiliary Branch Hon. Secretaries, 22 May 1941, RSPCA Archives CM/80. My grateful thanks to the RPSCA for granting me permission to quote from this.

141. Minutes of quarterly meeting of the RVC council,12 January 1939; 23 June 1939. In the months before the war the College and NVMA were still discussing a scheme to protect their status (and level of animal treatment) and refrained "from committing themselves too deeply" to ongoing collaboration. Editorial, "The NVMA and the PDSA of the Poor," *Veterinary Record*, 15 April 1939, 482–83. See also Gardiner, "'The Dangerous Women' of Animal Welfare."

142. Steele-Bodger, "Presidential Address," *Veterinary Record*, 11 October 1941, 589–90. The Ministry had asked the Ministry of Agriculture and the Ministry of Food to take over the rural scheme. It then changed its mind regarding the urban scheme but all the ministries disowned "dealing with animals of economic value on farms" and said NARPAC should close down.

CHAPTER EIGHT

1. M20 C Hendon 27 August 1941 TC 79/1 E, Mass Observation.

2. Thanks to Philip Howell for his comments.

3. R. G. W. Kirk, "In Dogs We Trust?" According to the *Daily Mirror*, sporting dogs were also needed by harassed gamekeepers for estates "over-run" by foxes and badgers. Terriers too, if they were good "ratters," could be of use against "the worse rural pest of all." Press cutting, "Wanted— Dogs," *Daily Mirror*, 29 June 1942, in MAF 84/61, National Archives.

4. R. G. W. Kirk, "In Dogs We Trust?," 7.

5. This "voluntary" measure was contrasted with reports that in Germany dogs not deemed to be useful in explicit war work were destroyed. Lind af Hageby, *Bombed Animals*, 36.

6. Battersea Dogs and Cats Home, *Report of the Committee for 1940*, 1.

7. RSPCA, *119th Annual Report*, 1942, 11.

8. Cummins, *Colonel Richardson's Airedales*, 165.

9. R. G. W. Kirk, "In Dogs We Trust?," 7.

10. By way of contrast the American approach emphasized conditioning through punishment. Note on a visit to British war dog training center, 13 March 1945, p. 2, WO 205/1173 TNA as cited in R. G. W. Kirk, "In Dogs We Trust?," 7.

11. This contrasts, for example, with the routine practice of the RAF today. The two dogs Brus, a Belgian Shepherd, and Blade, a German Shepherd, who had guarded Prince William, second in line to the British throne, were summarily killed after the prince left his role as a search and rescue pilot in north Wales. Larisa Brown and Sara Smyth, "Two guard dogs that protected Prince William on RAF duty are destroyed days after he quits because they couldn't be redeployed or re-homed." http://www.dailymail.co.uk/news/article-2424123/Guard-dogs-protected-Prince -William-RAF-duty-destroyed-days-quits.html visited 27 April 2015. For a fascinating account of what happened to the dogs who had guarded the Berlin Wall and disputes about the extent of their violent behavior and ability to integrate or not into family life, see Schneider, *The German Comedy: Science of Life after the Wall*, 208–12. Thanks to Marilyn Kinnon for drawing my attention to this.

12. Eileen Woods in Schweitzer, *Goodnight Children Everywhere*, 246–47. Thanks to Val Horsfield for drawing my attention to this.

13. See a "depressing footnote" to the Nazi Holocaust in a recent article that argues that there is the "likelihood" that guard dogs in concentration camps carried out their attacks on Jewish prisoners "out of loyalty and probably love for their human companions." Tindol, "The Best Friend of the Murderers," 119–120.

14. Press cutting, *Daily Mail*, 28 October 1944; cutting, *Star*, 11 October 1944, in HO 186 /2671.

15. Press cutting, "a daily paper," 17 December 1944, in HO 186 /2671. Jet is also memorialized today near where he is buried in Calderstones Park in Liverpool.

16. HO 186/2572. Jet was declared temporarily unfit because of his injury. Many dogs would be presented as war heroes before the King and Queen in Hyde Park in the farewell parade for Civil Defence Services in June 1945. MEPO2/6489 Farewell parade in London for members of Civil Defence Services 10 June 1945, National Archives.

17. Memorandum W. B. Brown, The use of dogs to assist in the location of trapped casualties, 9 January 1945, HO 186 /2671.

18. Cats' acute sense of smell did not desert them in war. Bob, the tabby cat with honey-colored eyes, for example, was wont to refuse to eat fish he deemed off. Thus he declined to eat stale, smelling, cod and even the stray cats to whom it was offered refused to eat it. Bob was later rewarded with "passable whiting" (Cox, diary entry, 11 September 1942). But when food was not abundant this skill could also prove beneficial for humans, as a story told by the poet Stephen Spender, working as a fire fighter in northwest London, revealed. One of the men, Fadden, had

been delighted with the Rock Eel he had acquired and had kept it in the fridge for two days to show off to others. However it started to stink and the cook declared it off, declaring, "Go and get the cat. Cats always know. If a fish ain't good they won't touch it. Go and get Nigger [*sic*]." The cat duly arrived: "Everyone watched while Nigger sniffed at the fish and then turned away. Fadden was disgusted and took the fish out to the dustbin. The others experienced a sense of deep atavistic exaltation that the cat had shown its powers of divination." Spender, *World within World*, 267.

19. Edward Heslop Smith, "For Members of the Wardens' Services Only," *Poplar Civil Defence Wardens' Organisation Bulletin* 67, Victory Issue, typescript, 10, Tower Hamlets Archive.

20. Photo file of Rip. Rip ARP dog and Post B 132 Southill St, Poplar, MOI photos 1–19. Tower Hamlets Archive.

21. PDSA, *Annual Report 1939 to 1945*, 26.

22. He was nevertheless also awarded a Dickin medal for bravery in 1945 that he wore until his death in 1948. "Dogs Bravery Medal Fetches Top Price," *Veterinary History* 15, no. 2 (2010): 171. Rip's medal fetched £24,250.

23. Birke and Hockenhull, "Journeys Together," 82.

24. Birke and Hockenhull, "Journeys Together," 83.

25. Kipps, *Sold for a Farthing*, 19, 20, 25.Thanks to Helen Tiffin who not only told me about the book but lent me a precious copy previously belonging to a deceased friend.

26. Kipps, *Sold for a Farthing*, 18.

27. Kipps, *Sold for a Farthing*, 31–32.

28. Kipps, *Sold for a Farthing*, 30.

29. Kipps, *Sold for a Farthing*, 18.

30. Kipps, *Sold for a Farthing*, 43.

31. Kipps, *Sold for a Farthing*, foreword (unnumbered) and 57–58.

32. Kipps, *Sold for a Farthing*, 43.

33. All quotes above from same article. CPL, "War Workers," *Cat*, July 1940, 111–12.

34. CPL, "Secretary's Comments," *Cat*, September 1940, 143–44.

35. Lind af Hageby, *Bombed Animals*, 36. Animal welfarists were also keen to highlight the paradox of Germany banning the use of the gin trap to trap wild animals, such as rabbits, "on account of its cruelty," arguing: "Is it not . . . something of a paradox and of a reproach that while we are fighting a crusade against brutality and oppression we should ourselves be guilt of subjecting helpless and innocent creatures to many hours of torture in the gin trap?" Letter from K. Ramsbottom of UFAW to the *Times*, 13 November 1939, 2.

36. Partridge, *A Pacifist's War*, 13 March 1942, 128.

37. Matheson, "The Domestic Cat as a Factor in Urban Ecology," 131.

38. Letter Mr. Thomson Home Office re suggested script of Stone's broadcast 10 October 1939 HO 186 /1417.

39. Matheson, "The Domestic Cat as a Factor in Urban Ecology," 130–31.

40. A separate category /definition of feral cats is not included. Matheson, "The Domestic Cat as a Factor in Urban Ecology," 132.

41. This was thought to be a lower figure than normal owing to "food-supply difficulties." Matheson, "The Domestic Cat as a Factor in Urban Ecology," 131–32.

42. G. Cox-Ife, Editorial, *Cats and Kittens* (April 1944): 1.

43. Lind af Hageby, *Bombed Animals*, 38.

44. In different ways animal imagery was used by Peter Conway. In language reminiscent of nineteenth-century explorers, the doctor described his observations of people in London shelters. For example, "The group seemed barely human. I could not help thinking, as I look at them, of a monkey mother with her young; and there was nothing disparaging in the thought. It was, I think, the pathetic suggestion of near-humanity and protection." War conditions seemed a not inappropriate context for blurring the human and animal and for conveying vulnerability. Conway, *Living Tapestry*,15.

45. Letter to Mervyn from Bill 15 September 1940. Haisman and Snellgrove, *Dear Merv . . . Dear Bill*, 83.

46. Dame Joan Varley as quoted in Maev Kennedy, "Sex, Fear and Looting: Survivors Disclose Untold Stories of the Blitz," *Guardian*, 5 October 2006, 9.

47. Inter alia Diana Cooper was the wife of Duff Cooper, then employed at the Ministry of Information.

48. Cooper, *Autobiography*, 569.

49. Vera Brittain, *England's Hour*, 267. A similar sentiment is found in Nicolson's diary. Describing bathing in his lake at Sissinghurst he projected his feelings about the disaster that had occurred in September 1939: "I could scarcely believe that the swans were being sincere in their indifference to the Second German War." Nicolson, *Diaries and Letters*, 4 September 1939, 25.

50. Jill Watts, Personal account written at request of the author, July 2009.

51. Cox, diary entry, Sunday 15 November 1942.

52. Broad and Fleming, *Nella Last's War*, Saturday 22 March 1944, 110–12.

53. Broad and Fleming, *Nella Last's War*, 23 July 1940, 58.

54. I am well aware that the quote originates with Claude Levi-Strauss, "Natural species are chosen not because they are 'good to eat' but because they are 'good to think.'" [Les espèces sont choisies non commes bonnes à manger, mais comme bonnes à penser.] It is often translated as good to think with. (From *The Savage Mind*, 1962.)

55. Tennyson Jesse, *London Front*, Letter 5 March 1940, 287.

56. Tennyson Jesse, *London Front*, 287.

57. Cox, diary entry, 3 and 5 September 1939.

58. Cox, diary entry, 5 September 1939.

59. Woman Mill Hill F40C 11 July 1941 Dogs in Wartime Pilot Survey 1/B.

60. M45 D Euston Pilot Survey 11–14 July 1941 Dogs in Wartime 1/B.

61. M40C Euston Pilot Survey 11–14 July 1941 Dogs in Wartime 1/B.

62. M40D Euston Pilot 11–14 July 1941 Dogs in Wartime 1/B.

63. M50D Euston Pilot 11–14 July 1941 Dogs in Wartime 1/B.

64. M20 C Hendon 27 August 1941 TC 79/1 E, Mass Observation.

65. Hodgson, *Few Eggs and No Oranges*, 11 June 1944, 480.

66. Foreword to Cox, diary.

67. M45B no. 28, 27 August 1941, Survey of non-dog owners 1E. He had had a dog three years before. Mass Observation.

68. Matt and Stearns, *Doing Emotions History*, 1.

69. Nussbaum argues, "We can come as close to [first-hand reports] as possible by focusing on a detailed narrative account of the emotions of particular animals, made by an observer who has unusual empathy and unusual awareness of the specific capacities of the animals in question." *Upheavals of Thought*, 92.

70. Bekoff is discussing a paper by Miho Nagasawa and his colleagues entitled "Oxytocin-Gaze Positive Loop and the Coevolution of Human-Dog Bonds" in the journal *Science*. http://www.huffingtonpost.com/marc-bekoff/dogs-humans-and-the-oxyto_b_7081010.html visited 20 April 2015.

71. Bentham, *The Principles of Morals and Legislation*, chapter 18, section 1, as quoted in Kean, *Animal Rights*, 22.

72. "Very few scientists have acknowledged, researched, or even speculated about animal emotional states." Masson and McCarthy, *When Elephants Weep*, 19–20.

73. Birke and Hockenhull, "Journeys Together," 96.

74. Broad and Fleming, *Nella Last's War*, 10 November 1942, 216–17. This also covers the block quote above.

75. Bradshaw, *In Defence of Dogs*, 207.

76. Bradshaw, *In Defence of Dogs*, 223. He has suggested that both cats and dogs have a relationship with a human keeper that is "fundamentally affectionate." Bradshaw, *Cat Sense*, 191. Bekoff is

more circumspect: "While we need animals, many animals would surely do much better without us." Bekoff, *The Emotional Lives of Animals*, 19. Philosophers too have started to explore animal emotions. Thus Mark Rowlands has argued that animals "can" be moral subjects (p. 33) and that "certain animals arguably show themselves to be concerned with the welfare or fortunes of others." *Can Animals be Moral?*, 8.

77. Howell, "At Home and Astray," 83.

78. Lees-Milne, *Ancestral Voices*, 25 August 1942, 92. Thanks to Anne Marshall for first introducing me to the work of this diarist.

79. Benson, "Animal Writes," 3.

80. Klemperer, *To the Bitter End*, entry for 15 May 1942, 64. Thanks to Brenda Kirsch for drawing my attention to these diaries.

81. Klemperer, *To the Bitter End*, 16 March 1942, 3.

82. Klemperer, *To the Bitter End*, 15 May 1942, 63–64.

83. Klemperer, *To the Bitter End*, 18 May 1942, 66–68.

84. Klemperer, *To the Bitter End*, 19 May 1942, 67.

85. Klemperer, *To the Bitter End*, 19 May and 22 May 1942, 67.

86. Thus Treasury Bill, allegedly renamed the Munich Mouser since he had been inherited from Chamberlain, continued to prowl offices of high state during the war. When the cat was found dead in the Foreign Office in July 1943, killed in mysterious circumstances, Sir John Martin, Churchill's private secretary, noted that they were avoiding publicity for fear of being flooded with black cats from all over the country to take his place. S. J. Martin, *Downing Street*, 4–5, 32, 106. Fearing that the animal had been thrown on the ash can, Churchill said that he would have been ready to give the Munich Mouser a burial in the garden of no.10. Eden, *The Reckoning*, 339, as quoted in S. J. Martin, *Downing Street*, 107.

87. Dilks, *Churchill and Company*, 44–45. Thanks to Roger McCarthy for drawing my attention to this. Nelson was evacuated with Churchill to Chequers, the Prime Minister's official residence on the outskirts of London, in October 1940, though Nelson was back in London by July 1943, waking up the Private Secretary of Churchill at 4 a.m., "flopped in at the window" when he had only gone to bed at 3. Unsurprisingly the Private Secretary declared, "I don't love Nelson." S. J. Martin, *Downing Street*, 106.

88. Dilks, *Churchill and Company*, 44–45.

89. A version can be found at http://www.bbc.co.uk/schoolreport/25751787 visited 8 December 2015.

CHAPTER NINE

1. Email from the former RSPCA Information and Records Officer Chris Read to author 17 May 2007.

2. Script of Christopher Stone radio broadcast 19 November 1939, HO 186/1417.

3. There was a caveat at the time. Those without conventional qualifications whose principal livelihood had been drawn from veterinary practice were allowed to continue if they had practiced for seven of the former ten years. Comben, *Dogs, Cats and People*, 222–23; http://trust.rcvs.org .uk/heritage-and-history/history-of-the-rcvs/

4. Outside the home, research into more intensive forms of farming was given an impetus due to shortages in wartime food production: Artificial insemination was a key development. The first artificial insemination unit had been established at Cambridge in 1942 after attacks on Atlantic convoys with the need for increased food production at home. It had been previously rejected by the government owing to opposition from religious organizations on moral grounds and from pedigree bull breeders as they thought it would ruin their business. Within 10 years a high proportion of dairy cows were bred in this way. Polge, "The Work of the Animal Research Station, Cambridge"; Woods, "The Farm as Clinic."

5. Dr. Reg Woolridge, then president of the NVMA, set up in 1942 the Veterinary Education Trust and in 1947 the Canine Health Centre in Kennett near Newmarket with the first director S. F. J. Hodgman from a south London practice, which in turn led to the British small animal veterinary association. Jones, "A Short History of British Small Animal Practice," 123.

6. B1654 Male Widower 78, Summer directive 2009, Animals and Humans Directive, Mass Observation.

7. Bekoff, *The Emotional Lives of Animals*, 21.

8. Fudge, *Pets*, 39.

9. Montague, *Let the Good Work Go On*, 10.

10. Battersea Dogs Home, *Annual Report 87*, 1947, 11.

11. In addition some 2,500 "owned" dogs and 2,000 cats were killed. Battersea Dogs Home *Annual Report 87*, 1947. The reports do not give a breakdown for reasons for destruction.

12. Minutes of Windsor, Uxbridge, Hillingdon RSPCA, 7 August 1946.

13. Arthur Frank, *The Wounded Storyteller* (University of Chicago Press, 1995), 22, as quoted in Irvine, *My Dog Always Eats First*, 7.

14. Originally a site in Hyde Park Corner was sought but this was given instead to the Empire Memorial Gates. Ward-Jackson, *Public Sculpture of Historic Westminster*, vol. 1, 187.

15. In earlier memorials, for example, in Scotland's National War Memorial in Edinburgh Castle or in Sydney's commemoration of the war dead in its own Hyde Park, there are humans, dying alongside horses or lining up together to do their common duty. See Kean, "Britain at War"; "Animals and War Memorials"; "Commemorating Animals: Glorifying Humans?"

16. There is one cat thought to represent Simon, the cat who served on HMS Amethyst and kept the ship mouse free during the Yangtze river incident in 1949. He is buried in the PDSA cemetery.

17. Animal Aid, *Animals: The Hidden Victims of War*.

18. Burt, "Reviews: The Animals' War Exhibition."

19. Kean, *Animal Rights*, 169–74; Leinon, "Finnish Narratives of the Horse in World War 11"; Litten, "Starving the Elephants"; I. J. Miller, *The Nature of the Beasts*.

20. This statement is on the back of the memorial.

21. There is also a bush in memory of Simon, the cat on HMS *Amethyst*, at the National Memorial Arboretum. It should be noted that it is not a "closed" memorial site but memorials continue to be erected.

22. Sarah Lowe et al., "The Impact of Pet Loss on the Perceived Social Support and Psychological Distress of Hurricane Survivors," *Journal of Traumatic Stress* 22, no. 3 (2009): 244–47 as quoted in Potts and Gadenne, *Animals in Emergencies*, 236.

23. Potts and Gadenne, *Animals in Emergencies*, 240.

24. See, amongst many examples, the story of Theo awarded a Dickin medal posthumously. Even the usually disdainful *Guardian* has carried such stories. Richard Norton-Taylor, "An Inseparable Pair: Dog Dies after Handler Is Killed," *Guardian*, 3 March 2011; "The Sun's Hero Dog Award," *Wag*, The Dogs Trust, summer 2011 (pages unnumbered).

25. As Alex Mutch, the rescuer of Dave, the ill-treated dog he swapped for a packet of flares, explained, "He was going to be our little troop dog while we were there but when I told my sister that he would be probably shot when we left she decided to set up a campaign to save him." Miranda Bryant, "Marine Saves Dog from Torture in Afghanistan," *Evening Standard*, 28 April 2011, 32–33. See also http://www.nowzad.com/about/our-mission-in-afghanistan/

26. See Benjamin, "Theses on the Philosophy of History."

27. As Nella Last wrote on 31 August 1939; cited in File Report 621, 11. Thanks to James Hinton for this reference.

28. Townsend, *The Family Life of Old People*, 253, 261.

29. Townsend, *The Family Life of Old People*, 12.

30. Email from the former Information and Records Officer Chris Read to author 17 May

2007. I hasten to add that the current staff and RSPCA executive member Richard Ryder have been extremely helpful and open and professional in their approach. I remain very grateful for the access to unpublished material not routinely available to researchers.

31. Kirby and Moss, *Animals Were There*, 18–19.

32. As I write (December 2015) the Conservative government is attempting to curtail the RSPCA's hitherto statutory right to undertake prosecutions, especially against hunters killing foxes in a manner banned by the Hunting Act 2004.

Bibliography

PUBLISHED BOOKS AND ARTICLES

Addison, Paul. "National Identity and the Battle of Britain." In *War and the Cultural Construction of Identities in Britain*, edited by Barbara Korte and Ralf Schneider, 225–40. Amsterdam: Rodopi, 2002.

Addison, Paul, and Crang, Jeremy A., eds. *Listening to Britain: Home Intelligence Reports on Britain's Finest Hour May to September 1940*. London: Bodley Head, 2010.

Age Exchange Reminiscence Group. *Londoners Remember Living through the Blitz*. Edited by Pam Schweitzer. London: Age Exchange, 1991.

Alanbrooke. *War Diaries, 1939–1945: Field Marshal Lord Alanbrooke*. Edited by Alex Danchev and Daniel Todman. Berkeley: University of California Press, 2001.

Alger, Janet M., and Steven F. Alger. *Cat Culture: The Social World of a Cat Shelter*. Philadelphia: Temple University Press, 2003.

Allan, Roy, and Clarissa Allan. *The Essential German Shepherd Dog*. Letchworth: Ringpress Books, 1994.

Andrews, Maggie, and Janice Lomas, eds. *The Home Front in Britain: Images, Myths and Forgotten Experiences since 1914*. Basingstoke: Palgrave Macmillan, 2014.

Animal Aid. *Animals: The Hidden Victims of War*. Tonbridge: Animal Aid, 2006.

"Animals A.R.P." *Picture Post*, 7 December 1940, 22–23.

Animal Studies Group. *Killing Animals*. Chicago: University of Illinois Press, 2006.

Anon. *Front Line 1940–1941: The Official Story of the Civil Defence of Britain*. London: HMSO, 1941.

Anon. *A Woman in Berlin*. With an introduction by Antony Beevor. London: Virago, 2005.

Ash, Edward C. *Puppies: Their Choice, Care and Training*. London: John Miles, 1936.

Ashton, Paul, and Hilda Kean. *Public History and Heritage: People and Their Pasts*. Basingstoke: Palgrave Macmillan, 2012.

Bachelard, Gaston T. *The Poetics of Space*. Translated by Maria Jolas. Boston: Beacon Press,1994.

Baker, Steve. *Artist / Animal*. Minneapolis: University of Minnesota Press, 2013.

Balshaw, June, and Malin Lundin. *Memories of War: New Narratives and Untold Stories*. London: University of Greenwich, 2010.

Beardmore, George. *Civilians at War: Journals 1938–46*. Oxford: Oxford University Press, 1986.

Bekoff, Marc. *The Emotional Lives of Animals*. Novato, CA: New World Library, 2007.

Bell, Amy Helen. *London Was Ours: Diaries and Memoirs of the London Blitz*. London: I. B. Tauris, 2008.

Bell, Ernest. "British War Dogs." *Animals' Friend* 27, no. 3 (December 1920): 25-26.

Bell, Ernest, and Harold Baillie Weaver. *Horses in Warfare.* London: Animals' Friend Society, 1912.

Benjamin, Walter. "Theses on the Philosophy of History." In *Illuminations,* edited by Hannah Arendt, 247-49. London: Fontana, 1992.

Benson, Etienne. "Animal Writes: Historiography, Disciplinarity, and the Animal Trace." In *Making Animal Meaning,* edited by Linda Kalof and Georgina F. Montgomery, 3-16. East Lansing: Michigan State University Press, 2011.

Best, Geoffrey. *Churchill: A Study in Greatness.* Oxford: Oxford University Press, 2003.

Bion, Wilfred R. "The War of Nerves: Civilian Reaction, Morale, and Prophylaxis." In *The Neuroses in War,* edited by Emanuel Miller, 180-200. London: Macmillan, 1940.

Birke, Lynda, and Joanna Hockenhull. "Journeys Together: Horses and Humans in Partnership." *Society and Animals* 23, no. 1 (2015): 81-100.

Bowker, G. H. "When the War Is Over." *Animals' Defender* (March 1940): 89.

Bradshaw, John. *Cat Sense: The Feline Enigma Revealed.* London: Allen Lane, 2013.

———. *In Defence of Dogs.* London: Allen Lane, 2011.

Brander, Michael. *Eve Balfour: The Founder of the Soil Association and Voice of the Organic Movement.* Haddington: Gleneil, 2003.

Brantz, Dorothee, ed. *Beastly Natures: Animals, Humans, and the Study of History.* Charlottesville: University of Virginia Press, 2010.

British Union for the Abolition of Vivisection (BUAV). *The National Health Service Act and Vivisection.* Bromley, Kent: BUAV, 1947.

Brittain, Vera. *England's Hour.* London: Macmillan, 1940.

Broad, R., and S. Fleming, eds. *Nella Last's War.* Bristol: Falling Wall Press, 1981.

Burlingham, Dorothy, and Anna Freud. *Young Children in War-Time: A Year's Work in a Residential War Nursery.* London: G. Allen and Unwin, 1942.

Burney, Ian. "War on Fear: Solly Zuckerman and Civilian Nerve in the Second World War." *History of the Human Sciences* 25, no. 5 (2012): 49-72.

Burt, Jonathan. "Conflicts around Slaughter in Modernity." In *Killing Animals,* Animal Studies Group, 120-44. Chicago: University of Illinois Press, 2006.

———. "The Illumination of the Animal Kingdom: The Role of Light and Electricity in Animal Representation." *Society and Animals* 9, no. 3 (2001): 203-28.

———. "Invisible Histories: Primate Bodies and the Rise of Posthumanism in the Twentieth Century." In *Animal Encounters,* edited by Tom Tyler and Manuela Rossini, 159-72. Leiden: Brill, 2009.

———. "Review of Cary Wolfe, *Zoontologies* and *Animal Rites.*" *Society and Animals* 13, no. 2 (2005):167-70.

———. "Reviews: The Animals' War Exhibition." *History Today* (October 2006):71.

Burton, David. *Bexhill in World War Two.* Bexhill-on-Sea: Bexhill Museum Association, 1998.

Calder, Angus. *The Myth of the Blitz.* London: Pimlico, 1992.

———. *The People's War.* London: Cape, 1986.

Calder, Ritchie. *Carry on London.* London: English Universities Press, 1941.

Cato [Michael Foot, Frank Owen, and Peter Howard]. *Guilty Men.* London: Victor Gollancz, 1940.

Clabby, John. *A History of the Royal Army Veterinary Corps, 1919-61.* London: J. A. Allen, 1963.

Cockett, Olivia. *Love and War in London: A Woman's Diary 1939-1942.* Edited by Robert Malcolmson. Stroud: History Press, 2008.

Comben, Norman. *Dogs, Cats and People: A Vet's Eye View.* London: Thames and Hudson,1955.

Conway, Peter. *Living Tapestry.* London: Staples Press, 1946.

Cooper, Diana. *Autobiography.* Salisbury: Michael Russell, 1979.

Cornish, F. J. *Animals of To-day: Their Life and Conversation.* London: Sweeley, 1898.

Cousens, Frederick. *Dogs and Their Management.* 3rd ed. London: Routledge, 1934.

Cronin, J. Keri. "'Can't You Talk?' Voice and Visual Culture in Early Animal Welfare Campaigns." *Early Popular Visual Culture* 9, no. 3 (2011): 203-23.

Croxton-Smith, Arthur. *British Dogs*. London: Collins, 1946.

——. *Tailwaggers*. London: Country Life, 1931.

Croxton-Smith, Arthur, and others. *Animals Home Doctor: Encyclopaedia of Domestic Pets*. London: Amalgamated, 1934.

Cummins, B. D. *Colonel Richardson's Airedales: The Making of the British War Dog School 1900-1918*. Calgary, Alberta: Detselig, 2003.

Darnton, Robert. "The Workers Revolt: The Great Cat Massacre of the Rue Saint-Severin." In *The Great Cat Massacre and Other Episodes in French Cultural History*, 75-104. London: Penguin, 2001.

Dashper, Katherine. "The Elusiveness of 'Feel' in the Horse-Human Relationship: Communication, Harmony and Understanding." Paper presented at Cosmopolitan Animals, Institute of English Studies, University of London, UK, October 26-27, 2012.

——. "Tools of the Trade or Part of the Family? Horses in Competitive Equestrian Sport." *Society and Animals* 22, no. 4 (2014): 352-71.

Demarne, Cyril. *The London Blitz: A Fireman's Tale*. London: Parents' Centre, 1980.

Dilks, David. *Churchill and Company: Allies and Rivals in War and Peace*. London: I. B. Tauris, 2012.

Dobson, Alan S. *The War Effort of the Birds*. Leaflet no. 100. London: Royal Society for the Protection of Birds, n.d.

Donaldson, Sue, and Will Kymlicka. *Zoopolis: A Political Theory of Animal Rights*. Oxford: Oxford University Press, 2011.

Douglas, Nina, Duchess of Hamilton and Brandon. *The Chronicles of Ferne*. London: Animal Defence Society, 1951.

Eley, Geoff. "Finding the People's War." *American Historical Review* 106 (2001): 818-38.

Field, Geoffrey. "Nights Underground in Darkest London: The Blitz 1940-1941." *International Labour and Working Class History* 62 (2002): 11-49.

Fielding, Steven. "The Good War: 1939-1945." In *From Blitz to Blair*, edited by Nick Tiratsoo, 25-52. London: Weidenfeld & Nicolson, 1997.

Finn, Frank. *The Budgerigar*. London: Feathered World, [1925?].

——. *Pets and How to Keep Them*. London: Hutchinson, 1907.

Finney, Patrick. *Remembering the Road to World War Two: International History, National Identity, Collective Memory*. London: Routledge, 2011.

Fitzgibbon, Constantine. *The Blitz*. London: Corgi, 1974. First published 1957.

FitzGibbon, Theodora. *With Love*. London: Century, 1982.

Folkes, John, ed. *Dogs, Goats, Bulbs and Bombs: Esther Rowley's Wartime Diaries of Exmouth and Exeter*. Stroud: History, 2010.

Foster, Rodney. *The Real Dad's Army: The War Diaries of Col. Rodney Foster*. Edited by Ronnie Scott. London: Pension, 2011.

Fudge, Erica. "A Left-Handed Blow: Writing the History of Animals." In *Representing Animals*, edited by Nigel Rothfels, 3-18. Bloomington: Indiana University Press, 2002.

——. *Pets*. Stocksfield: Acumen, 2008.

——. "What Was It Like to Be a Cow? History and Animal Studies." In *The Oxford Handbook of Animal Studies*, edited by Linda Kalof, 1-14. doi:10.1093/oxfordhb/9780199927142.013.28.

Galsworthy, Ada. *The Dear Dogs*. London: William Heinemann, 1935.

Galvayne, Sydney. *War Horses Present and Future; or, Remount Life in South Africa*. London: R. A. Everett, 1902.

Gardiner, Andrew. "The 'Dangerous' Women of Animal Welfare: How British Veterinary Medicine Went to the Dogs." *Social History of Medicine* 27, no. 3 (2014): 466-87.

Gardner, George. *Cavies or Guinea Pigs*. London: L. Upcott Gill, 1913.

Garfield, Simon, ed. *We Are at War: The Remarkable Diaries of Five Ordinary People in Extraordinary Times*. London: Ebury, 2005.

Gilbert, Martin. *Second World War*. London: Phoenix, 2000.

Glover, Edward. "Notes on the Psychological Effects of War Conditions on the Civilian Population." *International Journal of Psycho-Analysis* 22 (1941): 132–46.

Goodall, Felicity. *Voices from the Home Front*. Newton Abbot: David & Charles, 2004.

Gordon, Sophie. *Noble Hounds and Dear Companions*. London: Royal Collections, 2007.

Gough, Paul. "'Garden of Gratitude': The National Memorial Arboretum and Strategic Remembering." In *Public History and Heritage: People and Their Pasts*, edited by Ashton and Kean, 95–112.

Gray, Ann, and Erin Bell. *History on Television*. Abingdon: Routledge, 2013.

Greene, Graham. *Ways of Escape*. London: Bodley Head, 1980.

Griffin, Alice. *Lost Identity: Memoir of a World War II Evacuee*. Alice Griffin, 2008.

Guerrini, Anita. *Experimenting with Humans and Animals*. Baltimore: John Hopkins University Press, 2003.

Haisman, Mervyn, and L. E. Snellgrove. *Dear Merv . . . Dear Bill*. Llandysul: Gomer, 1992.

Haldane, J. B. S. *A. R. P.* Left Book Club ed. London: Victor Gollancz, 1938.

Hall, Libby. *These Were Our Dogs*. London: Bloomsbury, 2007.

Harcourt-Brown, Nigel, and Chitty, John. *BSAVA Manual of Psittacine Birds*. 2nd ed. Gloucester: British Small Animal Veterinary Association, 2005.

Harrisson, Tom. *Living through the Blitz*. Harmondsworth: Penguin, 1979.

Hediger, Ryan, ed. *Animals and War: Studies of Europe and North America*. Leiden: Brill, 2013.

Henderson, Sir Nevile. *Hippy in Memoriam: The Story of a Dog*. London: Hodder and Stoughton, 1943.

Hennessy, Peter. *Never Again: Britain 1945–51*. London: Cape, 1992.

Hewison, Robert. *Under Siege: Literary Life in London 1939–1945*. London: Weidenfeld and Nicolson, 1977.

Hinchliffe, Steve, Matthew Kearnes, Monica Degen, and Sarah Whatmore. "Urban Wild Things: A Cosmopolitical Experiment." *Environment and Planning D: Society and Space* 23, no. 5 (2005): 643–58.

Hobday, Frederick. *Fifty Years a Veterinary Surgeon*. London: Hutchinson, 1938.

Hodder-Williams, John Edward. *Where's Master? By Caesar, the King's Dog*. London: Hodder & Stoughton, 1910.

Hodgson, Vere. *Few Eggs and No Oranges: A Diary Showing How Unimportant People in London and Birmingham Lived through the War Years 1940–45 Written in the Notting Hill Area of London*. Edited by Jenny Hartley. London: Persephone Books, 1999.

Hostettler, Eve. *The Island at War: Memories of Wartime Life on the Isle of Dogs, East London*. London: Island History Trust, 1990.

Howell, Philip. "The Dog Fancy at War: Breeds, Breeding and Britishness 1914–1918." *Society and Animals* 21, no. 6 (2013): 546–67.

———. *At Home and Astray: The Domestic Dog in Victorian Britain*. Charlottesville: University of Virginia Press, 2015.

Hribal, Jason C. "Animals, Agency, and Class: Writing the History of Animals from Below." *Human Ecology Review* 14, no.1 (2007): 101–12.

Hughes, Molly. *A London Family between the Wars*. Oxford: Oxford University Press, 1993.

Humphrey, George. *Eastbourne at War: Portrait of a Front Line Town*. Seaford: S. B., 1998.

Hunt, Karen. "A Heroine at Home: The Housewife on the First World War Home Front." In *The Home Front in Britain*, edited by Maggie Andrews and Janice Lomas, 73–91. Basingstoke: Palgrave Macmillan, 2014.

Hylton, Stuart. *Kent and Sussex 1940: Britain's Front Line*. Barnsley: Pen and Sword, 2004.

Irvine, Leslie. *My Dog Always Eats First*. Boulder, CO: Lynne Rienner, 2013.

Isaacs, Susan, ed. *The Cambridge Evacuation Survey*. London: Methuen, 1941.

Jackson, Julian. *The Fall of France: The Nazi Invasion of 1940* . Oxford: Oxford University Press, 2003.

Jackson, Kevin. *Humphrey Jennings*. London: Picador, 2004.

Jacobs, Nancy J. "The Great Bophuthatswana Donkey Massacre: Discourse on the Ass and the Politics of Class and Grass." *American Historical Review* 106, no. 2 (2001): 485–506.

James, Allan J. "A Visit to the Leipzig Veterinary College and Public Abattoir." *Veterinary Journal* 95 (May 1939): 174–77.

Jones, Bruce V. "A Short History of British Small Animal Practice." *Veterinary History* 15, no. 2 (2010): 93–135.

Jones, Bruce V., and Clare Boulton. "Robert Stordy 1873–1943." *Veterinary History* 16, no.4 (2013): 394–407.

Joseph, Michael. *Cat's Company*. 2nd ed. London: Michael Joseph,1946.

———. *Charles: The Story of a Friendship*. London: Michael Joseph, 1943.

Kean, Hilda. *Animal Rights: Political and Social Change in Britain since 1800*. London: Reaktion, 2000.

———. "Animals and War Memorials: Different Approaches to Commemorating the Human-Animal Relationship." In *Animals and War*, edited by Ryan Hediger, 237–62. Leiden: Brill, 2013.

———. "Britain at War: Remembering and Forgetting the Animal Dead of the Second World War." In *Mourning Animals*, edited by Margo de Mello. East Lansing: Michigan State University Press, 2016.

———. "Challenges for Historians Writing Animal-Human History: What Is Really Enough?" *Anthrozoos* 25, no. S1 (2012): 57–72.

———. "Commemorating Animals: Glorifying Humans? Remembering and Forgetting Animals in War Memorials." In *Lest We Forget: Remembrance and Commemoration*, edited by Maggie Andrews, Charles Bagot-Jewitt, Nigel Hunt, 60–70. Stroud: History Press, 2011.

———. "Continuity and Change: The Identity of the Political Reader." *Changing English* 3, no. 2 (1996): 209–18.

———. "An Exploration of the Sculptures of Greyfriars Bobby, Edinburgh, Scotland and the Old Brown Dog in Battersea, South London, England." *Society and Animals Journal of Human-Animal Studies*11, no. 4 (2003): 353–73.

———. "The Home Front as a 'Moment' for Animals (and Humans): The Animal-Human Relationship in Contemporary Diaries and Personal Accounts." In *The Home Front in Britain*, edited by Maggie Andrews and Janice Lomas, 152–69. Basingstoke: Palgrave Macmillan, 2014.

———. "Human and Animal Space in Historic 'Pet' Cemeteries in London, New York and Paris." In *Animal Death*, edited by Fiona Probyn-Rapsey and Jay Johnson, 21–42. Sydney: University of Sydney Press, 2013.

———. "The Moment of Greyfriars Bobby: The Changing Cultural Position of Animals 1800–1920." In *A Cultural History of Animals in the Age of Empire 1800–1920*, Vol. 5, 25–46, edited by Kathleen Kete. Oxford: Berg, 2007.

———. "Nervous Dogs Need Admin, Son." *Antennae* 23 (2012): 61–63.

———. "The Smooth Cool Men of Science: The Feminist and Socialist Response to Vivisection." *History Workshop Journal* 40 (1995): 16–38.

———. "Traces and Representations: Animal Pasts in London's Present." *London Journal* 36, no. 1 (2011): 54–71.

———. "Vets and Pets: Tensions between the Veterinary Profession, the State and Animal Charities in World War 2." Lecture at Centre for Animal Welfare, Department of Veterinary Science, University of Cambridge, 5 March 2012.

Kean, Hilda, and Paul Martin. *The Public History Reader*. Abingdon: Routledge, 2013.

Kete, Kathleen. *The Beast in the Boudoir: Petkeeping in Nineteenth-Century Paris*. Berkeley: University of California Press, 1994.

——, ed. *A Cultural History of Animals in the Age of Empire 1800–1920*. Oxford: Berg, 2007.

King, Elspeth, and Maggie Andrews. "Second World War Rationing: Creativity and Buying to Last." In *The Home Front in Britain*, edited by Maggie Andrews and Janice Lomas, 184–200. Basingstoke: Palgrave Macmillan, 2014.

Kinney, James, and Ann Honeycutt. *How to Raise a Dog in the City and in the Suburbs*. London: Hamish Hamilton, 1939.

Kipps, Clare. *Sold for a Farthing*. London: Frederick Muller, 1956.

Kirby, Elizabeth, and Arthur W. Moss. *Animals Were There: A Record of the RSPCA during the War of 1939–1945*. London: Hutchinson, n.d.

Kirk, Robert G. W. "In Dogs We Trust? Intersubjectivity, Response-able Relations, and the Making of Mine Detector Dogs." *Journal of the History of the Behavioral Sciences* 50, no. 1 (2014): 1–36.

Kirk, William Hamilton. *The Diseases of the Cat*. London: Bailliere, Tindall & Cox,1925.

——. *Index of Diagnosis (Clinical and Radiological) for the Canine and Feline Surgeon*. London: Balliere,1939.

Klemperer, Victor. *To the Bitter End: The Diaries of Victor Klemperer 1942–1945*. Translated by Martin Chalmers. London: Phoenix, 2000.

Kirkham, Pat. "Beauty and Duty: Keeping Up the Home Front." In *War Culture: Social Change & Changing Experience in World War Two*, edited by Pat Kirkham and David Thoms, 13–28. London: Lawrence & Wishart,1995.

Lane, Charles Henry. *All About Dogs*. London: John Lane, 1900.

Langdon-Davies, John. *Air Raid: The Technique of Silent Approach: High Explosives: Panic*. London: George Routledge & Sons, 1938.

Lees-Milne, James. *Ancestral Voices: Diaries 1942–1943*. London: Faber, 1984.

——. *Prophesying Peace, 1944–1945*. London: Chatto and Windus, 1977.

Leinon, Rutta-Marja. "Finnish Narratives of the Horse in World War II." In *Animals and War*, edited by Ryan Hediger, 123–50. Leiden: Brill, 2013.

Levine, Joshua. *Forgotten Voices of Dunkirk*. London: Ebury, 2010.

Lewey, Frank R. *Cockney Campaign*. London: Stanley Paul, 1944.

Li, Chein Hui. "Mobilizing Christianity in the Anti-vivisection Movement in Victorian Britain." *Journal of Animal Ethics* 2, no. 2 (2012): 141–61.

Light, Alison. *Mrs. Woolf and the Servants*. London: Fig Tree, 2007.

Lind af Hageby, Louise. *Bombed Animals . . . Rescued Animals . . . Animals Saved from Destruction*. Animal Defence and Anti-Vivisection Society, 1941.

——. *On Immortality: A Letter to a Dog*. 2nd ed. London: Lind af Hageby, 1916.

Linzey, Andrew. *Why Animal Suffering Matters: Philosophy, Theology, and Practical Ethics*. Oxford: Oxford University Press, 2009.

Litten, Freddy S. "Starving the Elephants: The Slaughter of Animals in Wartime Tokyo's Ueno Zoo." *Asia-Pacific Journal: Japan Focus*, September 21, 2009.

Lloyd-Jones, Buster. *The Animals Came in One by One*. London: Secker and Warburg, 1986.

Lukacs, John. *Five Days in London, May 1940*. New Haven, CT: Yale Nota Bene, 2001.

MacDonogh, Katherine. *Reigning Cats and Dogs: A History of Pets at Court since the Renaissance*. London: Fourth Estate, 1999.

Mackay, Robert. *Half the Battle: Civilian Morale in Britain during the Second World War*. Manchester: Manchester University Press, 2002.

MacNeice, Louis. *Autumn Journal*. London: Faber, 1996.

——. *The Strings Are False: An Unfinished Autobiography*. London: Faber and Faber, 2007.

MacNicol, John. "The Evacuation of Schoolchildren." In *War and Social Change in British Society in the Second World War*, edited by Harold L. Smith, 3–31. Manchester: Manchester University Press, 1986.

Madge, Charles, and Tom Harrisson. *Britain by Mass Observation*. Harmondsworth: Penguin, 1939.

Martin, Bob. *Bob Martin on Dogs*. 3rd ed. Southport: Bob Martin, [1920s?].

———. *How to Care for Your Dog and Cat in Wartime*. Southport: Bob Martin, [1939].

Martin, Sir John. *Downing Street: The War Years*. London: Bloomsbury ,1991.

Mason, James. *The Cats in Our Lives*. London: Michael Joseph, 1949.

Masson, Jeffrey, and Susan McCarthy. *When Elephants Weep: The Emotional Lives of Animals*. London: Cape, 1994.

Matheson, Colin. "The Domestic Cat as a Factor in Urban Ecology." *Journal of Animal Ecology* 13, no. 2 (1944): 130–33.

Matt, Susan J., and Peter N. Stearns. *Doing Emotions History*. Chicago: University of Illinois Press, 2014.

Mayer, Jed. "Representing the Experimental Animal: Competing Voices in Victorian Culture." In *Animals and Agency*, edited by Sarah E. Macfarland and Ryan Hediger, 181–206. Leiden: Brill, 2009.

McPherson, Susan, and Angela McPherson. *Mosley's Old Suffragette: A Biography of Norah Dacre Fox*. Angela MacPherson and Susan McPherson, 2010.

McShane, Clay, and Joel A. Tarr. *The Horse in the City: Living Machines in the Nineteenth Century*. Baltimore: Johns Hopkins University Press, 2007.

———. "The Horse in the Nineteenth-Century American City." In *Beastly Natures: Animals, Humans and the Study of History*, edited by Dorothee Brantz, 227–45. Charlottesville: University of Virginia Press, 2010.

Miller, Emanuel, ed. *The Neuroses in War*. London: Macmillan, 1940.

Miller, Ian Jared. *The Nature of the Beasts: Empire and Exhibition at the Tokyo Imperial Zoo*. Berkeley: University of California Press, 2013.

Millgate, Helen D. *Mr. Brown's War: A Diary of the Second World War*. Stroud: Sutton, 1998.

Montague, Frederick. *Let the Good Work Go On*. London: PDSA,1947.

Murray, J. K., W. J. Browne, M. A. Roberts, A. Whitmarsh, and T. J. Gruffydd-Jones. "Number and Ownership Profiles of Cats and Dogs in the UK." *Veterinary Record* 166 (2010): 163–68.

Nagel, Thomas. "What Is It Like to Be a Bat?" *Philosophical Review* 83, no. 4 (1974): 435–50.

National Air Raid Precautions Animals' Committee (NARPAC; under the auspices of the Home Office). *Wartime Aids for All Animal Owners*. London: NARPAC, [1939].

Nesbo, Jo. "Guardian Book Club." *Guardian*, May 3, 2014, 6.

———. *The Redbreast*. London: Harper Collins, 2012.

Newman, Jon, and Nilu York. *What to Do When the Air Raid Siren Sounds: Life in Lambeth during World War Two* . [Lambeth]: Lambeth Archives, 2005.

Nicolson, Harold. *Diaries and Letters 1930–1939*. Edited by Nigel Nicolson. London: Fontana, 1969.

———. *Diaries and Letters 1939–1945*. Edited by Nigel Nicolson. London: Fontana, 1970.

Nixon, Barbara. *Raiders Overhead*. London: Lindsay Drummond,1943.

Nussbaum, Martha C. *Upheavals of Thought: The Intelligence of Emotions*. Cambridge: Cambridge University Press, 2001.

O'Brien, Terence Henry. *Civil Defence*. London: HMSO, 1955.

Orwell, George. *The Complete Works of George Orwell*. Vol. 11, *Facing Unpleasant Facts 1937–1939*. Edited by Peter Davison, assisted by Ian Angus and Sheila Davison. London: Secker and Warburg, 1998.

———. *The Complete Works of George Orwell*. Vol. 12, *A Patriot After All 1940–1941*. Edited by Peter Davison, assisted by Ian Angus and Sheila Davison. London: Secker and Warburg, 1998.

———. "The English People." In *Collected Essays, Journalism, and Letters*, Vol. 3, *As I Please*, edited by Sonia Orwell and Ian Angus. London: Secker and Warburg, 1968.

———. *George Orwell: A Life in Letters*. Edited by Peter Davison. London: Harvill Secker, 2010.

Our Dumb Friends League (ODFL). *18th Annual Report*. London: ODFL, 1938.

Overy, Richard. *The Bombing War: Europe 1939-1945*. London: Allen Lane, 2013.

Padley, Richard, and Margaret Cole. *Evacuation Survey: A Report to the Fabian Society*. London: Routledge,1940.

Partridge, Frances. *A Pacifist's War: Diaries 1939-1945*. London: Phoenix, 1999.

Pegasus. *Horse Talks: A Vade-Mecum for Young Riders*. London: Collins, 1948.

Pemberton, Neil, and Matthew Warboys. *Mad Dogs and Englishmen: Rabies in Britain, 1830-2000*. Basingstoke: Palgrave Macmillan, 2007.

Perry, Colin. *Boy in the Blitz: The 1940 Diary of Colin Perry*. London: Corgi, 1974.

Pierce, Doris. *Memories of the Civilian War 1939-1945*. London: Temple, 1996.

Polge, Chris. "The Work of the Animal Research Station, Cambridge." *Studies in the History and Philosophy of the Biological and Biomedical Sciences* 38, no. 2 (2007): 511-20.

Porter, Mary Haskell. *Hastings in Peace and War 1930-1945*. [England]: Ferndale, 2002.

Potts, Annie, and Donelle Gadenne. *Animals in Emergencies: Learning from the Christchurch Earthquakes*. Christchurch, New Zealand: Canterbury University Press, 2014.

Pratt, Jean Lucey. *A Notable Woman: The Romantic Journals of Jean Lucey Pratt*. Edited by Simon Garfield. Edinburgh: Canongate, 2015.

Quester, George H. "The Psychological Effects of Bombing on Civilian Populations: Wars of the Past." In *Psychological Dimensions of War*, edited by Betty Glad, 201-14. Newbury Park, CA: Sage, 1990.

Radford, Mike. *Animal Welfare Law in Britain*. Oxford: Oxford University Press, 2001.

Reddy, William M. *The Navigation of Feeling: A Framework for the History of Emotions*. Cambridge: Cambridge University Press, 2001.

Richardson, Edwin Hautenville. *British War Dogs, Their Training and Psychology*. London: Skeffington & Son, [1920].

———. *Forty Years with Dogs*. London: Hutchinson, 1929.

Ritvo, Harriet. *The Animal Estate: The English and Other Creatures in Victorian England*. Cambridge, MA: Harvard University Press, 1989.

Robertson, Ben. *I Saw England*. London: Jarrolds, 1941.

Robinson, Keith. "Cats and Legislation." *Animals in Politics* 17 (August 1938), ODFL.

———. "Cats Must Be Taxed." *Animals in Politics* 18 (September 1938), article 16, ODFL.

[Robinson, Keith]. Editorial. *Animals in Politics* 20 (Spring 1939), article 12, ODFL.

Roodhouse, Mark. *Black Market Britain 1939-1955*. Oxford: Oxford University Press, 2013.

Rose, Nikolas. *Governing the Soul: The Shaping of the Private Self*. London: Routledge, 1990.

Rose, Sonya O. *Which People's War? National Identity and Citizenship in Wartime Britain 1939-1945*. Oxford: Oxford University Press, 2003.

Rosenzweig, Roy, and David Thelen. *The Presence of the Past: Popular Sites of History in American Life*. New York: Columbia University Press, 1998.

Rosman, Alice Grant. *Nine Lives: A Cat of London in Peace and War*. New York: G. P. Putnam's Sons, 1941.

Rothfels, Nigel. *Savages and Beasts: The Birth of the Modern Zoo*. Baltimore: John Hopkins University Press, 2008.

Rowlands, Mark. *Can Animals Be Moral?* Oxford: Oxford University Press, 2012.

Schmideberg, Melitta. "Some Observations on Individual Reactions to Air Raids." *International Journal of Psycho-analysis* 23 (1942): 146-76.

Schmideberg, Walter. "The Treatment of Panic." *Life and Letters To-Day* 23, no. 7 (1939): 162-69.

Schneider, Peter. *The German Comedy: Science of Life after the Wall*. London: I. B. Tauris, 1992.

Schweitzer, Pam, ed. *Goodnight Children Everywhere: Memories of Evacuation in World War II*. [London]: Age Exchange Theatre Trust, 1990.

Scott, Sir Harold. *Your Obedient Servant*. London: Andre Deutsch, 1959.

Sewell, Brian. *Outsider: Always Almost, Never Quite: An Autobiography*. London: Quartet, 2012.

Shaffer, Mary Ann, and Annie Barrows. *The Guernsey Literary and Potato Peel Pie Society*. London: Bloomsbury, 2009.

Sheial, John. "Wartime Rodent-Control in England and Wales." In *The Front Line of Freedom: British Farming in the Second World War*, edited by Brian Short, Charles Watkins, and John Martin. Exeter: British Agricultural History Society, 2006.

Sherley, A. F. *Sherley's Dog Book*. London: A. F. Sherley, 1930.

Shirer, William L. *Berlin Diary: The Journal of a Foreign Correspondent*. Abingdon: Taylor and Francis, 2002.

Smail, Daniel Lord. *On Deep History and the Brain*. Berkeley: University of California Press, 2008.

Smith, Carmen. *The Blue Cross at War*. Burford: Blue Cross, 1990.

Smith, Horace. *A Horseman through Six Reigns: Reminiscences of a Royal Riding Master*. London: Odhams, 1955.

Smith, Malcolm. *Britain and 1940: History, Myth and Popular Memory*. London: Routledge, 2000.

Sokoloff, Sally. "The Home Front in the Second World War and Local History." *Local Historian* 32, no.1 (February 2002): 22–40.

Spender, Stephen. *World within World*. London: Faber, 1977.

Spillane, J. P. "A Survey of the Literature of Neuroses in War." In *The Neuroses in War*, edited by Emanuel Miller, 1–32. London: Macmillan, 1940.

Stallwood, Kim. *Growl*. New York: Lantern, 2014.

Stansky, Peter. *First Day of the Blitz*. New Haven: Yale University Press, 2007.

Steedman, Carolyn. *Dust*. Manchester: Manchester University Press, 2001.

Stonebridge, Lyndsey. "Anxiety at a Time of Crisis." *History Workshop Journal* 45 (Spring 1998): 171–81.

Swarbrick, Nancy. *Creature Comforts: New Zealanders and Their Pets*. Dunedin: Otago University Press, 2013.

Swart, Sandra. "Horses in the South African War c.1899–1902." *Society and Animals Journal of Human-Animal Studies* 18 (2010): 348–66.

———. *Riding High: Horses, Humans and History in South Africa*. Johannesburg: Witwatersrand University Press, 2010.

The Tail-Waggers Club. *The Tail-Waggers Club*. London: The Tail-Waggers Club, [1931?].

———. *A Dog Owner's Guide*. London: The Tail-Waggers Club, [1931?].

———. *On to the Million*. London: The Tail-Waggers Club, [1931?].

Tansey, Elizabeth. "Protection against Dog Distemper and Dogs Protection Bills: The Medical Research Council and Anti-Vivisectionist Protest 1911–1933." *Medical History* 38 (1994): 1–26.

Taylor, Nik. *Humans, Animals, and Society: An Introduction to Human-Animal Studies*. New York: Lantern, 2013.

Tennyson Jesse, F., and H. M. Harwood. *London Front: Letters Written to America, August 1939–July 1940*. London: Constable, 1940.

Thomas, Donald. *An Underworld at War: Spivs, Deserters, Racketeers and Civilians in the Second World War*. London: John Murray, 2003.

Thompson, Edward P. *The Making of the English Working-Class*. 2nd ed. Harmondsworth: Penguin, 1980.

Thompson, F. M. L. *Victorian England: The Horse-Drawn Society*. Inaugural lecture, Bedford College, University of London, 1970.

Thomson, Mathew. *Psychological Subjects: Identity, Culture and Health in Twentieth-Century Britain*. Oxford: Oxford University Press, 2006.

Thornton, David William. *Hastings: A Living History*. Hastings: Hastings, 1987.

Tichelar, Michael. "Putting Animals into Politics: The Labour Party and Hunting in the First Half of the Twentieth Century." *Rural History* 17, no. 2 (2006): 213–34.

Tindol, Robert. "The Best Friend of the Murderers: Guard Dogs and the Nazi Holocaust." In *Animals and War*, edited by Ryan Hediger,105–22. Leiden: Brill, 2013.

Titmuss, Richard. *Problems of Social Policy*. London: HMSO, 1950.

Townsend, Peter. *The Family Life of Old People: An Inquiry in East London*. London: Routledge & Kegan Paul, 1957.

Trotter, Wilfred. "Panic and Its Consequences." In *The Collected Papers of Wilfred Trotter*, edited by Wilfred Trotter, 191–94. Oxford: Oxford University Press, 1941.

Turner, Ernest Sackville. *All Heaven in a Rage*. Fontwell: Centaur Press, 1992.

——. *The Phoney War on the Home Front*. London: Michael Joseph, 1961.

Vale, George. *Bethnal Green's Ordeal 1939–1945*. London: Borough of Bethnal Green Council, 1945.

Ward-Jackson, Philip. *Public Sculpture of Historic Westminster*. Vol. 1. Liverpool: Liverpool University Press, 2011.

Webb, Beatrice. *The Diaries of Beatrice Webb*. Edited by Norman Mackenzie and Jeanne Mackenzie. London: Virago, 2000.

Westall, Robert. *Children of the Blitz: Memories of Wartime Childhood*. London: Macmillan, 1995.

Wilbert, Chris. "What Is Doing the Killing? Animal Attacks, Man-Eaters, and Shifting Boundaries and Flows of Human-Animal Relations." In *Killing Animals*, Animal Studies Group, 30–49. Chicago: University of Illinois Press, 2006.

Williams, Mrs. Leslie. *Sidney Appleton's Handbooks for Animal Owners: The Cat: Its Care and Management*. London: Sidney Appleton, 1907.

Williams, Shirley. *Climbing the Bookshelves: The Autobiography*. London: Virago, 2009.

Wilson, David. "Racial Prejudice and the Performing Animals Controversy in Early Twentieth-Century Britain." *Society and Animals* 17, no. 2 (2009):149–65.

Wolfe, Cary. *What Is Posthumanism?* Minneapolis: University of Minnesota Press, 2010.

Woods, Abigail. "The Farm as Clinic: Veterinary Expertise and the Transformation of Dairy Farming, 1930–1950." *Studies in History and Philosophy of Biological and Biomedical Sciences* 38 (2007): 462–87.

Woolf, Virginia. *The Diary of Virginia Woolf*. Vol. 5, 1936–41. Edited by Anne Olivier Bell, assisted by Andrew McNeillie. Harmondsworth: Penguin, 1984.

Woon, Basil. *Hell Came to London*. London: Peter Davies, 1941.

Ziegler, Philip. *London at War 1939–1945*. London: Sinclair-Stevenson, 1995.

Zuckerman, Solly. *From Apes to Warlords: The Autobiography (1904–1946)*. London: Hamilton, 1978.

ARCHIVAL MATERIALS

Battersea Dogs and Cats Home, London

BBC Sound Archives, Caversham, Reading

Bishopsgate Institute, London

Blue Cross Archives, Burford, Oxfordshire: Ethel Bilbrough, diary

Cats Protection League (now Cats Protection)

Imperial War Museum Archives

London Borough of Camden Archives

London Borough of Havering Archives (covering the former Wanstead and Woodford Borough Council)

London Borough of Tower Hamlets Archives

Mass Observation Archive, University of Sussex

The National Archives, Kew

National Canine Defence League

Royal College of Veterinary Surgeons, London
RSPCA Hillingdon
RSPCA National Archive, Horsham
WW2 People's War. An archive of World War Two memories—written by the public, gathered by the BBC: http://www.bbc.co.uk/history/ww2peopleswar/

Index

Page numbers in italic refer to figures. See named non-human animals under different species.